IN SEARCH OF THE RELIGIOSITY IN RELIGION

SACRED THOUGHT, SACRED ACTION REVISITED

Jack Shechter

Printed in the United States of America

First Printing, 2020

ISBN 978-1-09833-797-1

Published by Oaks Press
Thousand Oaks, California

This book is for my grandchildren and their generation who, I hope, will regularly revisit the established thought and practices of our faith and people in search of the embedded core meaning and inner spirit.

CONTENTS

INTRODUCTION

The Objective of this Work

The quest that threads its way throughout this book, inherent in it in one way or another, is this: an effort to discern the core meaning and essential implications of a selection of Judaism's fundamental ideas, as well as to understand the basic intent of a set of its religious practices. What has led me to this undertaking through the years is encounter with the vexing problem of dissonance between unthinking faith and its rational affirmation, and between rote ritual and its spiritual intent. What do I mean by this?

Religion and life are inextricably interwoven as Judaism conceives it, which is to say that doctrine and practice must serve to guide, enrich and ennoble everyday life—personal and communal. Unfortunately, in too many faith quarters, religion takes on a life of its own, creating for its adherents a rarified, theoretical mental caste unrelated to real people in real life. Yet more, observance of the ritual regimen is often undertaken mechanically and for its own sake without realizing its intent, let alone actualizing its purpose in the business of everyday living.

The questions, "Why should we believe?" and "Why should we observe the mitzvot?" are often responded to with "because God said so" or "because that's the tradition." This merely prompts the questions, "Why did God say so?" or "Why does the tradition say so?" Of course, it is true that not everything can be explained via reason and that much in religion is a matter of faith. Nevertheless, the additional elements of reasoned analysis and critical thinking are called for, because, in the end, the religious enterprise is thereby enriched and enhanced

One of the major contributions to Judaism in our time by Martin Buber is the distinction he stressed between "religion" and "religiosity." Religion is the institutional, carefully structured, formal aspect of a faith community. *Religiosity is the inner meaning, the irreducible spirit and essence of the doctrine and practices of the faith community, that which constitutes the essential purpose of the institutional structure.* Thus, in Buber's landmark unpacking of the life and literature of Hasidism, he pointed out, that what the tzaddikim (spiritual leaders) considered decisive in the observance of religious ritual was the intent and spirit, the aim of the action, the inner purpose of the panoply of practices the faithful were engaged in. Each person was obliged to unite action with its purpose and thus develop wholeness as a truly religious personality.[1]

This is the thrust of the luminous body of teaching which flows from the inspired pen of Abraham Joshua Heschel. It was, indeed, to grasp the ideational essence and spiritual intent of Jewish practice. For example: "Prayer is an invitation to God to intervene in our lives," Heschel avers, "to let His will prevail in our affairs, to seek to be allied with what is ultimately right....It is necessary to make us aware of our backsliding and our opportunities."

And this about "religion" vis-à-vis "religiosity:" "Religion as an establishment must remain separate from government. Religiosity is a voice for mercy, a cry for justice, a plea for gentleness, virtues that must be kept apart. Let the *spirit* of prayer dominate the world, interfere in the affairs of man. Prayer is private, a service of the heart; but let concern and compassion, born out of prayer dominate public life." Heschel further emphasizes that "Jewish tradition insists that no religious performance is complete without the participation of the heart. It asks for *kavanah*, for inner intention and participation, not only for external action. *Kavanah* is awareness of the will of God."[2]

---

1. Buber, Martin. "Jewish Religiosity." *On Judaism.* Schocken Books, 1996; p. 80.
2. Heschel, Abraham J. *Between God and Man: An Interpretation of Judaism.* Free Press, 1997; p. 165.

Reason: A Tool

The writings here, then, are designed to unpack, to "excavate," if you like, what Buber and Heschel have perceived as the "religiosity" of Judaism's faith assertions and religious practices. The basic tool employed in this endeavor is what Moses Maimonides has called "reason," which, in turn, he emphasized, can lead to spiritual affirmation and focused ritual action.

Bakhya Ibn Pakudah, a renowned Jewish philosopher of the Middle Ages, in his *Duties of the Heart*, speaks of this vital human attribute. Faith, he says, must be joined with the intellect, not be blind and unreasoning. Tradition alone, without the support of proof, is sufficient for those who are not able to study. But, "if you are a man of intellect, you are obligated to use your own faculties to gain knowledge of the truth, so that your faith and conduct may rest on a foundation of tradition, reason, and personal understanding."[3]

So, too, Maimonides, the equally renowned author of *The Guide for the Perplexed*, speaks disparagingly of people who consider it "a grievous thing that reasons should be given for any law," that intellect is employed in examination of the commandments and laws. They think that in doing so, people might consider the laws as deriving from human intellectual reflection rather than from God. On the contrary, Maimonides asserts that the laws were accepted by man because *he understands their utility* on the basis of the dictum in Deuteronomy 6:24, "For our good always that He might preserve us alive, as it is at this day." And further, Deuteronomy 4:6 emphasizes, "observe them faithfully, *for that will be proof of your wisdom and discernment* to other peoples, who, on hearing all these laws, will say: 'Surely *that great nation is a wise and understanding people.'"[4]

3. Pakudah, Bahya Ben Joseph Ibn, et al. *Duties of the Heart*. Yeshivath Beth Moshe, 1999.
4. Maimonides, Moses. *The Guide for the Perplexed*. Dover, 1956; 3:31.

Maimonides is indicating that God views His people as intelligent human beings not only because He gave them the laws, but also because they knew *why* they were given. Further, when we seek out reasons for our beliefs and practices, we parry the taunts that we owe all allegiance to an irrational faith in which God tends to be seen as a tyrannical ruler imposing arbitrary precepts and laws on His subjects. And so, we believe and practice, not merely because we are commanded, but also because for these we have good reason:

הָאֵל הַנִּכְבָּד וְהַנּוֹרָא הַזֶּה–מִצְוָה לְאַהֲבוֹ וּלְיִרְאָה אוֹתוֹ, שֶׁנֶּאֱמַר: „וְאָהַבְתָּ אֶת ה' אֱלֹהֶיךָ", וְנֶאֱמַר: „אֶת ה' אֱלֹהֶיךָ תִּירָא" וְהֵיאַךְ הִיא הַדֶּרֶךְ לְאַהֲבָתוֹ וּלְיִרְאָתוֹ? בְּשָׁעָה שֶׁיִּתְבּוֹנֵן הָאָדָם בְּמַעֲשָׂיו וּבְרוּאָיו הַנִּפְלָאִים הַגְּדוֹלִים וְיִרְאֶה מֵהֶן חָכְמָתוֹ שֶׁאֵין לָהּ עֵרֶךְ וְלֹא קֵץ, מִיָּד הוּא אוֹהֵב וּמְשַׁבֵּחַ וּמְפָאֵר וּמִתְאַוֶּה תַּאֲוָה גְדוֹלָה לֵדַע הַשֵּׁם הַגָּדוֹל, כְּמוֹ שֶׁאָמַר דָּוִד: „צָמְאָה נַפְשִׁי לֵאלֹהִים לְאֵל חָי".

It is our duty to love and revere this honored and revered God, as it is written: "You shall love the Lord your God...You shall revere the Lord your God."[5]

Now, what is the way that leads to the love of Him and the reverence for Him? When a person contemplates His great and wondrous acts and creations, obtaining from them a glimpse of His wisdom, which is beyond compare and infinite, he will promptly love and glorify Him, longing exceedingly to know the great Name of God, as in Psalm 42:13: "My whole being thirsts for God, the living God."[6]

Elizabeth Barrett Browning famously put it this way: "Earth is crammed with heaven, and every common bush afire with God but only he who sees takes off his shoes."

The mood of biblical psalmody is captured in a phrase from Isaiah: "Lift your eyes on high and see who has created these things."[7] Indeed, the more we delve into the makings of the

---

5.   Deuteronomy 6:5, 13.
6.   Maimonides, Moses. *Mishne Torah*; 3:4.
7.   Isaiah 40:26.

natural world and the wonder of the human physical body and soaring spirit, the more awe-inspiring these and their Architect reveal themselves to be.

In our own time this emphasis remains etched into the Jewish consciousness. I recall vividly the procedure Professor Mordecai Kaplan instituted before each class lecture at the Rabbinical School of the Jewish Theological Seminary. He opened with the words of the moving *Ahavah Rabbah* prayer which is recited before the Shema at each Shabbat and Festival service:

> Our Father, instill in us the desire to understand and discern, to listen, learn and teach in order to observe, perform, and fulfill the teachings of Your Torah in Love.

Herein is the purpose of these writings. The stress is on the inherent meaning and spiritual intent of aspects of Jewish thought and practice. This so that Jewish ideas might be more personally meaningful than heretofore, and selected rituals more successfully operative in the lives of our people in our time. Reasoned ideology, the process that has been labeled *ta-amay hamitzvot*, "reasons for the commandments," is our method.

This book consists, in part, of selections from my previous books, *The Land of Israel, Journey of a Rabbi* and *The Idea of Monotheism*, and articles published elsewhere. In some cases, they have been revised in perspective, expanded or condensed. I have included, as well, the Hebrew texts of the passages originally cited in English. In addition, a set of new pieces has been included especially in the area of ritual and prayer.

I need to point out to the reader of these essays that each is a separate, self-contained unit of thought which stands on its own—although, as we shall see, general thought lines unite them. Thus the reader will find some of the same material in a number of the essays. This is because of the obvious need to maintain the flow and coherence of an individual essay.

A personal note: for the most part, the criterion employed for inclusion of the materials in this volume is their having emerged from my own personal experience as student and father, rabbi and professional educator. Thus what I have done here is to review, analyze and reflect on that which I have personally practiced and the ideas I have wrestled with over the years.

SACRED THOUGHT

Moses at Mount Sinai took the book of the covenant and read it aloud to the people. And they said na-aseh v'nishma, "We shall do and we shall listen" (Exodus 24:7). Not in the ordinary translation would wisdom have us read these words— "we shall do and we shall listen"—but in the more original and more fundamental meaning of the word nishma: And we shall do and we shall understand (what we do).

—Abraham J. Heschel

– One –

WHY IS MONOTHEISM OF SUCH GREAT IMPORTANCE?

שְׁמַע יִשְׂרָאֵל ה' אֱלֹהֵינוּ ה' אֶחָד

Hear, O Israel, the Lord our God, the Lord is One.

—Deuteronomy 6:4

אֲנִי מַאֲמִין בֶּאֱמוּנָה שְׁלֵמָה, שֶׁהַבּוֹרֵא יִתְבָּרַךְ שְׁמוֹ,
הוּא יָחִיד, וְאֵין יְחִידוּת כָּמוֹהוּ בְּשׁוּם פָּנִים,
וְהוּא לְבַדּוֹ אֱלֹהֵינוּ, הָיָה הֹוֶה וְיִהְיֶה.

I believe with complete faith that the Creator, blessed be His name, is a unity, and that there is then no unity in any manner like His, and that He alone is our God, who was, is, and will be.

—Maimonides Mishne Torah
Hilkhot Yesodai Hatorah 1:2

The Shema

For more than two thousand years, the Shema declaration has been recited twice daily by devout Jews. The Jewish child is taught the verse as soon as he can learn to speak. The Jew repeats it on his deathbed if he is able to utter any sound at all. The Jewish martyrs recited it as they made ready to give their lives for their faith. Throughout the ages, it has been the most powerful single declaration of the significance of the Jewish religion. So,

9

too, at the conclusion of every religious service this is chanted: "And the Lord shall be King over all the earth; on that day shall The Lord be One, and His name One."[1]

Why, indeed, is this declaration so important?

I have posed that question to many Jews on many occasions and rarely have received coherent answers. In one instance, for example, I asked a Ph.D. psychologist, observant Jew and regular Shabbat service attendee to estimate how many times in his lifetime has he recited the Shema, which proclaims the Oneness of the Deity. His response: "Probably some five thousand times." I then asked, "What does the Oneness of God mean? Why is it so important?" To which he stammered something about God overseeing the world. This accomplished man did not know what the Oneness of God connoted, even though he has recited the Shema in synagogue, at home, and at bedtime some five thousand times! Though I have no statistical data to prove it, I venture to say that such is the condition among most Jews in our time.

The content of a previous book of mine, *The Idea of Monotheism*, contains some answers to the question about the importance of the Oneness of God. Here I seek to offer a summary of the ideas' fundamental significances.

When juxtaposed with the paganism of the past, the notion of the absolute Oneness of the Deity harbors three fundamental principles for all time:

I. ONE GOD MEANS ONE HUMANITY

הֲלוֹא אָב אֶחָד לְכֻלָּנוּ הֲלוֹא אֵל אֶחָד
בְּרָאָנוּ, מַדּוּעַ נִבְגַּד אִישׁ בְּאָחִיו ?

Have we not all one Father? Did not one God create us? Why do we break faith with one another, profaning the covenant of

---

1. Zekhariah 14:9.

our ancestors?

—Malachi 2:10

Once a great naval ship sailed into port. On the hillside overlooking the sea a crowd had gathered to watch it enter. Among them was a young lad, who waved to the ship. An adult asked the boy to whom he was waving. He replied, "I am waving to the captain of the ship." The man asked, "Do you think the captain of such a great ship would notice a young lad like you?" "I am sure of it," said the lad. "Why?" the adult asked, to which he responded, "The captain of the ship is my father."

God is our "Father," as it were, and we are His children. When God told Moses to lead the Israelites to freedom, He told them to say to Pharaoh: "My child, my first born, Israel."[2] When Moses commanded the Israelites not to lacerate themselves nor divide themselves into factions, he said: "You are children of the Lord your God."[3]

One God created all human beings. All are His children and all are brothers and sisters. Hence, all human beings are, in the nature of things, members of one family. As we shall see, the many "fathers" of paganism, by contrast, render many different families unconnected to each other.

The One God's people, members of one family, kinsmen made of the same basic stuff that gives them life, is that which binds them together. This bond creates a sense of solidary among all members of the family. It is a deep-rooted feeling that prompts responsibility for one another, which motivates protection of the family's weak and oppressed members, which gives rise to a decided drive for justice, and for love and compassion for kinsmen. According to biblical dicta, such behavior is mandatory because it is God, the Father's, will: "You shall love your neighbor as yourself. I am The Lord."[4]

---

2. Exodus 4:22.
3. Deuteronomy 14:1.
4. Leviticus 19:18. A special note: The *Webster Collegiate Dictionary* defines

Further, humane behavior is called for because all humans were created "in God's [the Father's] image,"[5] which is to say that even as the One Father evinces love and mercy, justice and compassion for His creatures, so must these attributes be replicated by all members of the human family. According to Rabbi Akiba, "It was by a special love that it was made known to man that he was created in the image of God, as it is said: 'For in the image of God made He man.'"

Leo Baeck has captured, I believe, the essential spirit of this notion:

> We cannot attribute to ourselves that high nobility which we consider to be ours without also attributing it to others. Were it not essentially theirs, it could not be ours. We are created in the image of God and that which we are, they are as well... My neighbor is the other man, and yet he is not the other; he is different from me, and yet the same: he is separated from me, and yet united with me... He is understood by me only if like me, he is viewed as having been created in the image of God. In the belief in the One God, the meaning of his life, as of mine, is revealed.[6]

II. ONE GOD MEANS ONE MORALITY

שֹׁפְטִים וְשֹׁטְרִים תִּתֶּן לְךָ בְּכָל שְׁעָרֶיךָ
וְשָׁפְטוּ אֶת הָעָם מִשְׁפַּט צֶדֶק: לֹא
תַטֶּה מִשְׁפָּט, לֹא תַכִּיר פָּנִים.
צֶדֶק צֶדֶק תִּרְדֹּף לְמַעַן תִּחְיֶה

---

the adjective "kind" as "affectionate, loving," "of a sympathetic or helpful nature," "of a forbearing nature: gentle." And then it defines "kind" as a noun: "family, lineage." When these two definitions are combined, a religious message clearly emerges: kind behavior and family/lineage are interwoven—"Be kind because you are kindred," you are of the same family, you are linked by lineage because you are children of One Father.

5. Genesis 1:27.

6. Baeck, Leo. The *Essence of Judaism.* Schocken, 1987.

You shall appoint judges and officials in all your gates...and they shall govern the people with due justice. You shall not judge unfairly: you shall show no partiality...Justice, justice shall you pursue, that you may thrive.

—Deuteronomy 16:18-20

One God means that there is *one* standard for moral and ethical living—one moral code whose source and authority is the One God. Thus, even as Monotheism means there is only one God, there can be but a single moral system for human beings. This is what is meant by what has been described as "ethical monotheism." The God idea presupposes certain moral values to be adopted by men and women: "Even as He is gracious, so be you gracious; even as He is merciful, so be you merciful, even as He is holy, so be you holy."[7] These values, along with the set of moral and ethical ones depicted in scripture as the will of the one God, are human obligations. Taken together, they represent the single standard for human moral behavior. In a word: as Monotheism means the One God, it thus means the one command, the one righteousness, a single moral path.

By way of contrast, multiple gods means multiple divine wills espousing multiple contradictory yet obligatory moral codes. Thus Monotheism constitutes a protest against the double morality preached and practiced before its advent. Then there was one special moral code for rulers and another for the ruled, one for the great and one for the small, one for the strong and one for the weak, be they weak in power or weak in spirit. Hence, the pursuit of justice, for example, is applicable to *all* of God's children whose "Father" is the One God. It is applicable at all times, in all places and to all cultures and tongues. Indeed, Bahya Ibn Pakudah, in his commentary on Deuteronomy 16:20, emphasized that the double use of the word "justice" teaches that justice must be reached for under all circumstances, whether to

---

7. Talmud, *Shabbat*; 133a.

one's profit or loss, whether in one's words or actions, whether dealing with a fellow Jew or a non-Jew. Regarding this principle, there can be no competing gods to teach otherwise.

Thus, Scripture states in God's name: "You shall not render an unfair decision: *do not favor the poor or show deference to the* rich; judge your neighbor fairly."[8] Further: "Hear out your fellow men and decide justly between any man and a fellow Israelite or a stranger. You shall not be partial in judgment *Hear out low and high alike*. Fear no man for judgment is God's."[9]

By way of stark contrast, the Babylonian Code of Hammurabi, commissioned by the pagan god of justice, the sun god *Shamash*, had a different take on this subject. The law of justice was applied differently to a nobleman than to a commoner (a member of the lower class such as an ox driver or a slave). Thus, the law of "an eye for an eye, a tooth for a tooth" (*lex talionis*) was a scaled punishment: penalty for its infraction was based on social status:

> If a man has destroyed the eye of a member of the aristocracy, they (the court) shall destroy his (the perpetrator's) eye. If he has destroyed the eye of a commoner, he (the perpetrator) shall pay one mina of silver. If a seignior (a man of high rank) knocked out the tooth of a seignior of his own rank, they (the court) shall knock out his (the perpetrator's) tooth. If the seignior knocked out a commoner's tooth, he (the perpetrator) shall pay one-third mina of silver."
>
> Indeed, Hammurabi's god hardly advocated fair justice, although he did place greater value on an eye over a tooth![10]

---

8. Leviticus 19:15.
9. Deuteronomy 1:16-17.
10. Pritchard, James B., and Daniel E. Fleming. *The Ancient Near East: An Anthology of Texts and Pictures*. Princeton University Press, 2011; p. 175, 196-201.

Especially significant is the fact that King Hammurabi claims that the sun god, Shamash, commissioned him to write his code; later he says that it was the god Marduk, the head god of Babylon, who did so. Now, these two gods played different roles in the lives of the people. Shamash was the promoter of justice, and Marduk was the director of the land—and they had different, often clashing, requirements for the people's lives, as the code's content demonstrates.[11] This was a system of law inherently unstable, inconsistent and ultimately unsustainable.

III. ONE GOD MEANS ONE DESIGN

אֱלָהַיָּא דִּי־שְׁמַיָּא וְאַרְקָא לָא עֲבַדוּ
עֹשֵׂה אֶרֶץ בְּכֹחוֹ
מֵכִין תֵּבֵל בְּחָכְמָתוֹ
וּבִתְבוּנָתוֹ נָטָה שָׁמָיִם

Their gods did not make heaven and earth. He (God) made the earth by His might, who established the world by His wisdom, and by His understanding stretched out the skies.

—Jeremiah 10:11-12

The heavens declare the glory of God;
*   the skies proclaim the work of His hands.*
Day to day they pour forth speech;
*   night to night they communicate knowledge.*
There is no speech, there are no words,
their voice is not heard.
Yet their music carries throughout the earth
*   their words to the end of the world.*

—Psalm 19:2–5

Be open to the great wonders of nature, familiar though they may be. But men are more wont to be astonished at the sun's

---

11. Ibid., p. 163, 165.

eclipse than at its unfailing rise.

—Moses Hayyim Luzzato

Belief in the Unity of God opened the eyes of man to the unity of nature, in that there is a harmony in the structure of things because of the unity of their Source. The natural world has wondrous order and system, a basic dependability and stability. Discernible rules are embedded in it making possible scientific study of the world based on the ability to rationally analyze its phenomena and predict probable outcomes.

On the other hand, a world divided among various gods— one of sun and another of moon, one of fire and another of water, one of flood which destroys and another of beneficent rain which nourishes the earth, one of scorching desert and another of frigid tundra, one of earthquake and another of sturdy terrain—such a world is confusing, tension-filled for different followers of the different gods, rendering the astonishing unity of the natural globe beyond human capacity to explicate.

Indeed, the Shema, the supreme declaration of the Jewish faith, tells us that when we assert that there is only one God, we are affirming that *unity is at the heart of the cosmos and that conflict is not woven into the fabric of the universe.*

A wise observer of the natural world described it this way:

> Night falls on one hemisphere, only that a new day may fell upon another. The bee sucks its sweetness from the flower, but at the same time, fertilizes it with the pollen she has unconsciously carried away on her body from some other flower. The sun draws up the water from the ocean in the form of vapor; the vapor becomes, a cloud; the cloud empties itself as rain; the rain replenishes the river, which empties into the ocean. Light and darkness, sunshine and storm, growth and decay all point to a mysterious unity in the universe, to a world that has been planned and is controlled by One Mind.

This perspective prompts us to affirm that the unity of nature is a result of a unitary will—a Single Designer and it enables the human mind to discern universal laws applicable everywhere, to wit:

The ecological chain that keeps the natural world in constant balance.

The law of gravity that makes it possible to rationally study the world and fashion plans for it.

The stability of the cosmos that made possible Einstein's historic studies, which relied on exact mathematical formulae governing time and space.

The design of the human body is the same everywhere. Thus the body can be studied and cures prescribed in one place and era and applied everywhere and at all times.

Two great persona—one a famed scientist and the other a famed religionist—have articulated the core concept regarding this matter:

Albert Einstein: What a deep rationality inherent in the structure of the world, and what a longing to understand even a small glimpse of the reason revealed to the world there must have been in Kepler and Newton to enable them to unravel the mechanism of the heavens in the long years of lonely work.

Abraham Joshua Heschel: In whatever way we try to conceive the reality of nature, it is given to us as a meaningful whole ruled by strict principles. They are intrinsically rational if our minds are capable of grasping them. But if rationality is at work in nature, there is no way to account for it without reference to the activity of a supreme intelligence.

Why is Monotheism of such basic importance? Because it teaches us that there is *one* humanity, *one* standard of morality and *one* design in all the world.

ADDENDUM

Affirmation of the One-God idea has had many profound consequences. What follows is but one of them.

Franz Rosenzweig's Transformation: The Realization of God as One

Franz Rosenzweig was one of the great Jewish thinkers of the twentieth century. He also pioneered an approach to Jewish adult education that has had a profound influence on all serious ventures in this realm of Jewish learning in modern times, including the ones employed by this writer throughout a rabbinic career and as a university educator.

Rosenzweig was the son of cultured German parents whose Judaism was primarily motivated by the prevailing anti-Semitism of the late nineteenth and early twentieth centuries. An astute and sensitive student, he entered university in 1905, concentrating on philosophy, history, and the classics. During this period, several of Franz's relatives and friends, feeling that their Judaism was outdated and irrelevant to their lives, converted to Christianity. He, too, contemplated conversion. At first he resisted, but after much soul searching, decided to take the step. However, a sense of honor and loyalty to his own people motivated him to convert in the manner of the earliest Christians—after first living, if only briefly, as a Jew.

He enacted his resolve by attending High Holy Day services at a small orthodox synagogue in Berlin. The experience of Yom Kippur transformed him. He realized that the Jew, though united with his brethren in prayer, stands utterly alone before his God. He is nothing other than man, and God is judge of the world. Franz heard anew: "Hear, O Israel, the Lord our God, the Lord is One," and then, "The Lord He is God" chanted seven times. With this declaration, followed by the sounding of the shofar, Franz experienced the drama of the Day of Atonement finding in it a resolution.

Rosenzweig left that service a changed person. What he thought he could find in the church only he had found that day in the synagogue. He revoked his decision to become a Christian, declaring: "It no longer seems necessary to me and no longer possible." It was clearly a radical personal experience. He explained that *he understood what the church means to the world, namely that the believer can reach the Father through Jesus;* but *"the situation is quite different for the one who does not have to reach for the Father via an intermediary because the Father—the one and only God—is already with him."*[12]

The profound experience in that Berlin synagogue persuaded Franz Rosenzweig that he was indeed a Jew—and it propelled him from that point on to seek to recover Judaism for himself and for many others like him. The circumstances that led to Rosenzweig's return to Judaism continued to influence his personal religious ways and his highly influential theological views.

---

12. Glatzer, Nahum Norbert. *Franz Rosenzweig: His Life and Thought.* Schocken Books, 1961; p. 28.

– Two –

THE DIVINITY IN MAN
Is Monotheism Compromised?

וַיִּיצֶר ה' אֱלֹהִים אֶת הָאָדָם עָפָר
מִן הָאֲדָמָה. וַיִּפַּח בְּאַפָּיו נִשְׁמַת חַיִּים
וַיְהִי הָאָדָם לְנֶפֶשׁ חַיָּה

The Lord God formed man from the dust of the earth, and He blew into his nostrils the breath of life, and man became a living being."

—Genesis 2:7

Transcendence and Immanence

The notion of God's transcendence—His total independence of the world and of humanity, and simultaneously of God's immanence, His abiding presence in the world and humanity, constitute, in essence, the same basic notion. That is to say, God's immanence, important, of course, as the notion is in Jewish thought, means that we can know God via His wondrous works, the manifestations of Him in the world, but never as He is in Himself.[1] He, in His essential nature, is wholly apart from the world, which is another way of affirming His transcendence. This represents the normative Jewish notion about God and the world. The chasm,

---

1. As the Shabbat prayer has it, "They depicted You, not as You are, but as you do: Your acts, Your power." *The Anim Zmirot*, "Song of Glory," by Rabbi Yehudah He Hassid, thirteenth-century CE.

between the Deity, as such, and humanity abides.[2]

With the burgeoning of the mystical realm of thought in Judaism and especially of the Kabbalah, God's relationship to the world and human beings is seen in a different light—a non-normative light. This points to the idea that divinity somehow inhabits the human being—a "Divine Spark" lodges in a person. Thus, the chasm, the abyss, is bridged.

The God Within

The notion that something of the Divine somehow lodges in a human being had long been hinted at in one form or another in earlier Hebrew sources.[3] It appeared to be rooted in a persistent effort to bridge the gap—what some have called the "yawning chasm," between the Creator and His creatures. This effort continued in the face of the traditional Jewish notion of God's transcendence combined with His immanence, which notion, no matter how parsed, did not satisfy. Yes, "knowing" God via His tremendous works, the wondrous manifestations of Him everywhere in the universe of nature and humanity, was indeed compelling. However, for many spiritual seekers this was not enough to slake the thirst of their deepest yearnings. They sought richer experience with the Divine, more direct and tangible connection. Their tradition on this score, many felt, seemed weak, inchoate, oblique. They needed more. They sought answers to questions such as these: can human beings truly communicate with a God who they know only via His works—indirectly? When human beings speak to God in prayer with their hearts and souls, is it a *personal* God who responds to their needs, their yearnings, their aspirations?

---

2. For a more detailed description of the distinction between God's transcendence and His immanence, and efforts to reconcile the two notions prior to the rise of the Medieval Jewish mysticism, see Shechter, Jack, *The Idea of Monotheism*, Hamilton Books, 2018; p. 106-117.
3. In Philo of Alexandria (20 BCE-50 CE) as well as in sections of rabbinic literature. See Shechter, Jack, *The Idea of Monotheism*, Hamilton Books, 2018; p. 114-117.

The notion of a personal God has long been an assertion of faith in the Jewish religious tradition despite the universally accepted idea that God's essence, as he is in Himself, cannot be known to man. Two earnest and articulate Anglo-Jewish thinkers in the modern era, Isidore Epstein and Jonathan Sacks, have sought to demonstrate how and why the idea of a personal God is equally a valid notion. God is personal, they argue, *because the idea has a practical purpose and meets human needs.*

Thus Epstein begins his effort by asserting that the whole Jewish religion revolves around the acceptance of the existence of a personal God. It is true, says Epstein, that the term "personality" is totally inadequate to describe the Deity; nonetheless *the notion must be maintained.* He writes: *"This must be insisted upon because we as persons could not have any relationship such as that which constitutes the essence of all religious belief, with any impersonal force."* An impersonal God who is too far away, removed from human concerns and needs would have no relevance to the lives of people in the here and now.[4]

Jonathan Sacks echoes Epstein on this matter: "God is more than a concept, an impersonal force, the God acknowledged by philosophers and scientists through the ages… For us he is also "the God of Abraham" who calls to us and who listens when we call to Him… An impersonal force cannot hear prayer. An "It" cannot forgive. Only one to whom we can say "you" can do these things.[5]

And so, the argument goes something like this: what, for example, would be the point of prayers if the worshippers did not believe that God listens and responds to them? Hence God is personal because humans need Him to be. His personalism validates our prayers, it meets our desires. He is personal because it is to man's benefit that He be so; it satisfies human needs. Put

---

4. Epstein, Isidore. *The Faith of Judaism.* Bloch Publishing Co., 1954; p. 137.
5. Sacks, Jonathan. *The Koren Yom Kippur Makhzor.* Koren Publishers Jerusalem, 2011; p. 160.

another way: we need to pray therefore God exists.[6]

In the end, this is a practical matter—and, one could argue, hardly a convincing argument.

In the Middle Ages there arose a set of Jewish religious mystics who spoke about a personal God in other terms, both provocative and unconventional. Read on.

The Zohar: The "Bible" of Jewish Mysticism (ca. 1290 CE)

Here the doctrine of a "Divine Spark" comes into full view in Jewish thought. The Zohar, generally considered to have been composed by the Spanish rabbi and Kabbalist, Moses de Leon (1250-1305), states clearly that the highest part of the soul—the *neshama*—comes from the world of the *sefirot*, which emanates from the *Ein Sof*, (God as He is in Himself).

> Rabbi Judah began his discourse by quoting the verse, "Let every soul praise The Lord" (Psalm 150:6). We have been taught that all souls are derived from that Holy Body and they animate human beings. From which place are they derived? From the place that is called Yah. "Which place is that?," asked Rabbi Judah. It is written: "How manifold are Thy works, O Lord. In wisdom hast thou made them all" (Psalm 104:24). We have been taught that all things are contained in that wisdom the spring of which flows into thirty-two paths; all things above and below are contained within it.[7]

Now, in the Zoharic scheme, there are ten *sefirot* (i.e., Divine emanations, powers, often visualized as "rays"). The three highest of these are *Keter*, crown (i.e., the Divine Will); *Hokhma* (i.e.,

---

6. This is similar to the argument often heard that there would be no obligatory moral code for humans unless one did not believe in the god of ethical Monotheism. We need such a binding code, *therefore* there is a God who is its authoritative source.
7. *Zohar II*, 1740.

Divine Wisdom); and *Bina* (i.e., Divine Understanding). In the above passage, man's soul is depicted as deriving ultimately from *Hokhma*, Divine Wisdom. This means much more than that God in His wisdom created man's soul. The *sefira* of wisdom is, in Zohar's thought, an integral aspect of the Deity. Although some Kabbalists view the *sefirot* as separate and distinct from God, *most classical Kabbalistic thinkers see them as an organic part of the Divine essence whose complex interactions with each other are merely indications of the One God's inner dynamism.* It is true that these ten *sefirot* relate to each other in ways that appear to disclose a degree of individual existence, yet they never attain the stature of independent entities. In fact, Kabbalistic texts warn against praying to them as if they were distinct gods.

In any event, since in this Zoharic construct the *sefira Hokhma* is viewed as an organic part of *Ein Sof* (God's essence) and hence partakes of inherent divinity, and the soul is derived from *Hokhma*, the consequence is clear: *the soul of man is derived from God Himself.* Man harbors divinity within.

Nakhmanides (1195-1270 CE)

This highly influential Spanish rabbi, philosopher and Kabbalist, in his commentary to the Pentateuch, also articulated the notion of divinity in man. On the classic verse Genesis 2:7, "Then the Lord formed man of the dust of the ground, *and breathed into his nostrils the breath of life*; and man became a living soul," Nakhmanides interprets the passage in the spirit of the Kabbalah:[8]

> This verse alludes to the exaltedness of the human soul, its essence and its mystical source. For it mentions God's full name (The Lord Elohim, The Lord God) in conjunction with it (i.e., the soul) and says, *"Kee Hu nafah "b'apav nishmat hayyim,"* that "He (God) blew into his (man's) nostrils the soul (the breath) of life."

8. See Hebrew and English translation and commentary in Mesorah Publications.

This is to inform us that the soul did not come from the physical elements as in Genesis 1:2, nor from the angels as in Genesis 2:1. Rather, it is from *ruah Hashem Hagadol, mipiv da-at utvunah* (Proverbs 2:6), "The spirit of the Great God from whose mouth comes knowledge and understanding" (Proverbs 2:6). *Ki hanofaykh b'apay aher mi-nishmato yitayno bo*," for when someone blows into someone else's nostrils, he gives him of his own breath.[9] This is what is said in Job 32:8, *v'nishmat shaddai t'vinaym*, "and it is the breath of the Almighty that gives them understanding."

From this passage, it is clear that Nakhmanides is stressing that man's soul is from God's own self since the passage is referring to the Kabbalistic doctrine that the soul comes from the *sefira Binah*, divine understanding, as an emanation from God. Indeed, according to Nakhmanides, there is a portion of the Divine in the soul of man.

Hayyim Vital (1545-1620 CE)

Rabbi and Kabbalist in Safed and the foremost disciple of Isaac Luria, Vital recorded his master's teachings and, following his (Vital's) death, his writings spread and had a powerful impact on various circles throughout the Jewish world. Vital elaborated on the theme of the divine soul.[10] The true man, says Vital, is not the body for this is known in Scripture as the "flesh of man." The pure soul is the real man, using the body as its garment. As a result of Adam's sin there came about a mixture of good and evil in all things so that *even the divine soul, hewn from the four Divine elements represented by the four letters of the Tetragrammaton*, became surrounded by an evil soul deriving from the forces of impurity and known as the evil inclination.

---

9. The term *neshama* means both "breath" and "soul." For further elaboration of the concept of man's soul originating in God's "breath," see Nakhmanides' *Nefesh Hahayyim*, I, chapter 15.

10. Shaaray Kedusha, *Gates of Holiness*. Sulzbach, 1758, Part I, Shaar I; p. 3a–4a.

Now the limbs of the physical body are garments for both the pure divine soul and for the impure evil soul. Thus when man uses his bodily limbs for sin he adds fuel to the forces of the impure soul. On the other hand, when he uses his limbs to perform good deeds, these nourish and sustain the pure divine soul enabling it to gain the upper hand over the unclean evil soul.

Vital proceeds to elaborate on the relationship of the soul, as described above, to the "upper world:"[11]

> *The greatness of man's soul has been described for it is a great light born of the light of the sefirot themselves.* This is the meaning of "you are children of The Lord your God."[12] For the children are in the category of a son who is completely attached to the father from whom he is descended. This is the mystery behind the saying that the Patriarchs are the "Heavenly Chariot" carrying the light of the sefirot which ride above without the mediation of any other light. Yet more: this is the meaning of the verse, "As the girdle clings to the loins of a man, so have I, The Lord, caused to cleave to Me the whole house of Israel.[13]

And so, from this we see that Vital affirms the notion of the divine in the soul of man. Moreover, as in the case of many of the Kabbalists, he sees Israel's role as central in the divine-human soul scheme based, as it is, on the notion that Israel on earth mirrors the heavenly pattern.[14]

Shabbetai Sheftel Horowitz (1561-1619 CE)

A native of Prague, a practicing physician and a highly regarded student of Kabbalah, Shabbetai Horowitz considered Moses Cordovera, the major Kabbalist, to be his chief teacher. Horowitz

---

11. Ibid., part III, Shaar II and III, p. 25b–29a.
12. Deuteronomy 14:1.
13. Jeremiah 13:11.
14. For similar views, see Bahya ben Asher, Menashe ben Israel and Elijah de Vidas in Shechter, Jack. *The Idea of Monotheism*, Hamilton Books, 2018; p. 122-123.

authored a famous book at the beginning of which he writes:

> It is known that the souls of the people of Israel are "a
> portion of God from above." The verse, "For the portion
> of The Lord is His People," hints at this. The term "por-
> tion" is to be taken literally. A portion separated from
> something is in every way like the thing from which it
> has been taken, the thing being whole and the total
> which is naturally greater than the part separated
> thereof. But in essence the whole and the part are identi-
> cal.
>
> In the same way there is no difference or distinction
> between the soul of man and God, except that God is the
> whole. He is the all-embracing light, the infinite, unend-
> ing great light, whereas *the soul is the portion and a spark
> separated from the great light*. As King Solomon says, "the
> spirit of man is the candle of The Lord." He means to say
> that man's soul is a candle, a spark deriving from God's
> light.

Clearly Horowitz follows in the footsteps of his Kabbalah
predecessors: Cordovera, Vital, de Vidas and others. He is particularly noted for the special prominence he gives to the notion
of the "Divine Spark," placing it, as he does, at the very beginning of his chief book.

Horowitz was quite conscious of the provocative character of
his notion of Divinity residing in a human being as compromise
of God's total Oneness. And so he added a cautionary note to his
readers, warning them not to jump to conclusions about a complex and difficult theme. He proceeds to alter his view and states
that what he meant to say was that man's soul does not derive
from the *En Sof*—from God Himself—but from the *sefira* of wisdom.

To this Louis Jacobs reacts, asserting that the *sefira* doctrine
Horowitz invokes here comes perilously close to compromising
the absolute Oneness of God. This is because *the very emphasis of
the sefirot being at one with the* En Sof *imparts to them inherent*

divinity. Thus, to assert that the human soul's divinity stems from a *sefira* is asserting that it is rooted in the Godhead itself. [15] Indeed, Gershom Scholem asserts, "The *sefirot* of Jewish mystical theology have an existence of their own; they form combinations, they illuminate each other, they ascend and descend. They are far from being static. What we have here is something like a real process of life in God." Hence, to posit the independent character of such phenomena and at the same to see them as being one with the *En Sof*—the Divinity itself—is to posit independent phenomena as divine, and this appears to contravene the basic monotheistic doctrine. As we have indicated previously, Scholem sums up this perplexing issue:

> "The Zohar, indeed the whole of the Kabbalistic mystical ideology, reflects a very ancient heritage of the soul, and it would be too much to say that this mystical heritage has everywhere been successfully integrated into the doctrine of Monotheism."[16]

Shneur Zalman of Liadi (1745-1812 CE)

In Shneur Zalman, the founder of the Chabad movement within Hasidic Judaism, we encounter a highly developed theological system based on the notion of a "Divine Spark" in man. He relied especially on Hayyim Vital, the chief expounder of the Lurianic Kabbalah school. In his magnum opus, *The Tanya*, Shneur Zalman speaks of the two souls which every Jew possesses: the "animal soul" and the "Divine soul."[17] The animal soul is the vital source of his desires and appetites, and is constantly at war with the Divine soul, the portion of God within man.[18] Here is how he describes the Divine soul:

---

15. For Jacob's comments, see Shechter, Jack. *The Idea of Monotheism*, Hamilton Books, 2018; p. 126.
16. For Scholem's comments, see *Major Trends in Jewish Mysticism*. Schocken Books, 1941; p. 224-225.
17. Shneur Zalman. *The Tanya*. Kehot Publication Society, Ch. 2.
18. For more about the soul in the Jewish morning liturgy, see *Berakhot 60b*.

The second soul in Israel is an actual portion of God from above (*haylek Eloha mi-maal mammesh*), as it is said, "And He (God) breathed into his (man's) nostrils the soul (*neshama*) of life and man became a living being."[19] As the Zohar comments, "When one blows, it is from himself that he blows," that is to say, from his most inward essence for man ejects his most inward vitality when he blows powerfully.

In the same way the souls of Israel "ascended in God's thought" (i.e., were fashioned by God), as it is written "'Israel is my son, my first born,'"[20] and "You are children of The Lord your God."[21] This means that as the child derives from the "brain" (i.e., the semen) of the father so, as it were, the soul of every Jew is derived from God's thought and wisdom. *D'ihu hahim*, "For God is wise," and *Hu v'hahmato ehad*, "He and His wisdom are one," as Maimonides says: *Hu Hamada v'hu Hayodaya*, "He is the knowledge and the knower."[22]

This Tanya passage is referring to Maimonides' *Mishne Torah* 2:10 concerning the *Hilhot Yesoday Hatorah*, "The Laws Concerning the Fundamentals of the Torah." In the case of man, Maimonides asserts, what he knows is external to him; his knowledge and his life are separate elements. In the case of God, however, "He, His knowledge and His life are one from all sides and corners, in all manner of unity…Thus you could say: *Hu Hayodaya v'Hu Hayadua v'Hu Hadaya atzmah, hakol ehad,* "He is the knower, He is the subject of knowledge, and *He is the knowledge itself,* all is one. Now, Maimonides' purpose here was only to emphasize the total Oneness of the Deity in contrast to the plurality of man: *The Tanya, however, uses this passage for its own purposes, which is to stress that "wisdom" and "God" are one and the same. Thus when Shneur Zalman asserts that the soul stems from "wisdom," he is*

---

19. Genesis 2:7.
20. Exodus 4:22.
21. Deuteronomy 14: 1.
22. Shneur Zalman. *The Tanya.* Kehot Publication Society, Ch. 2.

asserting that the soul stems from God Himself.[23]

Shneur Zalman continues his thought line about the nature of wisdom. Such knowledge about God is difficult to comprehend. There are many gradations of souls:

> Nevertheless, the root of every soul, from the highest of all ranks to the lowest, all derive, as it were, from the Supreme Mind which is Heavenly wisdom. As in the illustration (if it is permitted to say this) of the child who stems from the brain (semen) of his father. Even the child's fingers and the nails are formed from the actual drop of brain (semen) which remains in the mother's womb for nine months, then descends from stage to stage until it changes so much that nails are formed, and yet it is still bound to and united with, in marvelous fashion, its first essence when it was part of the brain (semen) of the father...so it is with the root of men's souls: they remain bound and united with a wonderful and essential unity with their original essence and entity, namely the *Hohma Ila-ah*, the Heavenly Wisdom (God).[24]

And so, we conclude that, according to Shneur Zalman of Liadi, there is an actual portion of God in every human being.

Conscience

Another reading of the human psyche might well be understood as adumbrating a "Divine Spark" inhabiting the human being: viewing "conscience" from a religious perspective.

There appears that there is something, some factor *inside* man, that affects his attitudes and actions. Its concern is decisions about values, chiefly good and evil. It is generally thought of in

---

23. See *Mishne Torah*, Ch. 2, Law 10. This idea is also hinted at in Maimonides' *Guide for the Perplexed*, Vol. One, Ch. 68. See Scholem, Gershom. *Kabbalah*, "The Kabbalah and Pantheism." Dorset Press, 1987; p. 144-52, for a valuable survey of this subject—God in and out of the world and of mankind.
24. Shneur Zalman. *The Tanya*. Kehot Publication Society, Ch. 2.

a negative sense—a faculty that reminds us, by stimulating feelings of guilt and shame, that we are doing wrong. The troubled heart is a sign of conscience.

The term has been articulated in numerous ways by religionists of all persuasions. Thomas Aquinas: "Conscience is that which witnesses or binds, incites and accuses, stings and rebukes." Immanuel Kant: "There exists in the human psyche an *innate sense* of what is right or wrong." Martin Buber: "Conscience is *that court within the soul* which concerns itself with the distinction between what is good and what is not good." Milton Konvitz: "The heart of conscience is not a voice that speaks outside of man; rather, *it is an internal hearing agency so that man may listen to the voice of God.*"

Indeed, this is what the prophet Elijah experienced at Mount Horeb as the *Kol d'mama dakah*, "the still small voice" speaking to him when all alone, the silent voice reminding Elijah that he was in the presence of the Deity. It was not "the whirlwind, the earthquake, the fire"—external factors—that riveted the prophet's attention, but the voice of God within him telling him what he must do.[25] So, too, in the Unetaneh Tokef prayer in the High Holy Days liturgy, the shofar awakens the worshipper and urges him to "listen" to the "still small voice" urging him to change his ways.

And so, conscience is the Divine voice within a person which, when cultivated by religious action and focused thought, acts as a deterrent to bad behavior and/or as a stimulus for good behavior. George Santayana articulated this well when he said that a person's true self is revealed when he is all alone: would he/she be honest and aboveboard? How would one behave when he knows that no one is *watching*? This is what Jacob's father-in-law, Laban, had in mind when he said to Jacob, "May the Lord *watch* between you and me when we are out of sight of each other. If you ill treat my daughters or take other wives besides my daughters—*though no one else is about, remember, God Himself will be*

25. I Kings 19:11-12.

witness between you and me."[26]

Why does conscience work to nurture ethical behavior? Because *the matter in the end is between a person and his Maker. He stands ever in the presence of the Divine who is watching.* "For not a man sees (does God see); a man sees only what is visible, but *the Lord sees into the heart."*[27]

Here, then, is a phenomenon pointing in the direction of the Divine-in-human idea.

We have sought to trace the idea of a Divine Spark in man. Admittedly, the notion is unconventional in Jewish religious thought, but for all the emphasis in normative Judaism on the impassable gulf between the individual soul and God, this daring idea did emerge in some circles that the abyss had been bridged.

What are the Implications of the Notion that Divinity Resides in the Human Being?

We have depicted a highly charged idea found in a significant stream of Jewish thought concerning the place of the Deity in human life—the Divine Spark in man. Here we venture to explicate the implications of the idea that man harbors Divinity within his very being?

These can be discerned in the life of the individual as such, and as the individual relates to others.

The Significance of Self

When one is aware that Divinity is present within his very self, this inevitably confers on that person a sense of extraordinary self-worth. A person of faith sees God as possessing surpassing characteristics: He is merciful, compassionate, long-suffering, but also just and judgmental, stern and creative.[28] This means

---

26. Genesis 31:49-50.
27. I Samuel 16:7.
28. Exodus 34:6-7.

that these very characteristics lodge within the person, thus making him a persona of enormous quality and capacity.

Gershom Scholem points to the notion that if man is a "microcosm" of the Divinity—"a doctrine which found universal acceptance among the kabbalists"—then man is obviously capable of exerting influence on the world. "Indeed, it is this which bestows on him the enormous importance and dignity that the kabbalists went to great lengths to describe." It is because man alone was granted free will that he has the power to either advance or disrupt through his actions the enhancement of the unity of the world. "Man's essence is unfathomably profound." Even his physical structure is precious because it harbors God's likeness. This is why the body of a criminal condemned to death must he treated with reverence,[29] and Hillel taught that keeping one's own physical body clean is an act of reverence for its Creator.[30]

These affirmations about man's profound self-worth constitute the grounds for his role in the world. As Scholem articulates this mystical thought line, "Man's principle mission remained to bring about a *tikun* or restoration of this world, and to connect the lower with the upper, thereby 'crowning' creation by setting the Creator upon His throne and perfecting His reign over all His handiworks."[31]

Moreover, the awareness of Divinity within is the source of great inner satisfaction. An individual contemplating this phenomenon becomes profoundly conscious of the blessings Divinity in him confers. Thus, Abraham Isaac Kook avers:

> The greater you are, the more you need to search for yourself. Your deep soul hides itself from consciousness. So you need to increase aloneness, elevation of thinking, penetration of thought, liberation of mind—until finally your soul reveals itself to you, spangling a few sparkles of her light. There you find bliss, transcending all

---

29. Deuteronomy 21:23.
30. Leviticus Rabbah 34:3.
31. Scholem, Gershom. *Kabbalah*; p. 153.

humiliations or anything that happens. Then you gather everything, without hatred, jealousy, or rivalry. The light of peace and a fierce boldness manifest in you. The splendor of compassion and the glory of love shine through you. The desire to act and work, the passion to create and to restore yourself, the yearning for silence and for the inner shout of joy—these all band together in your spirit, and you become holy.[32]

Rav Kook echoed Isaac of Akko, the thirteenth century mystic, who wrote, "Whoever attains the mystery of cleaving to God will attain the mystery of equanimity."[33] And Abraham Abulafia, another influential mystic, similarly spoke about the deep personal satisfaction that awareness of Divinity within confers:

You feel an extra spirit arousing you, flowing over your entire body, bringing pleasure. It seems as if fine balsam oil has been poured over you from your head to your feet—once, maybe more. You are overjoyed, in delight and trembling: the soul in delight, the body in trembling.[34]

The Significance of Others

If a person is aware that Divinity abides within a human being as such—within all human beings—as a fundamental aspect of their nature, it follows that he must treat with honor the Divinity both he and others harbor. Why? Because he is obliged to honor Divinity as such—a basic obligation for a man of faith; thus the principle: man must treat his fellow man with reverence and respect.

This is a conception of far-reaching importance in Jewish

---

32. *Orot Hakodesh* 3:270 as per Matt, Daniel Chanan. *The Essential Kabbalah: The Heart of Jewish Mysticism.* Harper-Collins Publishers, 1995; p. 124.
33. Ibid; p. 118; Maimonides, Moses. *Meirat Einayim,* 1753; p. 218.
34. Abulafia, Abraham ben Samuel. *Otsar Eden Ganuz.* Amnor Gros, 2000; see Idel, "The Mystical Experience in Abraham Abulafia." p. 188, as per Matt, Ibid., p. 111.

thought. *Reverence for God is shown via reverence for man.* The fear one must feel of offending or hurting another must be as of ultimate importance as one's fear of God for Divinity inheres in that other. An act of violence against an innocent other is a desecration of the Divinity within the violated. To be arrogant toward another person is to be blasphemous toward God: "He who oppresses the poor blasphemes his Maker. He who is gracious to the needy honors Him."[35] The Midrash stresses: "You must not say, since I have been put to shame, let my neighbor be put to shame, for in the likeness of God He (God) made that neighbor.[36] The Rabbis teach that he who sheds the blood of another human being is considered as though he diminished the Divinity.[37]

Martin Buber illustrates this dictum via two examples in Scripture. Cain and David both murdered (David—indirectly—"slew Uriah the Hittite via the sword"[38]), and both are called to account by God. Cain attempts evasion: "Am I my brother's keeper?" He is a man who shuns the dialogue with God. Not so David, who answers, "I have sinned against The Lord."[39] This is the true answer, says Buber: whomever one becomes guilty against, in truth, becomes guilty against God.[40]

---

35. Proverbs 14:31.
36. Genesis Rabbah 24:7.
37. Mekhilta to Exodus 20:16.
38. 2 Samuel 12:9.
39. Cain: Genesis 4:9; David: 2 Samuel 12:13.
40. Buber, Martin. *On Judaism.* Schocken Books, 1996; p. 220.

– Three –

WHEN *IS GOD IN OUR MIDST?*

וַיִּבְרָא אֱלֹהִים אֶת־הָאָדָם בְּצַלְמוֹ בְּצֶלֶם
אֱלֹהִים בָּרָא אֹתוֹ זָכָר וּנְקֵבָה בָּרָא אֹתָם

And God created man in His image, in the image of God He created him; male and female He created them.

—Genesis 1:27

In our previous essay, "The Divinity in Man" (#2), we pointed to the notion held by some that Divinity in inherent in the human being. Which is to say that man by nature harbors a drive for genuine faith and positive spiritual action motored, as it were, by a "Divine Spark." However, according to another perspective on the matter in Jewish religious sources, there is the idea of a "Divine Image": man's disposition for faith and positive religious action which is *not* innate. Rather, such a disposition must be actively cultivated by man himself by the way he acts. Thus to assert that man was created in God's image essentially means that he has the *capacity and potential* to be a reflection of Divinity by the way he conducts his life in the world of the here and now. The Midrash[1] explains the Prophet Isaiah's proclamation (43:12), "You are my witnesses, saith the Lord, and I am God" this way: "If you are my witnesses, I am God, but if you are not my witnesses, then I am not."

What follows seeks to elucidate such active cultivation and the earnest intention it requires.

---

1. *Sifri Deuteronomy* 33:5.

The Divine Image

There is a major biblical concept that appears to parallel the Divine Spark in man we have depicted. In Genesis 1:27 we hear, "And God created man in His image, in the image of God He created him; male and female He created them." Now the two notions—the Divine Spark (*nitzutz*) and the Divine Image (*zelem*)—are manifestly different. The former denotes Divinity intrinsic to man, inherent in the human being (though, to be sure, it can be diminished by man's evil behavior). *The latter—the Divine Image—is conferred on man by man himself via his own actions.* Gershom Scholem stressed the point of their dissimilarity. He indicates that unlike the Divine Spark, the *zelem* is developed by the practical efforts of man. Scholem quotes the mystical way Moses de Leon, the author of the Zohar, makes this point: "The purpose of the *zelem* in man is to exhibit its powers and abilities in the world. When it descends into this world it receives, via man's own actions, power to guide this vile world and to undergo a *tikkun* of "the above and the below," for it is of high rank. *And when it is in this world, it perfects itself, which was not the case in the beginning before its descent.*"[2]

How Does One Demonstrate His/Her Being an "Image of God"? By Imitating His Ways.

This is the import of the regnant dictum Moses was instructed to convey to the people: "You shall be holy for I, The Lord, your God, am holy."[3] This means that man's holiness is acquired via imitation of God's ways. Thus when the Midrash speaks of "walking in God's ways," it is averring that just as God is called merciful so are you to be merciful; and just as God is compassionate, so are you to be compassionate.[4] To act as God acts in mercy and love, Dr. Heschel observes, is the way to reflect God's

---

2. Scholem, Gershom. *Kabbalah*, p. 159.
3. Leviticus 19:2.
4. Sifre to Deuteronomy 11:22.

likeness within the human actor.[5] *Man becomes what he worships:* "Says the Holy One, Blessed be He, he who acts like Me shall be like Me." Says Rabbi Levi ben Hama, "Idolators resemble their idols (Psalm 115:8); how much more must the servants of The Lord resemble Him."[6] Maimonides in his code, the Mishna Torah, observes that the reason God is called by the prophets "long suffering," "merciful," "righteous," upright," etc. (Exodus 34:5-7) is so that man is to replicate these qualities in his life with the result that *he becomes actually God-like.*[7]

And yet, Heschel observes,[8] God's likeness may be—alas, very often is—defiled and distorted. Man must recognize and preserve this likeness but he fails. The consequence: "I have placed the likeness of My Image in them and through their sins I have upset it," God declares.[9] But there is hope. The Midrash interprets the verse in Deuteronomy 1:10 as if it were written, "Lo, today you are like the stars of heaven, but in the future you will resemble the Master."[10] *The likeness is broken, but it is not utterly destroyed. Man retains the potential to reflect God's image.*

When Does One Become an Image of God?

Scripture relates that the patriarch Abraham and his household had just undergone circumcision. This was a sign of the covenant between him and his descendants and God for all time. It was a bond between the Hebrews with the Power that governs the universe, along with a pledge later undertaken by Abraham's descendants to a life of faith, a life characterized by morality and justice It was a bond Abraham affirmed when he performed the circumcision rite; Genesis 18:1 then tells us, "And the Lord appeared to him by the oaks of the Mamre as he sat by the opening of the tent in the heat of the day." Both Rashi and Nakhmanides

---

5. Heschel, Abraham Joshua. *Man's Quest for God*; p. 126.
6. Deuteronomy Rabbah 1:10.
7. Hilchot Deot 1:16.
8. Heschel, Abraham Joshua. *Man's Quest for God*; p. 127.
9. Talmud, *Moed Katan*, 15b.
10. Deuteronomy Rabbah 1:10.

link God's appearances to Abraham with the patriarch's act of circumcision. Nakhmanides put it this way:

> The Torah narrates that the Lord appeared to Abraham
> while he was still recovering from his circumcision in or-
> der to inform us that no prophetic revelation was here in-
> volved. Abraham did not fall on his face or pray. Never-
> theless this vision was vouchsafed to him purely as a
> mark of honor to him.[11]

Take note: the sage is telling us that God usually appears to a
person in the Bible with a message, a blessing, a promise, a demand. Not here. He just appears at this particular juncture. God
appeared in Abraham's midst *when* the effort and sacrifice involved in carrying out the rite of circumcision took place. *The Divine is activated when human beings themselves perform acts of high
purpose.* Indeed, Abraham had just connected his people to an exalted cause; he committed them to a life of exemplary living via
the deed of circumcision *and it was at that point that God appeared to
him.* It is at that point that Abraham reflected God's image.

In the same passage we hear of Abraham sitting at the door of
his tent extending warm hospitality to three strangers who appeared nearby. We then read that *at that point* God appeared to
Abraham with no demands; He came to him because a person
reached out to help his fellowman. The Zohar remarks about the
three men who came to Abraham "in the heat of the day:"

> When the world below is ablaze with desire for the world
> above, the upper world will descend to the lower, and
> both will unite and permeate each other in man.[12]

Nakhmanides cites additional examples of this phenomenon:

- Moses and Aaron had led the Israelites through much difficulty and turmoil, instructed them in the appropriate
  rites of their faith with patience and precision, whereupon
  Leviticus 9:23 tells us: "And Moses and Aaron went into

---

11. Commentary to Genesis 18:1.
12. Buber, Martin. *On Judaism.* Schocken Books, 1996; p. 80-81.

the tent of meeting; and when they came out they blessed the people, and the glory of the Lord appeared to all the people." God's revelation is here accompanied by no message or command; *His presence is felt because of the quality of behavior on the part of Israel's leaders.*

- Genesis 32:2 tells how Jacob had just made peace with his father-in-law, Laban. Then as they were about to part we're told: "And the angel of God appeared to him (Jacob)." No message, no promise is delivered. *God met a person here because that person made peace with another.*

The holiest item in the ancient sanctuary was the Ark. It contained the most sacred of objects—the tablets on which were written God's words. Above the Ark were two figures, cherubim. The Torah says that "their faces were turned to one another."[13] The sages interpret the meaning of the posture of these figures as lovers intertwined.[14] And it was *between the two cherubs* that God spoke to Moses. The message: God speaks *where and when two persons turn their faces to one another in love,* and embrace generosity and care. God's presence is, of course, everywhere, but not everybody is ready to receive it. When we open our "I" to another who is "thou," that is where God is present, where He speaks, where He lives.

The poet Jiri Langer tells that when he was a youngster he initially thought that the two square dots in the siddur indicating the conclusion of a thought were the monogram for God's name. His teacher told him: "no, no, Urele, that does not mean the name of God. Only when there are two sitting nicely side by side, where one looks on the other as an equal—*only there is the name of God;*

---

13. Exodus 25:30. Note: It needs to be noted that the images of physical creatures in a place of worship had to be a risky matter given Scripture's prohibition of such. Yet to this day still, even in some of the most orthodox synagogues (including the one in which I grew up), the Ark contains two lion figures facing each other usually with tablets of the ten commandments in between.

14. Yoma 54a.

where one is under the other and the other is raised higher—there the word of God is not.

Rabbi Meir used to say the Holy one calls us, saying: Guard your mouth from all transgression, purify and sanctify yourself from fault and iniquity, and *if you do so, I, God, will be with you everywhere.*[15]

A midrash: The Holy One said to Israel: What do I seek of you? All I ask is that you love one another, and honor one another, and respect one another, and that there be found in you neither transgression nor theft nor anything ugly, so that you do not become tainted. As it is said:…*walk humbly with your God.* Read it this way: *Walk humbly, and your God will be with you.*[16]

The rabbis taught: there are three partners in every person, the Holy One Blessed be He, the father and the mother. When a person honors his father and his mother, the Holy One Blessed Be He says, "I view them as though I had dwelt among them and they had honored Me."[17]

Conclusion

Divinity within a person is activated by man's own actions.

Martin Buber confirms this perspective inherent in the Bible. According to Buber, it is in the earnest intention and high quality of a person's worldly deeds that he experiences communion with God. God is an unknown being beyond the world only for the indolent, the decisionless, the lethargic, the man enmeshed in his own designs:

> *For the man who chooses, who decides, who is aflame with his goal, God is the closest, the most familiar being, who man through his action realizes ever anew, experiencing thereby the mystery of mysteries.*[18]

---

15. Berakhot 17a.
16. Micah 6:8.
17. Kiddushin 30b.
18. Buber, Martin. *On Judaism.* Schocken Books, 1996; p. 81.

– Four –

WHAT MAKES THE LAND OF ISRAEL "HOLY?"

A significant facet of study about the sanctity of space has projected the notion that the "holiness" of concrete place is a cultic one with mythological characteristics: God Himself lives in the land, as it were, and it is that which renders it "holy." It is inherently so. Another facet of study about the subject views it differently: it is human beings' "holy action" which renders sanctity to land. That is, man's behavior on the land in response to divine moral and religious dicta is the determining factor. Land is not inherently holy. It is conferred on by religiously faithful human beings.

This essay explores the twofold dynamic and various issues that flow from it.

CONTENTS

b) Biblical Historical Factors

c) Biblical "Strategic" Factors

d) Rabbinic Perspectives

e) Anthropological and Psychological Perspectives

f) The Role of Memory

I. ON INHERENT HOLINESS

a) The Cultic Element in the Bible

This notion has mythological characteristics. It conceives divinity itself as dwelling within a specific locale. Because God is holy, His presence generates sanctity. Thus the land is holy and must, therefore, be maintained unmarred and undefiled out of reverence for God's presence (כָּבוֹד). God's territorial base is on earth—specifically on Mount Zion in Jerusalem as the site of His temple, "His abode" (בֵּית הִי) in the land.[1] The prophet Isaiah declared: וָאֶרְאָה אֶת אֲדֹנָי יֹשֵׁב עַל כִּסֵּא רָם וְנִשָּׂא וְשׁוּלָיו מְלֵאִים אֶת הַהֵיכָל, "I beheld my Lord seated on a high and lofty throne, and the skirts of His robe filled the Temple."[2] The survivor in Lamentations 2:1 is grief-stricken over the Babylonian destruction of Judean sovereignty and the defilement of God's Temple and cries out: וְלֹא זָכַר הֲדֹם רַגְלָיו בְּיוֹם אַפּוֹ, "He did not remember 'His footstool' on the day of His wrath." God consents to being met by His people at the physical tent of meeting at Shilo and Shechem. King Solomon invites the Lord to dwell on earth: בֵּית זְבֻל לָךְ מָכוֹן לְשִׁבְתְּךָ עוֹלָמִים, "in a stately house, a place where You may dwell forever."[3]

---

1. Isaiah 2:2 and Micah 4:1.
2. Isaiah 6:1.
3. I Kings 8:13, also see Orlinsky, Harry. "The Biblical Concept of the Land of Israel: Cornerstone of the Covenant Between God and Israel," in *The Land of Israel: Jewish Perspectives,* ed. L.A. Hoffman. University of Notre Dame Press, 1986; p. 52-53.

According to this perspective, the land is conceived of as holy irrespective of any human activity on it or experience with it. It has a life of its own, as it were. It is forcefully and vividly personified, as in Leviticus 20:22-26, which portrays the land as itself ejecting the Israelites when they are unfaithful to the commandments. Implicit in this is the notion of the place itself in action, that the Lord Himself inhabits it and causes the action. This is the import of Numbers 35:34: "You shall not defile the land in which you live, *in the midst of which I dwell*" (אֲשֶׁר אֲנִי שֹׁכֵן בְּתוֹכָה). Harvey Cox has described this notion that views nature as semi-divine:

> Pre-secular man lives in an enchanted forest. Its glens and groves swarm with spirits. Its rocks and streams are alive with friendly and fiendish demons. Reality is charged with mystical power that erupts here and there to threaten or benefit man.[4]

When a number of scriptural passages emphasize the centralization of the sacrificial liturgy, limiting it to one shrine only, they phrase the rationale for the move in terms of the presence of God there. Hence, even when the Hebrews were in exile in Persia, they prayed in the direction of Jerusalem in the hope that their supplications would he heard by the deity there.[5] In this way, Jerusalem retained its sanctity regardless of whether the Temple was standing and regardless of whether the supplicant was there physically. The city is thus sacred because God is present there; it is His "abode," His "throne," His "footstool," "the place where He dwells forever."[6]

---

4. Cox, Harvey. *The Secular City: Secularization and Urbanization in Theological Perspective*. Princeton University Press, 2013; p. 19
5. Daniel 6:11.
6. For a detailed exposition of the *Shekhina*, God's presence in special places on earth found in pervasive form in biblical and rabbinic literature, see Crim, Keith and Buttrick, George. *Interpreter's Dictionary of the Bible*. Abingdon Press, 1981; p. 317–319.

b) The Cultic Notion in the General Atmosphere

The conception of the deity dwelling in specific places has its analogues in non-Israelite cultures around the world. This appears to indicate that the notion was part of the Israelite religious mindset and practice in common with other religionists. It would seem, therefore, that embrace of the notion stemmed from shared human religious impulses and concepts of the deity. To cite but a few examples:

Greece

Vincent Scully in his monumental *The Earth, the Temple, and the Gods* has summarized the results of his studies about ancient Greek temples:

> I tried to show that all important Greek sanctuaries grew up around open altars which were normally sited where they are because *the place itself first suggested the presence of the divine being. Indeed, its natural forms were regarded as embodying that presence.* The Temple when finally built embodied it also, now in terms of the human conception of the divinity. Between the two kinds of shapes a fundamental counterplay developed, seen most richly in the late archaic and classic periods, which created an architectural balance of tensions between the natural and the man-made.

Scully explains that the core reason for these locales being considered hallowed was because they were favorable to the contemplation of the sky, which was an essential component of religious experience. Thus he proceeded to explore "the holiness of the earth" in his work, quoting a Homeric hymn: "well-founded earth, mother of all, eldest of all beings, Mother of the Gods, wife of starry Heaven."[7]

---

7. Scully, Vincent. *The Earth, the Temple, and the Gods: Greek Sacred Architecture.* Trinity University Press, 2013; Ch. 1, p. 8. See also "Scholar Theorizes on Pyramid Sighting." *Los Angeles Times*, 11 Dec. 1983. It speaks of natural locales such as mountain peaks and manmade objects such as

René Dubos supports Scully's thesis about the sanctity of place in his examination of the subject:

> Canterbury Cathedral, which was built on the site of a pre-Saxon monument, became a Christian shrine which has remained a focus of English life ever since. The same can be said, of course, for all the important religious and ceremonial sites of Asia and Europe—the hallowed places which in French are appropriately designated *hauts lieux* of civilization. The sanctity of place is as old as man's association with the caves of Altamira and Lascaux. Christianity never displaced completely the religion of nature; rather it built its own temples on sites where worship had been practiced from time immemorial.[8]

This phenomenon also obtained with regard to the local Israelite shrines in the land, those in Shechem, Shilo, Gilgal et al., which were originally sacred sites among previous pagan worshippers. This accounts for Deuteronomy's proscription of these places in favor of centralizing worship in Jerusalem as we have pointed out above.

Peru

In a report titled "Their Gods Resided There," published in the *Los Angeles Times*, we're told that more than twenty Inca sites on mountaintops in the Peruvian Andes were discovered during a four-year period by Johan Reinhard, an American anthropologist and mountain climber. The Incas who labored up these

---

the ziggurats in the Bible's tower of Babel episode. These have regularly stimulated the human imagination to view them as points of connection with the transcendent. Hans Goedicke, the internationally known Egyptologist, reflected the notion in terms of the Egyptian pyramids. "They are the only buildings," he said, "that have never disappointed me. The pyramid is the most perfect monument you can build. The amazing thing is that when you stand in front of it and look up toward the peak, it gives you the illusion of a road leading to the infinite."

8. Dubos, Rene Jules. *A God Within.* C. Scribners Sons, 1983; p. 118.

mountains, some higher than twenty-thousand feet, *were wor-shipping the mountains and the gods that they believed dwelled in and on them.*

At least fifty such mountaintops with Inca ruins, remains and artifacts indicative of active worship have been found on peaks from southern Peru to central Chile:

> The Incas and even peoples of the Andes before them thought the mountain gods determined the weather and controlled the springs, rivers and underground water sources vital to their harvests and animals. Offerings and sacrifices—sometimes human—made in the sacred places on the peaks were attempts to assure good weather, adequate rainfall and abundance of crops and herds.

Reinhard proceeds to document this mountain deity worship on the famous Machu Picchu and far beyond. *All the peaks in view were considered sacred by the Incas and are still revered by their Peruvian descendants today.*

The sacred *inti huatana* stone, long thought to be a sort of sundial, stands in the center of the complex surrounded by four sacred mountains. "I believe the stone had little to do with the sun," says Reinhard. "It probably represented, and was worshiped as, a major mountain deity in the region."

Present-day offerings to the mountain gods are made far beyond Machu Picchu. People in the Andes still sacrifice such things as coca leaves, grain, textiles and llamas to the deities. Just as in Inca times, ceremonies include ritual drinking and communal meals, followed by dancing and singing. Llama is a popular main course when it is used as part of the offering.

Human sacrifices may also still take place. In 1942 and 1945, children reportedly were sacrificed in Peru to prevent a drought. Villagers in the central part of the country still talk about human sacrifices from time to time, especially when a major tunnel or road that might anger the gods is being built.

On various summits, Reinhard has found grain, textiles and coca leaves used in Inca rituals. But the most unusual things he found were small human-like statues fashioned from Pacific Ocean seashells and outfitted with perfectly woven textile clothing. The Incas valued the red and white shells more than gold and considered them indispensable in ceremonies calling for rain.

Most impressive were the ruins of buildings and altar platforms on many of the peaks, some with walls five feet thick and sixteen feet long. On Chile's Llullaillaco, at 22,057 feet, one of the highest volcanoes and archaeological sites on earth, Reinhard found stone buildings, collapsed roofing, bits of ceramics, pieces of textile, firewood and a sacrificial altar. To build the altar on top of the Las Tórtolas in Chile, Reinhard estimates that at least four thousand baskets of gravel had to be carted fifteen hundred feet. Priests and their assistants were probably responsible for the building and maintenance of the lofty sites. They regularly scaled peaks more than twenty thousand feet high in leather sandals.[9]

Kenya

In another report, titled "Kenyan Home of God is Melting," we're told that from a tree-shaded plateau facing Mount Kenya the worshippers gaze anxiously at its melting ice cap and wonder: is God dead? The melting has been causing serious environmental devastation.

For those Kenyans who still practice tribal religions and revere Mount Kenya as the home of god, the environmental alterations have triggered a crisis of faith.

"This is where God lives and it is being destroyed," said one older Kenyan whose community continues to make sacrifices to the deity they believe resides on Mt. Kenya. He worries that the disappearing ice is a sign of God's

---

9. *Los Angeles Times.* April 15, 1984; p. 8.

fury. "God is very angry, and if things don't change, I fear he might abandon us forever."

The report goes on to describe the reasons for Mount Kenya having become a sacred place, and the forms of worship and sacrifice to the god who inhabited the place in the long past and into the present.

It's no surprise that Kenya's earliest settlers revered Mount Kenya. Shrouded in mist and covered year-round with a blinding carpet of snow, the mountain inspired awe and legend from every tribe that laid eyes on it. Scholars date the oral traditions surrounding Mount Kenya back as far as five hundred years, when tribes such as the Kikuyu and Meru arrived in the region. Life and worship centered on the mountain. They prayed facing Mount Kenya and oriented their homes toward the peak. Sacrificial animals were positioned to face the mountain before slaughter.

When he was a boy, said retired Catholic priest Joaquim Gitonga, seventy-six, everyone here in the village of Muranga marveled at the mysterious source of Mount Kenya's white tips. Living on the equator, no one in the village had any concept of ice or snow, so they assumed the brilliant white peaks were a sign of the mountain's divine nature.

Though how much of Mount Kenya's forest cover was lost is unclear, a 1999 Kenya Wildlife Service survey observed nearly twenty thousand acres of freshly logged terrain. Today around the base of Mount Kenya, stumps are nearly as common as trees. "This is a sin against God," said John Irungu, a local farmer who helps maintain a shrine where the first Kikuyus were believed to have settled.[10]

During a months-long period of drought a sacrificial goat was led to a bed of leaves at one of the shrines. One of the elders sang a prayer and the worshippers raised their hands toward the mountain. Before slaughter, the animal's head was gently

---

10. *Los Angeles Times*. November 10, 2009; p. 20.

positioned toward the mountain as a local prophetess in a multicolored headscarf predicted quick success. "It will rain," she said. "That I know. God is in this place."

As the service ended and worshippers drifted back to their homes, the sky was dear and blue. Weeks later, worshipers were still waiting for rain, and for God, their eyes turned hopefully toward the distant peak.

Bahrain

In 1983, a four-thousand-year-old temple was discovered on the island state of Bahrain, located off the coast of Saudi Arabia. The temple was described as the greatest monument of the ancient Dilmun civilization. According to the archaeologist Helmuth Andersen of Denmark, who supervised the excavation, the temple was believed to be dedicated to one of the three principle Sumerian deities — *Enki, the water-dwelling god of wisdom.*

A chamber for sacrifices to the god containing a central altar was located. Adjacent to it was a flight of carved steps leading down to Enki's pool, a deep stone-walled well built over one of the numerous underground springs of which Enki was also the god and *where he was believed to live.*

In these springs, which still supply contemporary Bahrain with much of its drinking water, lies one of the cornerstones of the Dilmun civilization. "With bounteous supplies of water from beneath the rock," Andersen said, "Bahrain was in ancient times an oasis of fertility in an otherwise desolate region. It was thus natural that the god ruling this vital source of water should be the principle deity of the Dilmun people."[11]

Mountains: Sinai and Zion

To return to the specific instance of Mount Zion as sacred and hence the city of Jerusalem as such. The sense of the presence of

---

11. "Laborers Discover Ancient Temple Site," *Los Angeles Times*, April 17, 1983.

the Deity in a direct way at this place is reflected in two Psalms in particular:

> The Lord is great and much acclaimed in the city of our God, *His holy mountain—fair-crested*, joy of all the earth, Mount Zion, *summit of Zaphon*, the city of *the great king. Through its citadels*, God has made himself known as a haven.[12]

Nahum Sarna explains "His holy mountain" to mean chosen by God as the place where the immediacy of His presence is to be most intensely experienced. Mount Zion as "fair-crested" as an image of a mountain rising to great height. Though hardly such in physical reality, the poetic phrase conveys the notion that this mountain is sacred because it is conceived to be a channel of communication between the world of the divine and the world of human beings. The designation of Zion as the "summit of Zaphon" is a place name which sees it as an equivalent to Mount Olympus, the special abode of the highest gods of Greek mythology, and hence Mount Zion as the abode of the God of Israel. As to the "city of the great King," this is a term for a sovereign in the language of the ancient Near East, a title reserved exclusively for the gods. Hence, the Deity in this Psalm is the God of Zion.[13]

And, Jon Levenson, in a striking interpretation of the phrase "through the citadels God made Himself known as a haven," sees it as a *visual* medium of God's revelation. It was the very sight of the temple in which the Deity resides that repelled Israel's foes.[14]

Note also Psalm 87 which Theodor Gaster re-translates as reflecting his understanding of the Psalm's meaning:

> It is the structure which *He Himself reared upon the holy*

---

12. Psalm 48: 2-4 (emphasis added).
13. Sarna, Nahum M. *On the Book of Psalms: Exploring the Prayers of Ancient Israel.* Schocken Books, 1995; p. 155-157.
14. Levenson, Jon Douglas. *Sinai & Zion: An Entry into the Jewish Bible.* Harper San Francisco, 1987; p. 149-151.

mountain. Yahweh loves the gates of Zion more than all of Jacob's dwellings. Glorious words apply to You, "City of God," (verses 1-3)…When it comes to Zion…He, yes *He, a heavenly being, it is that founded it* (verse 5) (emphasis added).[15]

The notion that the divine had actually built a temple which the god inhabited existed in biblical Israel's general environment. Egyptian temples, for example, were commonly held to have been designed by the gods. A Babylonian hymn to Enlil of Nippur hails him as the builder of his local shrine. Ishtar is said to have fashioned one of her major shrines in Nineveh. The Muslim tradition holds that the Kaaba, the sacred enclosure at Mecca was planned by the angels. And Exodus 15:7 speaks of "the place, O Yahweh, which You have made for Your abode, the sanctuary which Your own hands have established."

Now, according to both Gaster and Mircae Eliade, the "holy mountain" which God Himself reared is for a "heavenly being who founded it."[16] The Deity's presence on Mount Zion as per Psalm 48 contains a subtle but compelling allusion and is charged with deeper thought. What the Psalmists are really saying is that the habitation of God on Zion is the earthly counterpart of the glorious "mansion" which the Divine overlord is said to have built for Himself on the holy hill.

The comparison reflects a basic tenet of all ancient thought: things on earth correspond to things in heaven. The real has its counterpart in the ideal. What is on earth is a reproduction of a transcendent model. Thus the earthly cities of Babylon, Ashur and Susa were recognized in the constellations. During the Han period in China, popular thought traced an equivalent of the city in the stars. Jewish literature is replete with the "Jerusalem on High" counterpart of the "Jerusalem Below" which will eventually come down to earth.

---

15. Gaster, Theodor. *Myth, Legend and Customs in the Old Testament*. Harper Row, 1969; p. 766-768.
16. Psalms 97.

What is true of cities held good also for temples. Hammurabi says that the temple at Sippar corresponded to the one in heaven, and the same is affirmed concerning Esagila, the great temple of Marduk in Babylon. As for the people of Israel, the same concept prevailed; thus the models for the temple, the tabernacle, the sacred utensils, had been created by Yahweh who revealed them to His people, to be reproduced on earth.[17]

Mircae Eliade depicts this phenomenon:

> The Lord says to Moses: "And let them make me a sanctuary; that I may dwell among them. According to all that I show you after the pattern of the tabernacle, and the pattern of all the instruments thereof, even so shall you make it" (Exodus 25:8-9). "And look that you make them after their pattern, which was showed you in the mount" (Exodus 25:40). When David gives his son Solomon the plans for the Temple buildings, the tabernacle, and all the utensils, he assures him that "all this…the Lord made me understand in writing by his hand upon me" (II Chronicles 28:19). He must, then, have seen the celestial model created by Yahweh from the beginning of time. This is what Solomon affirms: "You have commanded me to build a temple upon your holy mount, and an altar in the city wherein you dwell, a resemblance of the holy tabernacle which you have prepared from the beginning" (Wisdom of Solomon 9:8).[18]

As for Heavenly Jerusalem itself, this: it was created by God at the very beginning of time, hence an ideal Holy city—ideal because it was not yet blemished by man, holy because God fashioned it. The earthly city of Jerusalem is its counterpart, a replication of it, if you like. To be sure, the latter was but an

---

17. Gaster, Theodor. *Myth, Legend, and Custom in the Old Testament.* Harper and Row; 1969, p. 766-768.
18. Eliade, Mircea. *Mystic Stories: The Sacred and the Profane.* East European Monographs, 1992; p. 60.

approximate reproduction of its transcendent model[19]; it could be—and was—polluted by man, but its model was incorruptible, permanently sacred for it was not involved in time. Hence something of this permanent sanctity is shared by its earthly counterpart. Jerusalem is thus a "holy city" in the full sense of the term.[20]

Finally, rabbinic literature has long recorded the normative Jewish theological vision of the future Jerusalem. Psalm 122:3 avers: "Jerusalem, built up, a city united together means the day will come when the earthly and heavenly Jerusalem will be fully united as one."[21]

c) The Dominant Biblical and Rabbinic Perspectives Which Differ from the Cultic

Notwithstanding all of the above data, careful analysis of Scripture and rabbinic literature reveals a dominant notion contrary to the cultic one. Gerhardt von Rad has emphasized that though the cultic notion of sanctity of the land informs much of the Pentateuchal legislation, "it nowhere appears in the Hexateuchal (i.e. the Five books plus Joshua) narrative on anything like on equal footing with the dominating historical perception." This also is the view of Yehezkel Kaufmann concerning the Hebrew Bible's general attitude about paganism that Israel encountered in its territory. Paganism's cultic character, which pictured the deity in mythic terms, gave way in Israel to the historical conception of the deity, which notion Kaufmann saw "as sovereign and self-sufficient."[22]

God's Name—Not God Himself

Indeed, the cultic notion is strongly negated by evidence in the

---

19. 2 *Barukh* 4:3-7.
20. Eliade, Mircea. *Mystic Stories: The Sacred and the Profane*. East European Monographs, 1992; p. 61.
21. Taanit 5a.
22. Rad, Gerhard von. *The Problem of the Hexateuch: and Other Essays*. SCM Press, 1984; p. 68f. For Kaufman on this, see Levenson, *Jon D. Sinai & Zion: An Entry into the Jewish Bible*. Harper San Francisco, 1987; p. 111.

book of Deuteronomy. Discomfort with localizing the Lord in Jerusalem and the temple is manifest. In times of religious syncretism when the exclusiveness of "the Lord" was called into being, Deuteronomy emphasized a program of strict concentration on a pure notion of the deity. Here we meet with striking statements about the Lord's name. *The Lord put his name* at the one place of Israel's worship, that he might "dwell" there:

- Look only to the site that the Lord your God will choose amidst all your tribes as His habitation, to establish His *name* there (12:5).

- Then you must bring every thing I command you to the site where the Lord your God will choose to establish His *name* (12:11).

- If the place where the Lord has chosen to establish His *name* is too far for you, you may eat (of your offerings) to your heart's content in your settlements (12:21).

In numerous other passages both in Deuteronomy and those reflecting the Deuteronomic influence, we hear the same emphasis on God's name—*not God Himself*—dwelling in a place. Examples: II Samuel 7:13, 1 Kings 5:19, 1 Kings 9:3, II Kings 21:4, II Kings 23:27, Jeremiah 7:12, II Chronicles 33:4. The Lord Himself is in heaven (Deut. 26:15), but His name "lives" at the place of worship.

According to von Rad, Deuteronomy is obviously attacking the older and more popular idea of the Lord's immediate presence at the place of worship and is substituting for it the theological differentiate between the Lord on the one hand and His name on the other, a severance that is carried through to the point of spatial separation.[23]

The notion of locating God in a specific place is further negated by other evidence in Deuteronomy's text. The second commandment (Deuteronomy 5:8) implies more than the prohibition

---

23. von Rad, Gerhard. *Old Testament Theology*. Harper & Row; 1965, p. 184.

of images; it implies rejection of all visible symbols of God, of the tendency to believe that He can be experienced physically in a particular place. Abraham Joshua Heschel has put it this way:

> The fundamental insight that God is not and cannot be localized in a thing was emphatically expressed at a moment in which it could have easily been forgotten: at the inauguration of the Temple in Jerusalem. At that moment, Solomon exclaimed: "But will God in very truth dwell on earth? Behold, heaven and the heaven of heavens cannot contain Thee…how much less this house that I have built!" (I Kings 8:27). God manifested Himself in events rather than things.[24]

Further, dominant Deuteronomy forcefully proclaims God's transcendence. In the worshipper's confession of obedience as he offers a tithe in his own locale he prays:

הַשְׁקִיפָה מִמְּעוֹן קָדְשְׁךָ מִן הַשָּׁמַיִם וּבָרֵךְ אֶת עַמְּךָ אֶת יִשְׂרָאֵל

Look down from Your holy habitation, from heaven, and bless your people Israel and the land which You gave to us, as You swore to our ancestors, a land flowing with milk and honey (26:15).

God does not dwell on the earth but in heaven; He views the earth and people from on high with His blessings and promises.

When in Deuteronomy 4:7 the people are told that their God is forever close, (i.e. "For what great nation is there that has a God as close at hand as is the Lord Our God whenever we call upon Him"), this means that such closeness is not physical but the result of man reaching out to Him *whenever* man does so, and from *wherever* he does so. Thus when Israel dwells in a strange land, she does not lose her relationship with God. In Deuteronomy 4:9 we read: "If you search *there* for the Lord your God, you will find Him, if only you seek Him with all your heart and soul."

---

24. Heschel, Abraham Joshua and Ruth Goodhill (translation). *The Wisdom of Heschel*. Farrar, Straus & Giroux, p. 240.

In classic rabbinical literature, as well, we find strong resistance to view God in spatial terms. Indeed, Rabbi Akiba did so when he averred that the Shekhina abides in the west, its preferred locale, the west possessing special sanctity being the abode of the Divine Presence.[25] However, it was Rabbi Ishmael who asked, "Is it possible for mortals to enshrine their Maker?" He rejected the notion that God's Presence could be spatially bound; rather "the Shekhina is everywhere."[26] That the Shekhina transcends space is similarly emphasized by Rabbi Yosi ben Halafta who said, "The Holy One is the place of the universe, but the universe is not His place."[27]

The desire to purge the notion of Divine Presence of its spatial connotations is reflected and highlighted in several sayings of the school of Rabbi Ishmael:

> You find that whenever Israel is enslaved, the Shekhina is with them, as it says, "In all their troubles, God is troubled" (Isaiah 63:9). This refers only to communal suffering. Where do we learn about individual distress? From the verse, "When he calls on Me, I will answer him; I will be with him in distress" (Psalm 91:15). Thus wherever Israel is exiled, the Shekhina is with them.[28]

Rabbi Yosi joined Rabbi Ishmael in an effort to free people from the notion that the Divine Presence depended on place. Even Mount Sinai, he declared, the site of the awesome encounters with God, enjoyed sanctity only at that specific point in time. So long as the Shekhina rested on the mountain, we read, "Whoever touches the mountain shall perish" (Exodus 19:12), but as soon as the Shekhina departed, all were permitted to go up to the mountain.[29]

Belden Lane has articulated this overall position:

---

25. *Bava Batra* 25a.
26. Ibid.
27. *Genesis Rabbah* 68:9.
28. Ibid.
29. *Mekhilta de-Rabbi Ishmael; Barkhadesh* 3; Taanit 21b.

Entry to a sacred place is always a matter of one's dynamic relationship with God alone. There is no unchangeable quality of holiness seen to reside statically in any given place. The site is not revered because of what it is in itself. While elements of scripture did adopt certain aspects of mythical space, Deuteronomy, seconded by the rabbis, viewed Israel as ultimately uncomfortable with the notion of primeval power being permanently possessed by a given locale. God was continually calling them, not back to a mythical Urzeit when a particular site was set apart as Sacred, but to a non-spatial reality discovered in faithfulness to God.[30]

Non-anthropomorphism

Heinrich Graetz has emphasized the non-anthropomorphic nature of the Judaic perspective on the land. Shlomo Avineri has summarized Graetz's view. He tells us that at the moment Judaism entered history, it appeared as protest, a negative force, a revolt against paganism; and this revolt is considered by Graetz the main historical characteristic of Judaism. Paganism is the cult of nature, while Judaism appears as the spirit, the antithesis of nature, and hence representing a more developed phase of historical development. *Pagans, according to Graetz, saw nature in its broader meaning as an immanent force acting out of its own power.* Even among the Greeks, with their sublimated notion of nature, god remains forever idealized nature, even in its highest stage of development where it is stripped of every animal and plant form and becomes humanized. The Olympian gods remain, just like ordinary mortals, subservient to the blind force of Tyche, the goddess of fortune.

To Graetz, Judaism is the exact obverse of this relation. *The*

---

30. Lane, Belden C. *Landscapes of the Sacred: Geography and Narrative in American Spirituality.* Johns Hopkins University Press, 2002; p. 28. Walter Harrelson adds that Israelite holy places were holy only "in virtue of the deeds of salvation associated with them." See his *From Fertility Cult to Worship.* Scholars Press, 1980; p. 6.

divine and the natural are separated, and nature becomes an object of divine activity; nature is considered as being created by God *ex nihilo.* God is omnipotent and is not Himself ruled by nature. It is before God that man is responsible for his actions. Judaism thus signifies man's emancipation from matter, and human responsibility becomes a possibility.[31]

Paganism is thus an immanent religion of nature, Judaism a spiritual religion of the transcendent. Pagan art is steeped in nature and is expressed in its being mainly figurative art, whereas Jewish art is poetic, verbal. Pagan man sees the deity in natural, physical form and molds it accordingly, whereas in Judaism one *hears* God. He appears as being mediated through consciousness and spirit. Pagans saw nature in its broader meaning as an imminent force acting out of its own power. Judaism protested that notion.

II. ON CONFERRED HOLINESS

a) The Basic Biblical Perspective

If holiness of land is not inherent, that the divine is not seen as actually located in a quasi-physical manner at a particular spot, what then are alternate ways to understand the land as holy? Biblical, rabbinic and other perspectives show us ways. These view places as hallowed *by human experience and association.* The sense of the numinous power in a locale is felt, due not to an indwelling of the divine, but by the evocation of intense religious emotion due to the place having been the scene of man's having had an experience with the divine—fervent worship or religiously motivated action. Put another way: it is via "holy experiences" or "holy action" that a place may be considered "holy land." It is "history" that hallows a locale.

The notion is attested to by a set of representative biblical incidents:

---

31. Avineri, Shlomo. *The Making of Modern Zionism: The Intellectual Origins of the Jewish State.* Weidenfeld and Nicolson, 1981; p. 25–26.

In Genesis 28:16-17, Jacob is en route to Haran where he has a dream about a ladder reaching from earth to heaven with angels ascending and descending on it and God standing beside him, promising offspring, land and blessing. Jacob is deeply moved and exclaims, "Surely God is present in this place...how awesome is this place (הַמָּקוֹם הַזֶּה); this is none other than the abode of God and this is the gateway to heaven."

In Exodus 3:5, Moses is at Mount Horeb/Sinai, where he encounters a burning bush that is not being consumed. There he hears the voice of God, who commands, "Remove your sandals from your feet" כִּי הַמָּקוֹם אֲשֶׁר אַתָּה עֹמֵד עָלָיו אַדְמַת־קֹדֶשׁ הוּא "for the place on which you stand is holy (ground)."

In I Kings 19:5-12 Elijah flees to the wilderness to escape the wrath of Queen Jezebel. The parallel of Elijah's experience with God to that of Moses at Mount Sinai/Horeb is manifest. First, Moses encounters God at a burning bush and first Elijah encounters God in his sleep under a "broom bush."[32] Moses neither eats nor drinks for forty days on the mountain[33] and Elijah neither eats nor drinks for forty days as he walks to "the mountain of God, at Horeb."[34] Moses "stands on the mountain"[35] and Elijah is told to "stand on the mountain before God."[36] The Lord "passes by" Moses[37] and "lo the Lord passed by" Elijah.[38] The Lord came to Moses in "thunder and lightning and a dense cloud"[39] and though Elijah experienced wind and earthquake and fire wherein God did not appear, the Lord did come to him in a *kol d'mama daka*, "a still small voice"—and as Moses had a "private audience" with the Lord,[40]

---

32. I Kings 19:5-7.
33. Exodus 34:28.
34. I Kings 19:8.
35. Deuteronomy 10:10.
36. I Kings 19:11.
37. Exodus 33:22.
38. Kings 19:11.
39. Exodus 19:16.
40. Exodus 20.

so did Elijah.[41]

And so, we surmise that even as Moses' encounter with the Lord at Sinai/Horeb conferred sanctity on that mountain at that moment in time, so did the parallel experience of Elijah at his moment in time confer sanctity on the mountain.[42]

In Joshua 5:15, Joshua is in Jericho, where he encounters a "captain of the Lord's hosts" standing before him who he greets warily at first. Realizing that the figure is a messenger from God sent to help in capturing Jericho for Israel, Joshua asks the messenger what he wills, to which Joshua is told in words similar to the ones Moses heard at the burning bush, "Remove your sandals from your feet, for the place where you stand is holy."

In Leviticus 18 a series of prohibitions of sexual abuses ends with an appeal to the people not to defile themselves with these abominable customs. "Do not defile yourself in any of those ways, for it is by such that the nations...defiled themselves. Thus the land became defiled and is called to account for its iniquity.[43] The same fate will threaten Israel if it becomes unclean and *makes the land with which it has been united unclean.*[44] In Deuteronomy 24:4, the sinful *people brings guilt on the land.* Numbers 35:33 requires a murderer be brought to justice *lest the blood he shed "pollutes the land,"* Jeremiah accuses Israel of having polluted the land through her whoredom.[45] Isaiah cries, *"The earth is defiled under its inhabitants* because they transgressed, violated laws, broke the ancient covenant. That is why a curse consumes the earth."[46]

Clearly these utterances are based on the belief in a direct connection between humans and the earth—a connection based on the nature of human behavior. Man is subject to the God who gave

---

41. I Kings 19:13-14.
42. Cohn, Robert L. *The Shape of Sacred Space: Four Biblical Studies.* Scholars Press, 1981; p. 53–54.
43. Leviticus 18:24-25.
44. Leviticus 18:28.
45. Jeremiah 3:9.
46. Isaiah 24:5-6.

them both the rules and the land upon which to live them; *hence his behavior has a direct influence—for good or for bad—on the earth itself. Indeed, the earth's sanctity is conditioned by human action.*

b) Biblical Historical Factors

Robert Wilken points out that the city of Jerusalem, originally one of Canaan's city—states, gave no signs of glory or grandeur. Only after it was conquered and subdued by King David in the tenth century BCE did it become an Israelite city. And only after David brought the Ark of the Covenant that had been housed in Shilo into Jerusalem did Jerusalem become a holy place. The Ark was the central sacred object of the twelve tribes, the symbol of God's presence in the midst of Israel. Therefore, holiness now—*not before*—was deemed to be present in the city. Further, it was later when the Ark was deposited in the inner sanctuary of the Temple built by King Solomon, that God's presence was deemed to be securely established in Jerusalem. *Thus this sacred city of the Bible was a creation of the Israelites.* Here is a clear example of human "holy action," if you like, conferring sanctity on a place.[47]

Robert Cohn spells out in more detail Wilkin's observation. He tells us that the prominent role of Jerusalem in biblical times as political and cultic center of Judah and in post-biblical times as a focus of Jewish territorial and spiritual aspirations makes it easy to forget that this *sacred center was not always sacred or a center for Israel.* A Jebusite fortress belonging to none of the tribes, Jerusalem in pre-monarchial days was a foreign enclave in the midst of the Israelite land of settlement. To appreciate the transformation which rendered this site God's "holy mountain, beautiful in elevation, the joy of all the earth,"[48] we must consider the geographical focus of those early days.

Not one but a multiplicity of centers characterized the settlement period. Each clan or tribe or group of tribes had its shrine.

---

47. Wilken, Robert L. *The Land Called Holy: Palestine in Christian History and Thought.* Yale University Press, 1992; p. 9–10.
48. Psalms 48:3.

Dan in the north, Shechem, Gibeon, Gilgal, Bethel in the center of
the country, and Hebron and Beersheba in the south, for instance,
could claim theophanies or various sacred objects which attracted
the allegiance of the surrounding inhabitants. Although many
such sites were undoubtedly inherited from Israel's Canaanite
predecessors, legend transformed them in the name of the Lord
and He was invoked and worshipped in them.

Clearly, none of these centers was the political or cultic locus
of order which Jerusalem eventually became. When King David
came to power he seized upon the plan which was to end the "center vacuum." Seven years after being proclaimed king in Hebron,
he captured Jerusalem in an apparent bloodless coup and made it
his personal possession, the "City of David."[49] It soon became the
capitol of an expanding empire, new home for the ancient Ark,[50]
and under Solomon, the site of the "house of the Lord." *In one master stroke, David transformed a foreign (Jebusite) hamlet, elevated his
capitol above tribal rivalries, and harnessed the power of the revered tribal
sanctum to sanctify the new city.*[51]

c) Biblical "Strategic" Factors

Sinai/Horeb, the mountain of Moses' transforming vision, came to
be forgotten. Indeed the site of Mount Sinai is unknown; its legacy
has endured but the physical place from which it originated has
long vanished from Israel's knowledge. How is it possible that the
encounter with the Transcendent and the great Moses did not render its concrete site sacred for all time? What does this puzzling
fact tell us?

Gunther Plaut surmises that the failure of the Jewish tradition
to preserve knowledge of the Sinai/Horeb concrete locale has its
deeper reason. The Torah states expressly[52] that the place of

---

49. 2 Samuel 5:7.
50. 2 Samuel 6:16.
51. Cohn, Robert L. *The Shape of Sacred Space: Four Biblical Studies.* Scholars
   Press, 1981; p. 64–65.
52. Deuteronomy 34:6.

Moses' grave remains unknown, and presumably, Plaut asserts, in order that it not become a place of pilgrimage, and the person of the lawgiver an object of adulation, even adoration. Plaut continues:

> Had the locale of Sinai become known as the "holy mountain" in later centuries, Jerusalem and the Temple could never have become the center of Jewish life for they would have been inferior in "holiness" to that other "sacred" mountain—Sinai. Sinai thus became either by design or happenstance a concept rather than a place, its universal importance heightened by the vagueness of its site, its timelessness unfettered by an identifiable place.[53]

Jon Levenson[54] amplifies Plaut's observation by pointing to its implication. Sinai did partake of a degree of sanctity because of Moses' experiences with God there, but for strategic reasons, the tradition blanketed it. How, Levenson asks, could the covenant theology attributed to Sinai be so pervasive in the developing religion of ancient Israel when the physical mountain itself ceased to play any role? To which he responds that other scriptural texts made it evident that *an experience like that of Moses was still possible but on a different mountain.*

Indeed, such an experience is depicted in Psalm 97. Here, as in Exodus 19, the account of the Sinaitic theophany, the atmospheric phenomena and pyrotechnics are stressed, rather than played down, as in the experience of Elijah at Horeb/Sinai. Here we see again the cloud and the fire and the lightning,[55] and we hear again the Lord's assumption of universal kingship and his humiliation and subjugation of other gods.[56] We hear even of the divine decrees of "judgments" that are so important in the Sinaitic

---

53. Plaut, Gunther. *The Torah: A Modern Commentary.* Union of American Hebrew Congregations, 1974; p. 520
54. Levenson, Jon D. *Sinai and Zion: An Entry into the Jewish Bible.* Winston Press, 1985; p. 90–91.
55. Exodus 19:16.
56. Exodus 19:4-6.

materials. *In Psalm 97, however, Sinai is not the focus, but a new mountain (Zion).*[57] *The traditions of the Lord's theophany, His earth-shatter-
ing apparition to man* (even, to some extent, His revelation of law)
*have been transferred from Sinai to Zion. In short, Sinai has not so much
been forgotten as absorbed.*

Levenson continues by pointing out that in the early poetry of
Israel it is from Sinai that the Lord acts;[58] but in most of its passages it is not from Sinai that He comes, but from Zion: "From
Zion, perfect in beauty, God shone forth. Our God came; He did
not fail to act. Before Him was a devouring fire; around Him it
stormed fiercely."[59] The transfer of the motif from Sinai to Zion
was now complete, so that the Lord came to be designated no
longer as "The One of Sinai" but as "He who dwells on Mount
Zion."[60]

And then Levenson concludes, "More than merely the name of
the mountain abode of the Lord is involved in the change. Zion,
unlike Sinai, was a known site in Israel. *The transfer of the divine
home from Sinai to Zion meant that God was no longer seen as being
experienced in an extraterritorial no man's land, but within the borders
of the Israelite community.*" And so, *for strategic reasons Sinai's sanctity was transferred to Zion.* Hence the sanctity of Jerusalem and the
Temple situated as they were on Mount Zion.[61]

d) Rabbinic Perspectives

Sanctity Via Observance of the Law

The Mishna articulates a similar thought line from the halakhic
point of view. Precisely because it was the land to which the law
most applied, the place gained in sanctity.

---

57. Verse 8: Zion.
58. Psalm 68:8-9.
59. Psalm 50:2-3.
60. Isaiah 8:18.
61. For a full discussion of this subject, see Shechter, Jack. *The Land of Israel:
    Its Theological Dimensions; a Study of a Promise and of a Land's "Holiness."*
    University Press of America, 2010; p. 223-225.

There are ten degrees of holiness. The land of Israel is holy. Wherein lies its holiness? In that from it they may bring the Omer,[62] the first fruits[63] and the two loaves,[64] which they may not bring from any other land.

Seven additional laws are then enumerated, laws that can only be observed in Israel's land. Here the Mishna is associating holiness of the land with Israel's fulfillment of a variety of prescribed laws (which we describe as "holy action"), and it is this action that confers sanctity on the place. W. D. Davies puts it this way:

> In each case—in the reference to the land, the walled cities, the wall of Jerusalem, the Temple Mount, the Rampart, the Court of Women, the Court of the Israelites, etc.—it is the connection with an enactment of the law that determines the degree of the land's holiness.

And Davies adds an illuminating point about the applicability of the law to the land in this Mishna that assures its special holiness. The implication is that Jewish sanctity is fully possible only in the land; outside of it only strictly personal laws can be fulfilled, that is, the moral law, sexual law, Sabbath law, circumcision, dietary laws, etc. Of necessity, outside the land, the territorial laws are necessarily set aside. The exiled life is therefore an emaciated life. Thus the laws applicable only to the land of Israel afford more opportunity to confer sanctity on it.[65]

After noting in detail the elements pertaining to agricultural work and produce outlined in Mishna Kelim 1:6-9 cited above and found elsewhere in scripture, Richard Sarason points to these as central to the relationship between the God of Israel, the Land of Israel and the people of Israel. He cites the singular attention the Mishna devotes to the *role of human action and*

---

62. Leviticus 23:10f.
63. Deuteronomy 26:2.
64. Leviticus 23:17.
65. Davies, W.D. *The Gospel and the Land: Early Christianity and Jewish Territorial Doctrine.* University of California Press, 1974; p. 55–60.

intentionality in this construct. In this, both territory and people are intersecting categories in the rabbinic mind.

The rules are directed exclusively to "native" Israelite society at home in her domain. They express a dynamic unity among the God who controls the land and rules over the people, the people who live on God's land and render God service through their work on the place, and the land that is under God's special providence and nourishes the people if they obey God's law.

Since, for the Mishna, the agricultural and other rules required for observance in the land apply only to the territories' Israelite inhabitants, *the sanctity of the land would appear to be relative to that of the People Israel; the Israelites, by inhabiting and working the land, would actively complete the land's consecration.*

In his concluding comment on this subject, Sarason appears to echo the observation of Davies about the laws applicable only to the Land of Israel affording more opportunity to confer sanctity on it:

> The various Mishnaic rulings maintain that through study of God's Torah and observance of God's commandments, the God of Israel can in fact be served by Jews anywhere and everywhere, but fully and perfectly only in the Land of Israel where additional land-bound commandments obtain, as Scripture ordains.[66]

Sanctity in the Fullest Sense

This notion that the fullness of Jewish life can be realized only in the Holy Land has long since been emphasized by the Rabbis:

The perspective of *Rabbi Moses ben Nachman (Nakhmanides)* has been articulated by Moshe Idel this way:

Dwelling in the Land of Israel becomes for Nakhmanides

---

66. Sarason, Richard. "The Significance of the Land of Israel in the Mishna," in Lawrence Hoffman, editor, *The Land of Israel: Jewish Perspectives*. University of Notre Dame Press, 1986.

not only a religious obligation but the single way to attain perfect Jewish life. The performance of the commandments in the Diaspora is, in Nakhmanides' view, a mere preparation intended to enable their true performance in the Land of Israel. Moreover, the Promised Land, being the only proper forum for a full religious life, the Jews must live in their own land even if this aim can be achieved through non-peaceful means. Nakhmanides considers this effort as one of the religious obligations incumbent upon every Jew and not a matter to be postponed until the Messianic era.[67]

Martin Buber retells the story in the Aggadah about the rabbis who go abroad to study and, no doubt, for other noble reasons. However, as soon as they arrive at the frontier, they are so taken by the thought of leaving the land that they weep, tear their clothes and return home with the cry, "Dwelling in the land of Israel outweighs all the commandments in the Torah"—an allusion to Deuteronomy 11:31-32 and 12:28, in which the fulfillment of the commandments and settlement in the land are linked. Says Buber:

> This reference to the Bible explains the ultimate meaning of the rabbis' cry: the true and perfect fulfillment of the commandments is possible only in the whole life of the people that settles in the land of Israel. Therefore, the settlement is the precondition of the true and perfect fulfillment of the commandments and thus it alone out-weighs them all for it alone makes the fulfillment of the others possible.[68]

Yet another articulation of this notion from the standpoint of the *Halakhah* comes from a work by Sol Roth: As a result of the

---

67. Idel, Moshe. "The Land of Israel in the Medieval Kabbalah," in Lawrence Hoffman, editor, *The Land of Israel: Jewish Perspectives*. University of Notre Dame Press, 1986; p. 175.
68. Buber, Martin. *On Zion: The History of an Idea*. Schocken Books, 1986; p. 53.

"Covenant Between the Parts,"[69] the ancient land of Canaan became the promised land. *It was subsequently invested, also by covenant, with sanctity: that is to say, the Jew became obligated to abide by the* mitzvoth ha-teluyot ba-aretz, *"the precepts that depend on the land."* In no other place can the Jew experience that (full) intimacy of involvement with the Divine Being that he can in the land he knows to be sacred (by virtue of his own obligatory "holy action," as it were, on the place).

Hence, the sanctity of both the people and the land is expressed in obligation. The people were invested with sanctity at Sinai when it accepted the Decalogue. *The land is sacred in the sense that it imposes obligations on the holy people which are not in force elsewhere.* The Holy Land directs a greater challenge to the Jew and inspires a deeper (and more comprehensive) response. Hence, the fulfillment by the Jew of his own spiritual potential and, simultaneously, his contribution to the wellbeing of mankind, ultimately depend on his presence on the land.[70]

Halakhic Criteria for "Sanctity"

There is another rabbinic formulation about the land, which indicates that human action confers (or does not confer) sanctity on Israel's place. The Talmud establishes criteria for the holiness of the land. The principle is קְדוּשָׁה רִאשׁוֹנָה קִדְּשָׁה לְשָׁעָתָהּ וְלֹא קִדְּשָׁה לְעָתִיד לָבֹא, "the first sanctification of the land (in Joshua's time) was meant 'for its time' and was not permanent." According to Maimonides, Joshua's sanctification of the territory was temporary in nature; it was abrogated upon destruction of the first Temple in 586 BCE and the subsequent exile because he came into possession of the territory by conquest. In contrast, the second part of this principle is קִדְּשָׁה לְשָׁעָתָהּ וְקִדְּשָׁה לְעָתִיד לָבֹו, "the second sanctification was for its time and sanctification for the time to come." This means that the second sanctification of

---

69. Genesis 15:17-21.
70. Roth, Sol. *Halakhah and Politics: the Jewish Idea of the State.* Ktav Publishing House, 1988; p. 27, 30.

the land (in Ezra's time) was meant both for its time and future time, i.e., was permanent; this was because Ezra came into possession of the territory not by conquest but via a peaceful return of the exiles from Babylonia. According to Maimonides, this rabbinic principle is the definitive law.[71]

Now, leaving aside the issue of whether or not the land's holiness was temporary or permanent (and how these criteria apply to specific locales in present day Israel), it is apparent that the rabbis viewed the human actions of Joshua and Ezra (who acted in response to what they considered God's will) as the factors that bestowed holiness on the land of Israel.

e) Anthropological and Psychological Perspectives

Jonathan Z. Smith makes essentially the same point about the conferral of sanctity on place from an anthropological perspective. In order for land to be one's very own, one must live together with it. It is when man dwells in relationship with his land that he transforms the place into the place of his people. It is history that makes the land truly mine. "It is that one has cultivated the land, dies on the land, that one's ancestors are buried in the land, that rituals have been performed in the land, *that one's deity has been encountered here and there in the land, that renders the place a homeland, a land of man, a holy land.*" Smith goes on to say that it was not just that the land was promised to Israel by God; it was also fought for and died for and was won. And it is the fighting and especially the dying that adds significantly to the other factors which, taken together, *"confers on the land its sacrality."*[72]

Ben Zion Bokser has captured the essence of this notion. In what sense can a land be "holy?" he asks. He responds that the land is a setting where man implements his designs and purposes. These enter into his culture and can either taint or hallow his

71. Yevamot 82b; Hagiga 3b; Hulin 7a; Maimonides' Laws of Voluntary Offerings 1:5.

72. Smith, Jonathan Z. *Map Is Not Territory.* Brill Academic Publishers, 1978; p. 109–110.

domain. When, for example, Adam rebelled in the Garden of Eden, the earth was cursed along with him. When the flood destroyed the generation of violence in the time of Noah, the earth was destroyed as well. Conversely, "when the people of a land adopt holiness as an ideal, the land is also touched with sanctity."

Every religion has a roster of holy places where special events reminiscent of its central faith have occurred and where these events can be recalled by constant re-living and re-experiencing. "In the case of Israel, the entire land of Canaan became a holy place because it was the physical setting for Israel's effort to build a holy nation in the image of the ideals set forth in the Covenant...*The land was an integral part of the culture created in it, and because holiness was the dominant ideal of that culture, the land itself became tinged with that holiness.*"[73]

Louis Jacobs has made this point from the psychological point of view. He tells us that the location of divinity in certain spots belongs to a primitive mode of thought. While there are traces of the idea in the Bible, Judaism nonetheless teaches that God is omnipresent and that He transcends the universe. Yet Judaism knows, too, of places especially hallowed: the synagogue, the Temple site, Jerusalem and the land of Israel as a whole. For modern Jews the most refined understanding of the idea of sacred places is not in the semi-magical way of seeing God as "present" in one place rather than another but in terms of psychological association. "The land of Israel," Jacob asserts, "does have, according to the *halakhah*, more holiness,' *kedusha*, than other lands but this should be interpreted in terms of the richer associations it has with the men who found God there. The land in which the patriarchs lived and the prophets taught is the idea which should be stressed. The same applies to the other sacred spots. Superstitious reverence for a particular piece of soil in itself should be rejected."

Jacobs then via analogy says that the Hebrew language is, similarly, the "holy tongue" not because it is God's special language.

---

73. Bokser, Ben Zion. *Jews, Judaism and the State of Israel*. Herzi Press, 1973; p. 45.

Historically considered, Hebrew is an ancient Semitic tongue with the strongest affinities to other Semitic languages such as Aramaic and Arabic and was not originally spoken only by the Israelites. Hebrew is the "holy tongue" by association, because it is the language of the Bible, the form in which the covenant between God and Israel first was expressed, the instrument by means of which the seers and prophets of Israel poured out their hearts to God, the key with which to unlock the spiritual treasures of the Jewish people.[74]

Another Psychological Perspective

The promise of a happy repossession of the motherland continued to keep Jewish hopes alive during centuries of exile and finally led to the third Zionade, which was implemented by modern Zionism. The returning Zionist sons were enflamed by a sacred zeal to fertilize Zion. *Hafrahat Hashmamot* or "making the desolate land bloom" was a major aspiration and a central slogan in the entire settlement effort.

The Israeli journalist and author Amos Elon drew attention to the interesting phenomenon in that the early Zionist settlers described their return to Zion not only in usual terms such as "homecoming" or "rebuilding" but also in stronger terms such as return to the "womb" of history or return to Zion the "betrothed." This led him to conclude that a "libidinous link with the soil" was taking place and that the old liturgical references to a mystical "betrothal" between Israel and the promised land was being given new personal and political meaning. Elon reported a statement by the old-guard Zionist leader Meir Yaari to his pioneer followers, in which he proclaimed that the land they tilled was their bride. Yaari compared the *halutzim* to a bridegroom who abandons himself in his bride's bosom or to the motherly womb of sanctifying earth.[75]

---

74. Jacobs, Louis. *A Jewish Theology*. Behrman House, 1973; p. 282.
75. Gonen, Jay Y. *A Psychohistory of Zionism*. New American Library, 1976; p. 18.

f) The Role of Memory

Imagine a large and totally bare room. It has only a floor, walls and ceiling. It is completely empty: no seats, no stage, no accoutrements, no people. Subsequently, people affix seats on the ground floor and in a three-tiered balcony, both sections for two thousand people. A stage is erected for a fifty-piece orchestra with a conductor at the podium; they are performing a Beethoven symphony. The heretofore totally bare and empty room is now a concert hall!

Alternately: imagine a totally bare and empty smaller room. It is subsequently occupied by some five-hundred people at a Shabbat religious service sitting in newly installed seats; an ark in which a revered Torah scroll containing "the Word of God" is installed; a rabbi is explaining Torah and a cantor and choir are leading the liturgy. The heretofore bare and empty room is now a synagogue!

The above-described two bare and empty spaces were not a concert hall or synagogue before human initiative took place there, were they?

Now consider this: the above concert hall has retained its accoutrements but is now empty—no audience, no orchestra, no conductor, no Beethoven. The synagogue remains furnished but also is empty—no congregants, no rabbi, no cantor, no choir, no liturgy. Yet when one enters the empty concert hall, one senses an aesthetic aura evoking the sound and feel of music. And when one enters the empty synagogue, one experiences a sense of reverence, assumes a posture of respect, hears the echo of prayer.

Why is this so? It is because of the *memory*, the awareness in one's mind and heart of what took place in times past in those spaces—of the orchestra and conductor, of the rabbi and cantor who functioned there. It is *recollection* of those activities that conferred the aura, the feelings one experiences even when the concert hall and synagogue are empty. We might put it this way: one *imagines* that a conductor is orchestrating a Beethoven symphony or that a rabbi and cantor are leading prayer in these places and thus the aura and reverential experience.

So it is with regard to the acquired sanctity of land/space. It is the activity of human beings, their historical experiences with God in the land, which renders the place "holy." And it is *the collective memory of those experiences*—on or off the land in history—that continued and continues to constitute the source of the land's sanctity. It is the memory of Israel's patriarchs' experience with God on the land in hoary antiquity; of the Israelite tribes inhabiting the place guided by a demanding yet loving God; and it is the memory of King David bringing the Ark of the Covenant to Jerusalem; of King Solomon completing erection of the Temple and placing the ark in the inner sanctuary; of the colorful ritual conducted by the priests and Levites at the Temple with its sacred instruments and sacrifices; of the three pilgrimages to Jerusalem by the Israelites; of the farmers' first fruits (*bekurim*) offering; of the great prophets walking the streets of the land's towns preaching God's word.

The role of history recalled as the way to understand the land of Israel as holy land has been articulated by Louis Jacobs this way:

> We find it hard to accept the view that Eretz Yisrael is a divinely promised land in a direct sense, because we have become accustomed to the dynamic view of Jewish history, including sacred history.
>
> On this view we need to be no less devoted to the land of Israel as the Holy Land, or indeed, as the Promised Land, provided we understand the holiness and the promise as conveyed through the historical experiences of our people.
>
> We would tend to see it as holiness and promise through association rather than divine fiat; through the fact that in this land and in no other did God reveal Himself to the prophets; that here and nowhere else did Israel see God on the throne with the seraphim singing "Holy, Holy, Holy"; that here Amos taught us justice and Hosea

love and compassion; that here Rabbi Yochanan Ben
Zakkai and Hillel and Akiba made the mighty attempt at
translating prophetism into a wondrous way of life
whose power has not abated....

This land and no other has become sacred to Jews
and a central feature of Jewish religion because of the tremendous associations between land and people and God
through a history of more than three thousand years.[76]

Martin Buber essayed that "all real living is meeting,"[77] that
the place of meeting serves always as the trigger of memory, the
occasion for hope. The physical locale forms the palpable context
around which a people's story grows. It is *the remembered* place
that excites and directs the imagination in its effort to understand the people's experience with its land-past and present—
whether physically at the place and elsewhere no matter how far
away.

Abraham Joshua Heschel connects Buber's notion of the intimate connection between place and memory to Israel's relationship to her place. He emphasizes the compelling role of memory
about Israel's life on the land. He asserts that after the destruction of Jerusalem, the city did not become a relic of the distant
past; it continued to live as an inspiration in the hearts and minds
of the people. Zion itself became a recurring theme in the liturgy,
at the wedding ceremony, at the circumcision rite, in the grace
after each meal, in the Amida prayer recited three times every
day, in the prayers for dew and rain:

> We are a people in whom the past endures, in whom the
> present is inconceivable without moments gone by. The
> vision of the prophets lasted a moment, a moment en-
> during forever. What happened once upon a time hap-
> pens all the time. Abraham is still standing before the
> Lord seeking to save Sodom and Gomorrah (Genesis

76. Jacobs, Louis. *A Jewish Theology*. Behrman House, 1973; p 58–59.
77. Buber, Martin. *I And Thou*. Simon & Schuster; 1970.

18:22). Nathan the prophet is still standing before David the king and saying, "You are the man" (II Samuel 12:7).[78]

A Pilgrimage to Palestine Through the Lens of Memory...In the Words of Harry Emerson Fosdick

The Holy Land's unique allurement lies in its antiquity. Palestine is the home of history. Acre, for example, ten miles north of Haifa on the seacoast, is a poor, shriveled town today with few visible reminders of its ancient glory, *but what ghosts walk its narrow streets and saii iis choked-up harbor!* To these walls the Hebrew tribesmen came and here one of the tribes twelve centuries ago was unable to dislodge the town's natives: "Asher did not drive out the inhabitants of Acco."[79]

Here walks the shade of Sennacherib, who seized the city before he marched on Jerusalem in Isaiah's day, and here came Alexander the Great conquering the world. From the heights a few miles to the north Jesus must have looked upon the town-called Ptolemais in Roman times—and perhaps he came here when he repaired to the coasts of Tyre and Sidon. Paul walked these streets, tarrying here a day with his fellow Christians, and before the second century was gone a Christian bishop had here his seat.

Then came the Moslems, in 638 A.D., within six years of Mohammed's death; and when, centuries afterward, the crusaders drove them out, Acre was for long their capital, the center of bloody sieges and hairbreadth escapes. Here Richard the Lion-Hearted is said to have slain five thousand Moslem captives whose ransom was not quickly paid; here Saint Francis of Assisi prayed; here Napoleon Bonaparte turned back baffled from the walls.

---

78. Heschel, Abraham Joshua. *Israel: An Echo of Eternity.* Jewish Lights Publishing, 1997; p. 60–67.
79. Judges 1:31.

Was there ever such a summary of history as Palestine affords? He who sees the land without eyes to see the long, astounding play that has been staged upon it has not really seen the land at all.[80]

---

80. Fosdick, Harry Emerson. *Pilgrimage to Palestine.* Curzon Press, 2007; p. 26–27.

– Five –

THE MIRACLE OF JEWISH SURVIVAL
Faith Nurtured by a People

A question: how was it possible for a people cast out of her land, without temple and cult and stated priests, without king and nationhood, to survive? These conditions, after all, are the usual, indispensable elements of the life of a people if it is to endure. In fact, for centuries Israel was deeply attached to her own land in which she encountered her God, in which she nourished her inner life, in which she had the opportunity to implement her faith in everyday life—in its social and economic, political and military facets. Without all this, how was it conceivable that such a people could persist as a distinct entity?

Survival Despite Absence of the Land: Religion

A basis for the answer to the above insistent question is provided by examination of Israel's relationship to the land embedded in the tradition prior to Israel's settlement in Canaan—a perspective subsequently adopted by the prophets. The prevailing notion was that *divinity was detached from soil.* As Salo Baron has put it:

> Since it would have been impossible to abstract God so abruptly from all locality, He remained the God of the desert long after Israel's settlement in Canaan. From the days of Debra to those of the writing Prophets, God

appears in poetic vision as having His seat at Mount Sinai, or Mount Seir, in the desert of Paran, or in other places—all outside Palestine. Not even the combined efforts of the kings and priests in Jerusalem to associate the divine presence with the Temple on Zion could succeed. Israel's God thus became definitely dissociated from exclusive residence on Israel's soil.[1]

The prophets Jeremiah and Ezekiel had the ground upon which to provide the answer to the question about *Israel's survival minus her land: Israel, indeed, could have a relationship to her God without the land she had inhabited, without temple and cult, without traditional nationhood*. Both assured her of this. The people could meet God and survive in the land of their exile if they sought Him there with their whole heart.

The Lord, Jeremiah explains, will visit the people in Babylon and fulfill His promises. He has plans for Israel's welfare to give them a future and hope: "Then you will call upon me and come and pray to me, *and I will hear you*. You will seek me and find me; when you seek me with all your heart *I will be found by you*, says The Lord, and I will restore your fortunes and gather you from all the nations and all the places where I have driven you and bring you back to the land from which I sent you into exile."[2]

And God speaks through Ezekiel and says: Though I removed them far off among the nations, and though I scattered them among the countries, *yet I have been a sanctuary to them in the countries where they have gone*. Therefore...I will give you (back) the land of Israel.[3]

Thus in the days of great suffering the idea of a people beyond state and territory was firmly established. It was their tenacious clinging to the One and Only God who could be accessed even in exile that made their survival as a people possible.

---

1. Baron, Salo. *A Social and Religious History of the Jews*. Columbia University Press, 1973; Vol. 1, p. 48.
2. Jeremiah 29:12-14.
3. Ezekial 11:16-17.

Yes, they continued to yearn for return to their ancestral land, and this was ever a source of hope for the morrow. Yet the people were without state or territory even in the days of Moses. What ultimately mattered was to obey the commands of The Lord *in all places*. Salo Baron has articulated the essential core thought of this "amazing" development in the life of the people Israel:

> New leaders arose. A transcendent and holy God, they taught, has selected the people of Israel as His holy nation, for reasons known only to Him. Through a life of holiness and, if necessary, of suffering, this people will continue to make known the name of God until the end of days, when all nations will recognize their error and worship the One God. In the meantime, Israel must keep aloof from these other nations, in order not to be contaminated by their errors and their unholy life. Such an aim can only be achieved by a full, specific, and peculiar law in all its ramifications. *The life thus demanded is necessarily artificial and contrary to nature in many ways [i.e., a people without its own land and all that goes with it]. Thus the Jew has to live, if necessary, in defiance of nature.*[4]

The answer to our question about Israel's survival without her land was thus planted. Here was a people in exile, scattered to the ends of the earth—a condition that under normal circumstances would inevitably lead to their being swallowed up by their surroundings. Why did this not happen? Major Jewish thinkers, each in his own way, echoed Baron, in answer to our question about exile. The following are summaries:

Nakhman Krochmal: God bestowed his grace upon the people of Israel—a grace for which we can find the reason neither in ourselves nor in any of the preceding generations....This grace presented us with a God idea that is supreme over all rational

---

4. Baron, Salo. *A Social and Religious History of the Jews*. Columbia University Press, 1973; Vol. 1, p. 164. See also "Emancipation from Sate and Territory," p. 16-25.

thought. We have always maintained this conception....The idea became engraved upon the tablet of our hearts and never departed from our history. Through it we have become teachers of the nations, and through it *we continue to exist to this day, and with it we shall be forever redeemed.*[5]

Heinrich Graetz: What prevented this ever-wandering people from degenerating into brutish vagrants or a vagabond horde of gypsies? The answer: during its desolate history of 1800 years in the diaspora, the Jewish people carried with it the Ark of the Covenant, which placed an ideal striving in its heart and transfigured the badge of shame on its garment with an apostolic radiance designed to educate the nations to the knowledge of God and morality.... Such a people for whom the present meant nothing and the future everything *which seemed to exist by virtue of its hope, is for that very reason as eternal as hope itself.*[6]

Yehezkel Kaufmann: What is the reason for the fact that the people of Israel persisted in being a people despite its being scattered among the nations?... When we examine the people's consciousness in the diaspora, we see that all of the values to which it clung were religious values—the language, the memories, the past with all its heroes, its destiny, race, customs—all were not secular matters but were sublimated and became religious values.... This all was the word and will of God with Israel as their bearer....As such, these were permanent values harbored by a permanent people.[7]

Jonathan Sacks: Jewry is not a mere secular people, an ethnic group, one of the myriad cultures in the anthropological lexicon of mankind. Had that been all there is to Jewish identity, there would be no Jews today. *No culture or ethnicity has survived two thousand years of dispersion and minority status.* Had the Israelites of ancient times not been moved by a religious vision, they

---

5. Meyer, Michael A (ed.). *Ideas of Jewish History.* Wesleyan University, 1975; p. 201.
6. Ibid., p. 231.
7. Ibid., p. 257.

would have assimilated among the Egyptians. Had they not carried the Torah with them into Israel, they may have won their independence, but they would today be numbered along with the Canaanites, Jebusites, Perizites, and the other peoples of the ancient Near East, remembered, if at all, as exhibits in museums. We are who and what we are because of a momentous faith.[8]

Survival Despite Absence of the Land: Religion Embedded in Peoplehood

All the above does not exhaust this subject nor fully answer the question posed: why the Jewish people's persistence in the diaspora?

The intimate relationship between the Jewish people and its faith is a basic phenomenon of Israel's history. G. Ernest Wright has pointed to this: "The Israelites point of view toward the apprehension of the Divine is to be seen, not primarily in abstract discussion of the merits of the one over against the many, but in the fact that the *God of the 'Bible is first of all the God of Israel,'"*[9]

Walter Eichrodt alluded to this as well when he pointed out that the idea of Monotheism took hold in the world because *it was embedded in the life of the people Israel who lived the idea and thus anchored it in the world.* It was not arrived at by philosophical speculation and thus an abstraction hovering about in thin air.[10]

And in the context of the Diaspora, Heinrich Graetz wrote for all the historians when he asserted that the God idea was, indeed, the core reason for Jewish survival outside of the land but this was *because it became lodged in a people who husbanded it.* The people lived on because it continually nurtured a sum of definite religious and moral ideals whose exponent was the Jewish people. Indeed, that people, once a nation in its own land, became *a virtual community*

---

8. Sacks, Jonathan. *Haggadah.* Continuum, 2007; p. 12.
9. Wright, G. Ernest. *The Old Testament against Its Environment.* SCM Press, 1950; p. 47.
10. Eichrodt, Walter. *Theology of the Old Testament.* Westminster Press, 1961; Vol. 1, p. 237.

scattered throughout *the space of the world*, bound now by a mystical sense of collective responsibility. Israel, said Rabbi Shimon bar Yokhai, is "like a single body with a single soul: when one part of it is afflicted, all feel the pain."[11] And so, nationhood, now gone, was replaced by peoplehood which became a working "substitute," as it were, a surrogate, however poor, for Israel's territory — a living people harboring and proclaiming the One living God.

A pronounced characteristic of Judaism, Graetz pointed out, was its drive to find concrete application for the most abstract and idealistic doctrine. Indeed, the unique God-idea was not left in the ethereal region of vacuous abstraction, but sought concrete embodiment in human life. Thus the Jewish people became the vital bearer of God's central position and role in the affairs of the world and humanity, this in the form of their ongoing life and practices as a community. The revealed God idea did not and does not exist for its own sake so that it might be known merely theoretically, but has a practical aim, that of promoting a temporal good life. "That it may be well with you on the land which the Lord your God gives you" is a phrase that recurs in the most diverse ordinances, for example, when Exodus 20:12 speaks of honoring father and mother, and Deuteronomy 22:6-7 forbids taking a mother bird together with her fledgling. Salo Baron amplifies this notion:

The seamless connection between Jewish peoplehood and its faith was felt at the very threshold of the history of both. It is no accident that among the oldest literary documents of the people are not only war songs, legends and tales such as are found in other civilizations, but primarily laws and religious and moral teachings. One of the oldest parts of the Bible is the so-called Book of the Covenant (Exodus 20-22-23:33) containing essentially civil and criminal laws. The Decalogue itself deals with creed only in the first two (or three) commandments, devoting all the rest to laws concerning the conduct of daily life.[12]

---

11. Sacks, Jonathan. *Haggadah*. Continuum, 2007; p. 63.
12. See Baron in Meyer, Michael A (ed.). *Ideas of Jewish History.* Wesleyan University, 1975; p. 339.

Thus the God idea was also a social and political idea. This accounts for the constant formation of Jewish communities throughout the diaspora period. These communities, often despite great distances, sought and found connections with the collectivities of fellow Jews, thus forming a distinct peoplehood. Driven to this condition by religious consciousness, this phenomenon took on the appearance of a life of its own.

One striking example of this was the *Vaad Arba Aratzot*, "The Council of Four Lands," which was the central body of Jewish autonomy in Poland between 1580 and 1764. The Four Lands were Great Poland, Little Poland, Podolia and Galicia. For these nearly two centuries until it was suppressed by the Polish government in 1764, the Council virtually governed the entire Jewish population of these provinces. Consisting of representatives of all the main communities concerned, the Council acted as a supreme court to decide on disputes between one community and another; to take measures for the safeguarding of Jewish rights when threatened by civil power; and to maintain the strict discipline which was necessary for the self-preservation of the Polish Jews.

The communities were reinforced by physical living enclaves, by historic memory, by an encompassing system of law, by a vast literature, by its own language, by an array of custom, by tenacious hope for resuming life in the land of her ancestors. Yet more, and especially significant, by geographical centers of authority such as in Babylonia, Spain, France and Germany, whose leaders were looked upon as arbiters of law and life for Jews in the far-flung regions of the diaspora.[13]

Yehezkel Kaufmann cautions not to overstate the independent character of this Jewish peoplehood. He stresses faith as the determining factor:

> The laws and way of life did not create the attachment of the people to the religious idea; they were its natural result, they were not means invented to preserve the people

---

13. Ibid., See Graetz; p. 336-337.

from extinction, but the result of a primary cause, the internal force which was the power of faith: the power of the fundamental idea of the existence of Israel, the bearer of the religion of God.[14]

Leo Baeck stressed this same point. He noted the sundering of Jewish peoplehood from the religion of Israel in the modern age. This was due, he pointed out, to the enlightenment and emancipation whereby the traditional religion of the Jews that he had so completely experienced in the past became blunted with the Jewish exodus from the old culture. The "history" of the people, its identity as a community, its purely political and social agenda, became dominant, with the religious element either absent entirely or a relatively minor component of this new condition. Baeck contended that this condition refused to concern itself with the ultimate meaning of the history of Judaism, that which gave Jewish life "its dynamic element and motive power." Baeck, in rather lofty language, articulated his reminder to the Jews in his time about that which characterizes authentic Judaism, its true strength, and the capacity of the Jewish people to persist in the past, the present and into the future, and that is:

> The incursion of the Infinite, Eternal, the One and unconditional into the finite, temporal, manifold and limited — and the spiritual and moral tension of the human fiber which is the result. Whatever ideas and hopes Judaism has created within its own sphere and beyond it emanate from here.[15]
>
> [To paraphrase: God has entered the world of the here and now, and mankind's spiritual and moral response to that phenomenon is the result. Whatever ideas and hopes Jews fashion emanate from that encounter.]

And then Baeck asserts, "The community and the transcendent were bound together. The narrow Jewish street knew that it is

---

14. Ibid., See Kaufmann; p. 252.
15. Ibid., See Baeck; p. 348.

encompassed by the world of Divine spheres...the renewal of this bond is Jewry's ordained task."

These factors, taken together, motored as they were by basic religious idea, as Kaufmann and Baeck and the historians emphasized, crystallized and strengthened diaspora Jewry's sense of peoplehood within the nations in which Jews lived — this all a people without the possession of soil and home-land, without geographical boundaries and state organisms. This is what Salo Baron meant when he said that diaspora life was "living contrary to nature," that is, living without a land of its own and all that goes with it. But it was a life lived as a people — a peculiar people indeed — which endured in the midst of, and, it must be said, in spite of the centrifugal vicissitudes of a stormy diaspora.

In sum, the Jewish people's tenacious, landless persistence is rooted in a double aspect that constitutes an essence of diaspora Judaism: knowledge of the One God and the sense of peoplehood that nurtures and propagates it. These two streams are inextricable; they interpenetrate and converge, making Judaism what it is and what it has always been in its long period of exile. As Martin Buber put it:

> Israel was and is a people and a religious community in one, and it is this unity which enabled it to survive in an exile no other nation had to suffer, an exile which lasted much longer than the period of its independence. He who severs this bond severs the life of Israel.[16]

ADDENDUM

Illustration of the status of Jewish peoplehood vis-à-vis Jewish religion can be located in the back-and-forth controversies and law-making in contemporary Israel. Are Jews considered authentically Jewish in the context of the modern state of Israel because of their adherence to their peoplehood or to their religion? And, is the latter the dominant factor forged by the historic Jewish psyche?

---

16. Buber, Martin. *Israel and the World*. Schocken Books, 1965; p. 249.

On one hand is the directive in 1958 of Israel's Ministry of the Interior stating this:

> Any person declaring in good faith that he is a Jew shall be registered as a Jew and no additional proof shall be required. [Regarding children the directive stated:] If both parents declare that the child is Jewish, the declaration shall be regarded as though it were the legal declaration of the child itself.

Thus peoplehood was determinative.

On the other hand, there were protests in and outside of Israel that such a ruling contravened Jewish law. That law defines a Jew as a person whose mother is Jewish or has been converted religiously to Judaism. Prime Minister Ben Gurion reacted. He sent a letter to 45 leading scholars in the Jewish world, one half of whom lived in the Diaspora. The vast majority opposed separating Jewish peoplehood and nationality from Jewish religion as the criterion for Jewishness.

Thus religion was determinative.

Then again on one hand were the Brother Daniel and Shalit cases. Daniel was raised and lived as a Jew but converted to Christianity. Shalit, a Jewish commander in Israeli's Navy, married a non-Jewish woman. When Daniel sought recognition as a Jew based on his peoplehood, the court ruled that the term "Jew" in the Law of Return "had secular meaning" and rejected the religious criterion for Jewishness. In the Shalit case, the court ruled that his children were Jewish even though their mother was not.

Thus peoplehood was determinative.

On the other hand, in reaction to the above two cases, the Israeli Knesset in 1970 accepted the definition of the term "Jew" as a person born of a Jewish mother or who had been converted religiously and who is not a member of another religion.

Thus religion is determinative.

Six

ON AN EARTHQUAKE
Taking the Bad with the Good

כְּשֵׁם שֶׁמְּבָרֵךְ עַל הַטּוֹבָה
כָּךְ מְבָרֵךְ עַל הָרָעָה

*Even as one recites a blessing for the good is one to recite a
blessing for the bad.*

—Berakhot 48b

*In Northridge, California, in January 1994, a devastating
earthquake struck a major sector of Los Angeles. Everywhere
people were perplexed by an event over which no one had control. Many sought guidance from Jewish tradition.*

*Rabbi Harold Schulweis, an eminent spiritual leader in
Los Angeles and throughout the country, swiftly penned a col-
umn for the Los Angeles Jewish Journal in which he sought to
make sense of the happening from a theological perspective.*

*This article, published soon after in the·Jewish Journal,
was my reaction to Rabbi Schulweis' argument.*

A Flawed Argument

I count myself among Rabbi Harold Schulweis' many admirers.
His theological insights and passionate patterns of action are the
stuff of legend in our community as well as throughout the country. However, I must offer my respectful dissent to his article
"Where Was God in the Earthquake?," which appeared in the

January 21 issue of the *Jewish Journal*. An earthquake of such devastating dimensions is for spiritually minded people far more
complex than Rabbi Schulweis would have us believe.

The essence of Rabbi Schulweis's message is this: God (*Elo-
him*) is the author of nature, the God of gravitation, of physical
laws, who determines how the world is. But God's role ends
there; He is not involved as nature relates to humanity. However, when it comes to humanity's reaction to the nature's devastating havoc wreaked on its world, God is *Adonai* who is not
responsible for this havoc, but rather functions in the lives of
people, prompting them to creatively cope and compassionately
deal with the effects of nature's fury.

What's the problem with this? It's certainly helpful to people
confused and anguished; its timely and "relevant" to the immediate situation; and it's conveniently soothing. But it is, in my
opinion, inconsistent, confusing theology, and ultimately unsat-
isfying. Let me explain.

To ask the question, "Where Was God in the Earthquake?" is
equivalent to asking, "Where is God in the physical universe?"
In the Jewish theological scheme of things, God is everywhere—
not just in the inspiring, beneficent and beautiful in nature—in
spring blossoms, aromatic plants and delicious fruit-but also in
the not so beneficent: in natural physical havoc as well. Indeed,
our prayerbook enjoins us not only to acknowledge God for our
food and clothing, for heaven's rain and rainbow, but also for
thunder and earthquake as well:

בָּרוּךְ אַתָּה ה׳ אֱלֹהֵינוּ מֶלֶךְ
הָעוֹלָם שֶׁכֹּחוֹ וּגְבוּרָתוֹ מָלֵא עוֹלָם

*Praised are you Lord our God, Master of the Universe, whose
strength and might fill the world.*

Our rabbinic tradition goes further and enjoins us to discern
God not only in that which human beings deem to be the good

things in life, but in the not so good as well. Rabbi Meir tells us:

כְּשֵׁם שֶׁמְבָרֵךְ עַל הַטּוֹבָה
כַּךְ מִבָרֵךְ עַל הָרָעָה

Just as one praises (God) for the good, so is one to praise (Him) for the bad.

Similarly, when a person dies, we are enjoined to ascribe to God wisdom in judgment:

בָּרוּךְ דַיַן הָאֱמֶת

Praised be the True Judge.

Is it not then, theological legerdemain to ascribe to God only the good and positive in our world but to remove Him from the picture when something bad happens? This way of thinking has us unabashedly thanking and praising God when we experience and benefit from the beauty and bounty of nature. It then has us conveniently disassociating Him from nature's havoc, thus visiting upon us tortuous inconsistency:

We laud God for the rain that waters the earth, which makes it possible to cultivate our crops thus enabling us to eat—and live. But when it rains too abundantly and the flood comes, we absent God from the picture.

We praise God for the moving air in the natural atmosphere, which gives us the very breath of life. But when the wind blows too strongly bringing on a hurricane, we hastily deal God out of the equation.

We stand in awe of God and thank Him as we watch the miracle of a normal and healthy baby emerge from a mother's womb. But when tragically a baby emerges malformed, a new insight springs to mind: in this God was not involved!

If Rabbi Schulweis would be just as unwilling to attribute to God nature's positive beneficence toward mankind as he is unwilling to attribute to God nature's negative manifestations toward humanity, then I would have no quarrel with him. If he is not—maintaining the belief that God is present only in the good things in our world and not in the bad—then I think his position is not only inconsistent insofar as classical Jewish theology is concerned, but flawed. How? It suggests a dualism wherein separate powers in the world appear to be functioning: one the source of the good (God) and another the source of the bad (Lucifer, Satan, the devil, a fallen angel, i.e. not God).[1] Thus an aspect of the world of nature (e.g., an earthquake) appears to function either at random or via a power other than God, a notion unacceptable to the religious mindset of the monotheist.

In Jewish theology, כְּבוֹדוֹ מָלֵא עוֹלָם, God's presence permeates the whole world—the natural and the human—not just part of it and not just some of the time, but all of it and at all times. The non-normative theology of Rabbi Schulweis, joined by so many earnest religionists in wake of the earthquake, provides balm, calm and some measure of meaning for perplexed minds and troubled spirits engendered by natural phenomena that hurts.

While this approach is quite understandable and seems to bring meaning to real problems, in the long run it evades the complexities, the mystery, the bittersweet, the existential reality of the often tragic pain of the world—the real world.

---

1. Fallen celestial upstarts, perpetrators of all manner of evil in heaven and on earth.

– Seven –

THE FAITHFUL MODERNIST
The Synthesis Between Tradition and Modernity

The faithful modernist embraces the traditional purpose of study that seeks religious guidance and affirmation. At the same time, he pursues the modern method and purpose of study that unearths striking and pertinent new data, values objectivity, and searches for spiritual meaning and affirmation. Both are indispensable and, combined, they produce an amplified and enriched "music of Jewish learning" of compelling and enduring value for all Jews who delve into the textual stuff of Judaism.

The Music in Jewish Learning

A favorite book of mine, one that has remained fixed in my mind, is Samuel Heilman's *People of the Book*. Dr. Heilman is a professor of sociology at Queens College in New York and a modern Orthodox Jew.[1]

He describes a study he undertook of the various *Chevra Shas* (Talmud study circles) in the New York area. These consist of interested laypeople who gather weekly to study and carefully

---

1. Heilman, Samuel. *The People of the Book: Drama, Fellowship and Religion.* University of Chicago Press, 1983.

examine the classic rabbinic texts and commentaries composed in Palestine and Babylonia some fifteen hundred years ago and earlier. The texts are entirely in Hebrew and Aramaic, but translated and discussed in English. Dr. Heilman wanted to discern the pattern and main characteristics of these learning enclaves, and what motivated the participants to be so deeply involved in what the contemporary Jew could justifiably consider arcane subject matter—compiled long ago and for another milieu.

Heilman himself attended one of these study circles for a full year. A novice in this kind of study, he attended the circle faithfully, listened intently to the proceedings and, as he himself said, had difficulty understanding the material. He had little background in Talmud, and his Hebrew/Aramaic was not strong. Yet he was diligent and persistent. When asked why he attended in this way, he responded, "I come here for the music."[2]

What I am discussing here is what I think Professor Heilman meant by "the music" of Jewish learning, which might yield some insight into the nature of study in the traditional Jewish mindset. I then describe the modern mode of study, how it differs from the traditional one—and what an affirming combination of the two modes produces: among other things, a faithful modernist.

The Role of Texts for Community

Let's first examine the difference between "reading" a Jewish text as moderns understand the word "reading," and "learning" (*lernen*, as the Yiddish has it) Jewish texts, the latter terminology used by traditional Jews.[3]

---

2. Ibid., p. 68–71.
3. This analysis of the difference between "reading" and "learning" is found in general form in the introduction to Holtz, Barry, *Back to the Sources: Reading the Classic Jewish Texts*, Summit Books, 1984). For detailed description of traditional "learning," or *lernen*, see Ibid., Heilman, "Looking into Lernen: An Introduction into the Talmud Study Circle," Ch. 1.

Reading is essentially a solitary activity. We sit alone as we read. We pause often, think to ourselves, mark up the book, take notes, go back and re-read a passage. It's usually quiet in our study or the library. We're enveloped in ourselves and in the people and ideas in the volume being examined.

Traditional Jewish reading is not reading in the modern sense. It's quite different. It's studying in a social context. Witness the Yeshiva. Here Jewish learning takes place in a hall amid a cacophony of voices. This is the *Beit Midrash* (the study hall). Here students study either in pairs or threesomes, reading out loud and talking animatedly back and forth. One who enters is immediately engulfed by the chatter and conversation of the learners.

I remember this experience vividly from my own school days at the Orthodox Yeshiva Chaim Berlin I attended through high school, from my college years at Yeshiva University, and from my son Reuven studying this way in the Yeshiva University *Beit Midrash* he attended for five years en route to receiving rabbinic ordination. The atmosphere is nothing like that of the silent home study or library carrel or the staid classroom we're accustomed to. Reading in the Yeshiva takes place amid an incessant din. It's reading in talk; it's reading by discussion; indeed, it's not reading at all—it's studying, it's learning, it's lernen.

What, then, is happening here? The study experience is not a solitary activity during which the person reflects on the text. Rather, *it's a way of communal communication. The Jew studies in order to become part of the Jewish people and to connect to its value system. Study here is a ritual act of the community.* This is what Professor Heilman meant when he talked about "the music" of the *Chevra Shas*. It was a learning environment that provided what he called "sentimental education."[4] This was a way for the Jew to connect to the Jewish community of the past as his own, and to gain access to the values of his tradition as embedded in that community—and to live out those values by the very act of study.

---

4. Ibid., p. 67, 97f.

I'm thinking of a furniture salesman I know. He works hard all day, comes home, has dinner, and announces to his household, "I'm going to the *Beit Midrash* to learn." He's really not all that interested in the subject of the accoutrements of the ancient *Beit Hamikdash* (temple), or the consequences to the owner of an ox who gored his neighbor's cow, or about a soon-to-be married virgin receiving two hundred *zuzim* (Jewish coins used in Roman Palestine) or a non-virgin one hundred *zuzim* as stipulated in the ketubah document.

When he studies Talmud this way, through discussion he is catapulted back into the talmudic world; time and place are erased and the student is back in the academies of Sura and Pumbedita in Babylonia fifteen hundred years ago. Here the learner joins in the discussions, voices his opinions, is refuted or defended by Ravina and Rav Ashi and the other great teachers and masters of other ages. This is the way the traditional student of today seeks to place himself vertically, as it were, within the Jewish tradition, continuing it into the present.

This kind of learning connects the student to the rich emotional world embedded in the classic texts. These are not just books on or off a shelf. They live in the context of hours of human give-and-take, of challenge and enlightenment in the framework of community. The texts here are interactive—in the way the reading is lively dialogue, in the way students speak in their *hevruta* (study circle) in which they debate and ponder the texts aloud.

The Role of Texts for Religious Experience

The classic texts of Judaism play yet another role in the life of the Jew: they point to the central religious facet of the Jewish enterprise. This is another basic reason why the traditional Jew studies his texts with such passion. He wants to know what God expects of him, how and why he ought to live as a diligent, faithful Jew. And so, the texts appear everywhere in his ritual life:

In the prayerbook... which abounds with material taken from the Bible, Talmud, medieval Jewish poetry, the Zohar, even from the theology of Maimonides; for example, the *Yigdal* hymn which contains the 13 principles of the Jewish faith, and the *Adon Olam* purported to be authored by the medieval Hebrew poet Solomon Ibn Gabirol, affirming the oneness of God.[5]

In the Torah readings... on the Shabbat and holy days, which have as their constant companions sections of the Pentateuch and Prophets. The biblical Song of Songs is chanted on Passover, the book of Ruth on Shavuot, Ecclesiastes on Sukkot, Esther on Purim, Lamentations on Tisha B'av. A rabbinic literary work, the Haggadah, is used on Passover, and on Hanukah medieval liturgical poems are read. The texts are always there—throughout the year and throughout the life cycle—in the rituals of birth, Bar and Bat Mitzvah, marriage and death.

In the home rituals... where, for example, the *Kiddush* chanted over wine on Friday evening is essentially composed of quotations from Genesis 2:1-3.

The role of the master teacher... tells about the religious context of traditional Jewish learning. It is no coincidence that the overseer of the *Beit Midrash* is called *mashgiakh rukhani* — "spiritual supervisor." This teacher is someone who guides the learner through the often difficult textual materials. He helps unravel thorny issues, prods the students to think for themselves, shows them a *derekh in lernen* — a methodology of study — and encourages interaction among his charges. The master here has a special kind of authority. It's an authority based on his personal piety, on his reputation for diligence, and especially on Torah-wisdom; it is based on his mastery of the biblical and rabbinic literary corpus, or on a profound grasp of a particular facet of this corpus. Indeed, Jews venerate the learned teacher, which continues the long tradition of respecting the instruction, the

---

5. The author of the *Adon Olam* has not been definitely established. Joseph Hertz in his *The Authorized Daily Prayerbook* (1946), p. 7, and Jonathan Sacks in his *The Koren Siddur* (Jerusalem: Koren 2009), p. 577, both cite the attribution of the poem by some to Ibn Gabirol.

insights, and the legal judgments of the sages of old.

In summary, the traditional mode of Jewish study is for the purpose of strengthening community (both "vertically," i.e., community of the past, and "horizontally" i.e., community of the present), and to re-experience the religious life and value system of those who preceded in time those who study.[6]

The Modern Mode of Study and Its Impact on the Traditional Mode

Up to this point, we've explored the traditional mode of Jewish study and learning. A core of Jews these days, as they delve into Jewish texts, remain fixed in that tradition. However, most Jewish students today do not remain so fixed. Most are highly educated in the secular methods of study; they've been reared in an educational system where study is much more like "reading"—alone at home or in a library, or in a university classroom that is usually a silent place where the instructor holds forth. This modern educational modality differs significantly from the traditional way.

One different way is study for historical information…

Biblical, rabbinic, liturgical and other Jewish literature have been and continue to be used as important sources of data about past history. They have been mined for knowledge about the language and literature, the life and religion, the culture and institutions of various early civilizations. To cite but a few examples:

Biblical archaeology has shone much light on ancient Canaanite and Egyptian religion and culture.

Plumbing the treasures of rabbinic literature, the prominent Talmudic scholar, Professor Saul Lieberman, has uncovered much about the Hellenistic world during the first three centuries

---

6. It should be noted that this essay does not attempt to identify how or when what is depicted here as the "traditionalist" model of study developed other than to say that this is the model associated with Ashkenazic study practice as of the eve of World War II.

of the Common Era. Thus, for example, *Kohelet Rabbah* 11:1 records a Gentile judge being credited with the just acquittal of a Jew. The Rabbis record the pagan emphasis on the value of hard work, a value Jews needed to emulate. Semi-proselytes were held by the Rabbis in high esteem. Some people of heathendom were viewed as good and honest.[7]

Study of biblical times has shed much light on nascent Christianity—what Jesus and the apostles, all of whom were Jews, imbibed from their Jewish roots.

Jewish scholars, such as the eminent historian Salo Baron, in his monumental study of the Jewish experience, have documented the great era of Islamic literary and cultural life during the Middle Ages. This flourishing period was shown to have impacted the Jewish Spanish "Golden Age," which produced a bevy of prominent Jewish poets, literary and philosophical figures such as Judah Halevi, author of the famous *Kuzari*.[8]

Moreover, those who study the history of Judaism via its literature in these ways need not necessarily be, nor, in fact, were and are practicing Jews. Indeed, they may not even be Jewish. Witness, for example, the seminal German Bible scholar Julius Wellhausen,[9] who helped reveal the actual complexity of the Pentateuch; William Foxwell Albright, the prominent archaeologist whose work has illumined many ancient biblical places and their characteristics based on his studies of the ancient Near East; Paul Lapp, my teacher of biblical history at the Pittsburgh Theological Seminary, who followed in Albrights's footsteps; John Bright, whose *History of Israel* has anchored the period of the Patriarchs in concrete history;[10] and George Foote Moore, whose

---

7. Lieberman, Saul. *Greek in Jewish Palestine*. Jewish Theological Seminary of America, 1942; p. 76–77.
8. Baron, Salo. *A Social and Religious History of the Jews*. Columbia University Press, 1969; Ch. 32.
9. Wellhausen's well-known hostility to Judaism ought not to morph into denial of his seminal contribution to unraveling the various sources of the Pentateuch
10. See Albright's *From the Stone Age to Christianity* (Baltimore: Johns

volumes on Judaism during the classical rabbinic period are themselves classics.[11] These scholars have opened up new and revealing vistas, and have deeply affected the ways in which a modern religious Jew studies, prodding him and her to look anew at many of the basic suppositions of traditional Jewish life and thought.

Another differing way is the focus on objective data . . .

The critically oriented Jewish scholar approaches the texts with an objective, critical eye, through a lens that sees things as they are, not as he wants the materials to be. Indeed, in this perspective, the Bible and rabbinical literature—all of Jewish literature for that matter—must be examined with critical care. For example, modern Bible scholars have discerned multiple strata in the biblical materials—not heretofore observed. Lawrence Boadt has succinctly summarized the essential character of the modern approach to study of the Pentateuch in this way:

> Drawing on the history of how the various strata came to be, the modern Bible student now could discover four different authors and their literary styles, and he could picture clearly the different times and places from which each source came. This analysis shows the development in which the early and mostly oral traditions of Israel were gradually written down and preserved in four documents, and then combined to make one Pentateuch. This is the famous documentary thesis known as JEDP (letters for each of the four sources) and accepted by the vast majority of modern students of Scripture.[12]

I would include among these critically oriented scholars in our time: Nahum Sarna, Mark Smith, Jon Levenson, Ziony Zevit,

---

Hopkins Press; 1957) Lapp's *Biblical Archaeology and History* (New York: World Publishing Company; 1969), and Bright's *A History of Israel* (Philadelphia: Westminster Press; 1981).

11. See G. F. Moore's three-volume *Judaism: In the First Centuries of the Christian Era*. Harvard University Press, 1954.

12. Boadt, Lawrence. *Reading the Old Testament*. Paulist Press, 1984; p. 94.

Benjamin Sommer, Michael Fishbane, and some dozen others whose work is contained in the collection found in the volume *Judaic Perspectives on Ancient Israel*. Their trenchant analytic writings in the world of biblical scholarship accept the documentary hypothesis as a given.[13]

In contrast to this perspective on the Pentateuch, the fundamentalist students of the Bible refuse to see these five books as they are, but rather as they want them to be, that is, that they are *in their entirety* the product of Moses at Mount Sinai, the work of this *single author* during *one specific time* in history. They do this by employing creative rabbinic exegesis and midrashic imagination, making scriptural texts to mean what their traditional faith prompts them to want them to mean.

The elements described here constitute the modern approach to scripture and rabbinic literature: the unearthing of historical information, the new view of the complexity of biblical writings, the consequences of the external contexts in which Jews have lived, the emphasis on objectivity. These do, indeed, render the modern approach different from the traditional study of texts by the pious Jew of the past, and the pious today in many quarters. For, as we have seen, in addition to the latter's study as a way to link to community, the traditional learner has another basic motive in mind as he approaches the texts: how does the God of Israel, the *Ribono Shel Olam*, the Master of the universe, want me

---

13. A selection of the works of these scholars:
- Sarna, Nahum. *Exploring Exodus: The Heritage of Biblical Israel.* Schocken Books, 1986.
- Smith, Mark. *The Memoirs of God.* Fortress Press, 2004.
- Levenson, Jon. Sinai and Zion: *An Entry into the Jewish Bible.* Harper, 1985.
- Zevit, Ziony. *The Religions of Ancient Israel.* Continuum, 2001.
- Sommer. Benjamin. *The Bodies of God and the World of Ancient Israel.* Cambridge University Press, 2011.
- Fishbane, Michael. *Sacred Attunement: A Jewish Theology.* University of Chicago Press, 2010.
- Neusner, Jacob and Levine, Baruch A. (eds.). *Judaic Perspectives on Ancient Israel.* Fortress Press, 1987.

to live? For him these texts communicate ultimate truth—truth about God, about the world, about what God wants of His people. Questions about historical reliability, about outside cultural, political and economic influences, about technical accuracy, are basically irrelevant to his overriding religious objectives. However, for the adherent of the modern approach to study, these objective factors remain quite relevant and unavoidably compelling.

In summary, the modern mode of study is more objective than the traditional mode generally and specifically with regard to Scripture. It seeks to see the Jewish experience and its literature in the context of the larger societies in which these have functioned, revealing in the process a good deal about the culture, religion and institutions of the non-Jewish world, and via these, in significant measure, of the Jewish world as well.

Can the Twain Meet?

Here, then, we have two apparently conflicting objectives in the study of Judaic texts—that of the traditional and modern, what I have called "lernen" and "reading." The question now is: can the two modes of exploration be seen as in unity with each other so that they, in fact, can strengthen rather than weaken each other? Indeed, can they be seen as in harmony rather than conflict, or must they remain in permanent tension?

A fascinating story about Yosef Yerushalmi, the late professor of Jewish history at Columbia University (a classmate of mine in the Rabbinical School at the Jewish Theological Seminary) appeared in the *New York Jewish Week*. The story reveals the unresolved tension between Yerushalmi's modern mode of historical studies that focuses on the objective facts of the Jewish experience versus the traditional view of Jewish history as influenced by the hand of Providence. After his passing, a heretofore unpublished and unknown novel that Yerushalmi wrote was published in *The New Yorker* magazine.[14] It concerned a character

---

14. Yerushalmi, Yosef. "Gilgul," *New Yorker*. 4 August 2011.

simply called Ravitch who is a scholar of Jewish history with a restless spirit who yearns for peace of mind. The article goes on to tell about Yerushalmi's book, *Zakhor*, which was about the tension between Jewish memory and Jewish history—and more broadly between the ancient, spiritual and religious life versus the modern, secular and academic one.

"Many Jews today are in search of a past," Yerushalmi wrote, "but they do not want the past that is offered by the historian."[15]

Yerushalmi, who taught at Harvard and Columbia, was never quite sure he wanted the history he had to offer either. He was religiously observant in his youth and later ordained at the Jewish Theological Seminary, but then abandoned the life of the pulpit for one of the professor's podium. The dilemma he faced was similar to Ravitch's: should he embrace the emotional pull of faith, or should he dismiss it and risk finding comfort in the facts?

"I think his life conflict was unresolved," Ophra, Yerushalmi's wife, said of the Ravitch character. And how about her husband, Yosef? Was the conflict unresolved too? "Perhaps," she ventured: "Like everyone, we all carry unresolved conflicts within us."[16]

And then there is Professor James Kugel, the long-time professor of Hebrew literature at Harvard University, and later at Bar Ilan University and a practicing Orthodox Jew. A highly creative and prominent scholar of biblical literature, Kugel in his *How to Read the Bible* describes both the traditional and modern modes of scriptural study, notes their fundamental differences, indicates that neither can be considered invalid and ignored, yet makes no effort to integrate the two in a way they might amplify and reinforce each other. To the contrary, he asserts in the closing pages of his book: "My own view is that modern biblical scholarship and

---

15. Yerushalmi, Yosef. *Zakhor: Jewish History and Jewish Memory*. University of Washington Press, 1983; p. 97.
16. *New York Jewish Week*, August 2011

traditional Judaism are, and must always be, completely irreconcilable."[17]

A faithful modernist cannot and need not accept this unresolved tension between the traditional and modern modes of study as exemplified by Professor Yerushalmi, nor can he accept the two modes as irreconcilable, as indicated by Professor Kugel. He agrees with Benjamin Sommer, Professor of Bible at the Jewish Theological Seminary, who equates Kugel's view on the irreconcilability of traditional Judaism and biblical scholarship with sticking one's head in the sand:

> An honest response (to critical biblical findings which challenge traditional faith) cannot be to pretend that the challenge does not exist. Nor can a Jewish response be to bifurcate, so that one has a Jewish soul and a secular mind, coexisting uneasily in a single body but not communicating with each other. A Jew is commanded to serve God with all one's mind, with all one's soul, with all one is. A Jew whose intellect believes that biblical criticism makes valid claims, but whose religious self pretends otherwise is rendering God service that is fragmented and defective."[18]

Both Professors Yerushalmi and Kugel represent those immersed in modern historical and biblical scholarly endeavor, yet are also persons of religious commitment rooted in the tradition. They see conflict between the two realms, but leave it unresolved. By way of contrast, here I search for an affirming relationship between the two realms. I believe that the two can be seen as in harmony with each other and also can and do strengthen one another. This hopefully will lead us to a unified modality embodied in what I have been calling the faithful modernist.

---

17. Kugel, James. *How to Read the Bible: A Guide to Scripture Then and Now.* Free Press, 2007; p. 681.
18. Sommer, Benjamin. "Two Introductions to Scripture: James Kugel and the Possibility of Biblical Theology." *Jewish Quarterly Review*, Vol. 100, No. 1. Winter 2010; p. 174.

What Does the Modern Study Approach Contribute to Harmony with the Traditional Approach?

1) Faith and basic traditional affirmations are often enhanced by modern critical thinking.

When, for example, a contemporary bible researcher detects multiple strata in the texts of the Pentateuch that reveal the hands of different writers and different eras in biblical life, we cannot conclude that the Pentateuchal texts are the product of a single hand and their provenance in but one period of time and clime. However, for the faithful modernist, what these researchers do show is that *the Divine speaks to humanity in all eras of Jewish life and to the many faithful in their own period and place who are attuned to God's will.* Indeed, genuine faith and basic traditional affirmations about the Divine role in human life are thereby enhanced rather than diminished.[19]

This is what is meant by the notion that the God of Israel is the God of history. The faithful modernist sees God as having manifested His presence and revealed His will not only in early biblical times, but in the prophetic era as well—in His communication with the great prophets, Isaiah, Jeremiah and Ezekiel, Amos, Hosea and Micah. Yet more: His presence and will were manifest when, earlier, God guided His people during the Exodus from Egypt—and into the Promised Land, when He went into exile with Israel in Babylonia, when He led His people back

---

19. Jeffrey Tigay in his foreword to Nahum Sarna's *Studies in Biblical Interpretation* (JPS, 2000), p. XII, writes this about Sarna's attitude about modern biblical criticism and its religious implications: "In its general outlines," Sarna has written, "the non-unitary origin of the Pentateuch has survived as *one of the finalities of biblical scholarship.*" Nor does Sarna see this as a problem for religious faith. "God can work through four documents as effectively as through one, unfolding His revelation in successive stages as well as in a single moment of time." He notes further that even the most traditional Jew must admit that this happened in the second division of the Bible, the Prophets, let alone the writings, which developed over several centuries.

to the land in the Persian era, when He girded the strength of the Maccabees during the revolt against the Syrian Greeks, when He was with His people during the traumatic period of Roman oppression...and on and on through the vicissitudes of the Jewish experience down through the centuries—including our own when His spiritual presence is seen to be in the midst of the people, teaching, sustaining and inspiring them as they delve into a vast literature-past and present.

Indeed, the tenacity of the Jew in the face of constant hostility, his survival, and the triumph of his spirit have their source in the faith that God guides and redeems. *The texts of the Jewish people explored by the modern scholar tell us that experience with the God of Israel in Mosaic times was but a crucial beginning.*

In this and similar ways, modern critical thinkers will not be put off or cavalierly dismissed in the name of tradition. Faith is not allowed to be jettisoned by blindness to the findings of the critical mind, which is one of God's marvelous endowments on His human children.

Abraham Ibn Ezra (1089–1167) was a prominent Spanish Jewish Bible commentator during the Middle Ages. His work occupies the standard editions of the Hebrew Bible. A guiding principle he employs in interpreting scripture was that the human intellect is a *malakh hashem*, "the mind, an angel of God" and he further emphasizes that "he who believes in something that contradicts the *sekhel* [that is, common sense, reason, logic] abuses the finest gift God has given him."[20]

Ibn Ezra echoed his famous Muslim predecessor, theologian and jurist, Abu Hamid al-Ghazali (1058-1111), who emphasized that *lo bara Hashem b'riah yoter nikhbedet min hasekhel*, "God has created nothing more distinguished than reason" (translated from the Arabic into Hebrew by Rabbi Avraham ibn Hasdai [ca.

---

20. See Ibn Ezra's introduction to his commentary on Genesis, where he surveys four different approaches to Bible commentary. In the third approach he says, "The Torah was not given to the unintelligent; the intellect must be the intermediary between man and God."

1230 CE], an enthusiastic scholarly partisan of Moses Maimonides who was a champion of rational thought in the pursuit of religious studies).

So, too, Thomas Aquinas (1224–1274), the preeminent spokesman of the Catholic tradition, who saw reason in harmony with faith. Indeed, reason, Aquinas emphasized, was a divine gift highly to be cherished, for it buttresses religious faith rather than undermines it. (Aquinas' notion of a Prime Mover/Causeless Cause demonstrated his reasoned thinking about the existence of God.)[21]

2) *Establishing core principles due to changing conditions does not alter the principles themselves.*

When the book of Leviticus ordains in great detail the content and methodology of the sacrificial system to be employed in the Temple,[22] it is clearly depicting the mode of worship of the Israelites after having settled in the Promised Land.

Indeed, the Temple built by King Solomon (ca. 920 BCE) began its service well over 300 years after the period of Moses (ca. 1300 BCE). Yet, the Bible in Leviticus asserts that the various specific details about the sacrificial system were ordained by Moses himself, which was, as noted, centuries before the Temple was in existence and the Israelite settlement in the land. Such a claim is in religious fundamentalist circles justified by a faith assertion, to wit: Moses could depict specific rules and regulations via prophecy, in this case meaning the capacity to predict detailed events and regulations centuries into the future.[23]

---

21. Aquinas, Thomas. *Summa Theologica.* "Question 2: The Existence of God, Article 2: Whether it can be demonstrated that God exists."
22. See, for example, Leviticus, chapters 5 and 9.
23. The final twelve verses of the book of Deuteronomy, unlike the body of the book that is covered in autobiographical style, speak of Moses in the third person, i.e., what occurred to and about him after he died. This indicates that these verses were not written by Moses. In fact, on Deuteronomy 34:1 Ibn Ezra explicitly says, "In my opinion, Joshua wrote from this verse on, for once Moses ascended the summit of Pisgah,

A faithful modernist, wedded as he or she is to rational thinking, avoids such a claim as a matter of principle, which clearly is
at odds with common sense, with reason, with logic. Rather, he
embraces the views of Ibn Ezra, al-Ghazali, Maimonides and
Thomas Aquinas, who do not allow statements of scripture to con-
tradict God's finest gift to man—his critical mind. *What the faithful
modernist does do in this representative instance is something strongly
affirmative religiously.* What Moses did was to hear the Transcendent bid him to establish *a basic principle of faith,* "You shall love the
Lord your God with all your heart and soul and might[24]—*ul'ovdo,*
and *"worship* the Lord with all your heart and soul."[25] This basic
principle—the obligation to worship, to thank and praise and be-
seech, to express dependence on a Power-not-human, on the One
and only God of the universe—was to be implemented by the later
stated leaders-priests of Israel. They were to employ the category
of the sacrificial system, which was the prevailing mode of worship in their own time and clime. And further, this principle of
recognizing the monotheistic God was to be implemented by the
religious leaders of subsequent generations when the sacrificial
system no longer obtained, again in accordance with the altered
ways of worship in those later times. And so forth into modern
times. As Benjamin Franklin wisely put it, "The ancients tell us
what is best, but we must learn what is fittest."

Such has been the pattern throughout Jewish religious history.
Indeed, the social and economic, political and religious conditions
inevitably change in the course of life's flow. *But, as a faithful modernist sees it, the core principles established in the Mosaic period do not.*
For it was in that seminal period launched, he contends, at Sinai,
that the obligatory principle of worship of the One God of Israel

---

when he died, he wrote no more." He then adds cryptically, "Or he
wrote prophetically about himself." About this Ibn Ezra says, "If you
understand the deep meaning of the twelve verses…you will recognize
the truth." See Sarna, Nahum. *Studies in Biblical Interpretation.* The Jewish Publication Society, 2000; p. 152.

24. Deuteronomy 6:5.
25. Deuteronomy 11:13.

was established, along with the other fundamental principles of the faith. What subsequent generations have done—and continue to do—was to adapt the principles then planted and do so in accordance with their own conditions in order to make the teachings relevant to the needs of those generations. Indeed, these subsequent adaptations were seen as implicit in the teachings of the Mosaic period.

Abraham Geiger has articulated this perspective in this way:

> The history of Judaism is wonderfully unique in that it spans a period extending from remote antiquity down to the immediate present. It is, therefore, not mere curiosity which acts as a spur to its study, not merely the desire to eavesdrop on the mystery of the origins of Judaism, but at least equally the desire to detect the extent to which all of its later development was essentially already inherent in the growth and flowering process of the original seeds. These beginnings are elusive…but without the revelation which only study of them affords, one can never succeed in gaining the proper insight into Judaism's subsequent history which lies more fully recorded before him.[26]

And later, Jonathan Sacks reinforced this perspective in striking modern terms, to wit:

> In the earliest stages of an embryo, when a fetus is still no more than a small bundle of cells, already it contains the genome, the long string of DNA, from which the child and eventually the adult will emerge. The genetic structure that will shape the person it becomes is there from the beginning. So it is with Judaism. Bible, Mishna, Talmud and Aggada, even what a senior disciple is destined to teach in the presence of his master, was already stated to Moses at Sinai.[27]

---

26. Geiger in Meyer, Michael. *Ideas of Jewish History.* Wayne State University Press, 1974; p. 169.
27. Sacks, Jonathan (ed.). *Koren Sacks Rosh Hashanah Mahzor.* Koren Publishers Jerusalem, 2011; p. xii. For a similar perspective, see Shneur Zalman

The faithful modernist does not need a literalist reading of scripture to establish for him abiding religious affirmation.

A practical result of this approach emerges: highly educated contemporary Jews who are "religious" by inclination yet have been profoundly influenced by modern/secular ways of learning, and are irrevocably committed to these ways, are persuaded to connect to the traditional fold. Why? Because, again, traditional religious affirmation and modern critical research have been found to be of one mind: *God's pervasive presence in the world and in the ongoing life of His people—and acceptance of His principal requirements on the part of that people.* The two realms are positively connected rather than being viewed at odds with each other.

3) The historical data modern scholars have unearthed provides new understanding of the phenomenon of adaptation and change that have contributed to Jewish sturdiness and survival through the ages.

Certain currently accepted—and rejected—beliefs and practices have, in fact, been molded and remolded as a result of the impact of new findings and perspectives developed in different periods of time and in various locales in the world. Thus historical studies reveal the adaptive nature of Judaism, its patterns of thought and action understood as responses to changing environmental conditions. Absent such ability to change and adapt to new times and climes, the Jewish enterprise would have become fossilized.

A personal experience might serve as an illustration of that which resists this necessity. While serving as a Rabbi in Pittsburgh, I once visited my alma mater, the Jewish Theological Seminary in New York, and was invited to a gathering of seminary faculty and their wives at the home of Rabbi David Weiss-Halivni, a leading scholar of rabbinics and another seminary classmate of mine. They wanted to hear about the various initiatives at my

---

of Liadi, *The Tanya*, chapter 2, p. 169f.

synagogue in Pittsburgh they had heard about, and I was eager to hear their take on some of the religious issues of the day.

The five faculty wives present were the following: a Ph.D. in library science; a prominent landscape artist; an editor of children's books; a Ph.D. in psychology; and a Ph.D. in biology.

I asked the group what they thought about women serving in the rabbinate, being counted to a *minyan* along with the men, receiving an *aliya* at services.

All five women were adamantly opposed, citing the traditional ban on these matters. When I pointed out that they, along with many women doctors and lawyers and college professors are active in the "outside" world, meet and work with professional men and women all the time, they each responded: the religious public domain is different. When I asked why it was different, their response was that the religious realm has a different set of criteria on these matters.

These truly accomplished professional women have not integrated their general and religious public domains—a puzzling dichotomy between the secular and religious ways of thinking and acting.[28]

Of course, these women, along with their traditional male counterparts, have not had the last word on these matters insofar as the faithful modernist is concerned. The latter points to the fundamental principle long since established in scripture: "And God created man in His image, in the image of God He created him; *male and female* He created them."[29] As such, both have equal status in God's eyes and, therefore, as a matter of principle, equal status in human eyes, both personally and in community. Hence, the *Zeitgeist* of the twentieth and twenty-first centuries, in contrast to that of the preceding centuries, has rightly led to the realization

---

28. For one analysis of this phenomenon, see Israel-Cohen, Yael. *Between Feminism and Orthodox Judaism: Resistance, Identity and Religious Change in Israel*. Brill, 2012.
29. Genesis 1:27.

that the place of women in general and in the religious realm in particular has changed. The faithful modernist thus applies the biblical principle of human equality to women along with men in the public domain, let alone the personal one. Indeed, he views such as clearly implicit in scripture's sacred dictum.

4) Modern studies in comparative religion have revealed striking similarities in sacred phenomena to that of the traditional notion.

Examples of this are sacred places considered to be of supreme importance due to experiences with the deity, mountains considered to be the abode of the deity, the view that one's own country is at the center of the earth, and law codes such as the Babylonian Code of Hammurabi (ca. 1880 BCE), which preceded in time the biblical codes and which have striking parallels to them.

In my book *The Land of Israel: Its Theological Dimensions*, I detail an aspect of this phenomenon. In a report titled "Their Gods Resided There," published in the Los Angeles Times, we're told that more than twenty Inca sites on mountaintops in the Peruvian Andes were discovered during a four-year period by Johan Reinhard, an American anthropologist and mountain climber, The Incas who labored up these mountains, some higher than 20,000 feet, *were worshipping the gods that they believed dwelled in and on those mountains and who communicated with them.*

At least fifty such mountaintops with Inca ruins, remains and artifacts indicative of active worship of the gods were found on peaks from southern Peru to central Chile documented this mountain deity worship on the famous Machu Picchu. Other archaeologists report that there are Kenyans who still practice tribal religion and revere Mount Kenya as the home of their god.[30]

To be sure, the content and implications of what occurred on

---

30. Shechter, Jack. *The Land of Israel: Its Theological Dimensions*. University Press of America, 2010; p. 180-181. The report referenced is in *The Los Angeles Times*, 5 April 1984, p. 8.

these mountains (about the notion of one's country's centrality, about the non-Israelite codes) are significantly different than the parallel biblical phenomena. Indeed, the extra-biblical notions have been refashioned in accordance with Israelite principles. However, the phenomena in which the contents are embedded are often strikingly similar.

For the traditionalist, this perspective opens up new vistas that soften ethnocentricity and invites a more inclusive approach. It offers place for others to share in the enterprise of religious development by suggesting that multiple ideational and ritual possibilities abound in the realm of religion. It induces such religionists to be open to the possibility that others—both within and without the Jewish fold—are in possession of compelling new knowledge and, more importantly, are equally affirmers of religious principle. When this perspective enters into the religious mindset of the traditionalists, the door of mutuality is jarred open so that "readers" and "learners" can see a way to value their different modes of study and a path found to appreciate the validity of other perceptions of the religious condition.

5) Contemporary critical research into the mystical strain in Judaism—the Kabbalah, Hasidism and its heretofore neglected literature—has revealed a great deal of spiritual and psychological value, which many modern religionists can and have embraced.

Thus, for example, Gershom Scholem, the founder of the modern study of Kabbalah, has elucidated a category of Jewish thought, prayer and ritual practice that pursues insights into what many view as God's nature, good and evil, and humanity's role in the cosmos. Further, the writings of Arthur Green on Hasidism, the scholarly work of Daniel Matt with his new translation of and commentary on the classic Zohar have opened up fresh and enriching vistas for today's student and has, thus, contributed much to strengthening the contemporary religious enterprise.[31]

---

31. See Scholem, Gershom. *Origins of the Kabbalah* (English translation by

6) Study tools

The modern study of biblical, rabbinic and subsequent Jewish literature presents another distinct result: its vast array of study aids, translations, maps, commentaries, dictionaries, encyclopedias, critical editions of texts, histories, comparative religion studies et al constitute a veritable treasure trove for all who wish to gain entry into the magnificent Jewish world of community and spirituality.

7) Finally, and especially significant, it is here where the modernist and traditionalist can meet in harmony on the basics of the religious enterprise.

When the faithful modernist internalizes and acts in the spirit of those two words, that is, he or she is truly "faithful and authentically "modern," and the two elements are integrated in his or her outlook on the religious enterprise of our time, a compelling notion occurs: he or she does not cavalierly negate the inner religious quest so evident in the traditional texts of the faith. To the contrary, he or she uses the critical, historical and other elements of modern study to elucidate the richness and personal relevance of the classic Jewish texts. He or she brings to bear the techniques and fruits of contemporary scholarship to illumine the depth and spiritual significance of this literature for the contemporary seeker.

Historian Yosef Yerushalmi has unearthed a fascinating document that illustrates what a modern critical scholar can and does contribute to the traditional religious perspective on the character of the Jewish enterprise through the corridors of history. Yerushalmi's now storied document demonstrates, I

Allan Arkush. Jewish Publication Society and Princeton University Press, 1987) and his *Major Trends in Jewish Mysticism* (Schocken Books, 1946); Matt, Daniel (and Wolski, Nathan and Hecker, Joel)'s *The Zohar: Pritzker Edition* (Stanford University Press, 2004-2017), and Green, Arthur *Tormented Master: A Life of Rabbi Nahman of Brazlav* (Schocken Books, 1979).

believe, that historical data illumines traditional religiosity.

In the dark year of 1942, Yerushalmi tells us, a German Jesuit scholar, Peter Browe, published *The Mission to the Jews in the Middle Ages and the Popes* in fascist Rome. The last chapter deals with the manifest failure of the Christian mission to achieve its total goal. Some Jews had been converted everywhere, in Spain, many, but medieval Jewry as a whole had not succumbed. This chapter, which Browe called "The Reasons for the Meager Success of the Mission to the Jews," is divided into three parts. The first is "The Reasons from the Christian Side"—namely, what was there in the Christian approach that precluded greater success? The second is "The Reasons from the Jewish Side"—to wit, what was there about the Jews that enabled them to resist?

At this point, Browe's hitherto consistent empiricism leaves him stranded. Having exhausted all the "reasons" he could find, Browe felt that the phenomenon was not fully comprehensible. And so, the last part of his chapter is entitled "The Reasons from God's Side." *Perhaps, in the end, God Himself did not want Judaism to be obliterated.* In conclusion, Browe wrote:

> This entire history of the Jewish people, its life and wandering throughout the centuries, the preservation of its race and peoplehood amid innumerable struggles and persecutions, cannot be explained out of purely political and sociological considerations...Only out of faith can we in some way understand the solution.[32]

In the same vein, historian Heinrich Graetz, long before Yerushalmi, wrote this:

> What prevented this ever-wandering people from degenerating into brutish vagrants or a vagabond horde of gypsies? The answer: during its desolate history of 1800 years in the diaspora, the Jewish people carried with it the Ark of the Covenant, which placed an ideal striving in its heart and transfigured the badge of shame on its garment with

---

32. Yerushalmi, Yosef. *Zakhor*. p. 90–91.

an apostolic radiance designed to educate the nations to the knowledge of God and Morality…Such a people for whom the present meant nothing and the future everything which seemed to exist by virtue of its hope, is for that very reason as eternal as hope itself.[33]

Conclusion

And so, we now come full circle. For the faithful modernist, a combination between the two modes of study—"reading" and "learning"—is his modus operandi. He embraces the traditional purpose of study that seeks religious guidance and affirmation. At the same time, he pursues the modern method and purpose of study that unearths striking and pertinent new data, values objectivity, and searches for spiritual meaning and affirmation. Both are indispensable and, combined, they can produce an amplified and enriched "music of Jewish learning" of compelling and enduring value for all Jews who delve into the textual stuff of Judaism.

---

33. Graetz in *The Ideas of Jewish History*. Meyer, Michael (ed). Behrman House, 1974; p. 231. See Meyer's introduction about this passage by Graetz in this volume, p. 218.

– Eight –

RELIGION CAN ENGENDER RAGE AS WELL AS RAPTURE

The task of this essay is to portray some of the hazards of reli-gious zealotry, and to analyze the basic reasons for the phe-nomenon and how it might be tempered. I do not write here about what might well be considered legitimate religious zeal-otry, which is an ardent pursuit of a religious way of life which enables its followers to cement collective cohesion, and which promotes moral and ethical principle. That issue requires an-other essay.[1]

Religious Zealotry: The Reality

At the Nicene Council of 325 CE, Christian leaders clashed vehe-mently over a satisfactory formula with which to express the re-lationship of Jesus to God. The Orthodox body defined Jesus as of *the same substance as God*. The moderate Arian party proposed the definition to be Jesus as of *similar substance with God*. The Or-thodox party prevailed and for years the church was split in war-ring factions, and the Arian "heresy" persisted in Europe for some 200 years.

Ultra-Orthodox Jews in contemporary times display fanatic behavior by hurling stones at cars riding through the Meah

---

1. For an incisive analysis of this subject, see King, Winston L. *Introduction to Religion.* Harper and Brothers, New York, 1954; Chapter VIII.

Shearim neighborhood in Jerusalem on Sabbath day. The "Day of rest," as these religious enthusiasts understand it, prohibits such riding, considering it a desecration.

And then there are Muslim Shiites and Sunnis who have been in violent conflict with each other for centuries due to the dispute over which individual properly or improperly assumed the mantle of leadership of the faith following the passing of its founder, Muhammad. There are those who criticize its founder in public who are often physically assaulted—and worse. Yet more: because of the deadly clash between Hindus and Muslims in India and the intense hatred among both religious groups for each other, separation between them was deemed a necessity and thus the Muslim nation of Pakistan was created.

The Jewish Experience

Biblical and post-biblical sources record instances of religious zealotry which has not engendered "rapture" but rather a kind of "rage" which, in truth, has brought about harm and hurt.

Scripture[2] tells us about Shechem, son of Hamor, chief of his country, who spotted Dinah, daughter of Jacob, was strongly drawn to her, took her, and cohabitated with her by force—a serious transgression. Her brothers, Simeon and Levi, were outraged and plotted and proceeded to kill all the males of Hamor's town, slew both Hamor and Shechem and took Dinah back. The other sons of Jacob proceeded to plunder the town, seized their flocks and donkeys, what was inside the town and outside, their wealth, children and wives, and what was in the houses taken as captives and booty. All of this because of a single transgression, odious as it was! What was father Jacob's reaction? Did he endorse his son's zealotry? Read on:

> Jacob said to Simeon and Levi, "You have brought trouble on me, making me odious among the inhabitants of the land, the Canaanites and the Perizzites. My men are

---

2. Genesis, Ch. 34.

few in number so that if they unite against me and attack me, I and my house will be destroyed." But they answered, "Should our sister be treated like a whore?"[3]

And later, when Jacob neared the end of his life, he assembled his sons for their final blessings. This is what he said to and about Simeon and Levi:

> Simeon and Levi are a pair; their weapons are tools of lawlessness. Let not my person be included in their council. Let not my being be counted in their assembly. For when angry they slay men, and when pleased they maim oxen. Cursed be their anger so fierce, and their wrath so relentless. I will divide them in Jacob, scatter them in Israel.[4]

The zealot Phineas slayed Zimri, a prince in Israel, who had relations with a Moabite woman, Cozbi, in public.[5] About this, the Talmud observes that had Phineas consulted beforehand about how to deal with the Zimri-Cozbi matter, about the law concerning it, he would have been told that his contemplated action would be considered murder, contrary to the law, and thus, he should not proceed to take Zimri's life. Indeed, the rabbis go on to say that if Zimri had defended himself by slaying Phineas, it would have been considered an act of self-defense and thus, he would not be guilty of murder. Clearly, the rabbis evince grave concern about this kind of religious zeal, a mindset ultimately to be rejected.[6]

So, too, Scripture implies and the rabbis assert the reason for the prophet Elijah's dismissal as a prophet. Elijah was indeed the herald of better days for Israel; he fought for social justice; he was a reconciler of families; he was a healer. But he was also overzealous. Indeed, no man is perfect—not even Elijah.

---

3. Genesis 34:30-31.
4. Genesis 49:5-7.
5. Numbers 25:1-15.
6. Song of Songs Rabbah 1:6; I Kings 19:10-16.

The rabbis were frank to express reservations about Elijah and some of his activities—actual in the Bible and fanciful in legend. Some considered aspects of his religiosity dubious and politically dangerous and sought to counter excessive veneration of him. For example, they cited Elijah's denunciation of Israel for having forsaken the divine covenant having so provoked God that He dismissed Elijah from His service and appointed Elisha in his place.[7] The "Chair of Elijah" at the circumcision ceremony is linked by the Rabbis to Elijah's complaint to God that "the children of Israel have forsaken Your covenant." The midrash interprets that to mean that Elijah had complained that the Jewish people had disregarded the commandment of circumcision and God, as it were, is said to have reacted:

> Because of excessive zeal for me, you have brought charges against Israel that they have forsaken my covenant; therefore (as a corrective measure) you shall have to be present at every circumcision ceremony.[8]

It cannot be gainsaid that passion and enthusiasm for one's faith and community are appropriate and necessary. Yet at times, such zeal can weaken the very cause for which one fought so zealously. The legendary Elijah himself, for all the praiseworthy aspects of his life and work, symbolizes that counterproductive way—the harmful aspect of unbridled passion.

And then there is the tragic story of the Bar Kokhba rebellion against the Roman administration in the Land of Israel in 132-135 CE. It was led by a group of the zealous who presumed to think that they were acting in the best interests of their people. Encouraged by the eminent Rabbi Akiba, they looked upon their leader, Bar Kokhba, as the "messiah" who would unburden them from the firm grip of Rome. Indeed, when Rabbi Akiba beheld Bar Kokhba, he exclaimed, "This is King Messiah," to which Rabbi Yochanan ben Torta retorted, "Akiba, grass will grow on your cheeks (i.e. you will be a long time in your grave) and he,

---

7. I Kings 19:10-16; Song of Songs Rabbah 1:6.
8. Sanhedrin, 81a.

the son of David, will not have come.[9] The fanatics, oblivious to all reality, to the impossibility of a small band of Jewish rebels prevailing against the mighty forces of Rome, ignored Rabbi Yochanan, sided with Rabbi Akiba and fought in vigorous rebellion. Rabbi Jonathan Sacks describes the result:

> The Bar Kokhba rebellion was a tragic error. It led to one of the greatest-ever devastations of Jewish life. The Roman historian Dio estimates that 58,000 Jews died in the fighting, "and countless numbers by starvation, fire, and the sword." Some 28 towns were destroyed and the countryside was laid waste. Jerusalem was razed to the ground and rebuilt as Aelia Capitolina, a Roman city, which Jews were forbidden to enter. The many sages who opposed Rabbi Akiba were, on this occasion, right.[10]

Hardly a contribution to the welfare of the Jewish people! Yes, indeed, people must learn about the negatives of religious fanaticism.

The Reasons for Religious Zealotry

Additional examples of religious zealotry could, of course, be cited—ancient, medieval, modern. While in the modern age in particular, there does exist in some places a degree of religious tolerance, it appears fair to assert that zealotry/fanaticism has been characteristic of religion in general. Zvi Hirsch Chajes, the Galician Talmudist and historian, remarked, "Just as faith in its highest sense is what unites people, so religion is what divides them." If this is so, why is this so? This is what needs to be explained.

We need to observe at the beginning of this inquiry that differences of viewpoint are a common experience and by no means limited to the religious sphere of human life. Philosophers in every culture have developed multiple systems of thought,

---

9. Lamentations Rabbah 2:2,4; Jerusalem Talmud 4:8.
10. See Telushkin, Joseph. *Jewish Literacy*. William Morrow, 2008; p. 136f.

many radically at odds with each other. Moral theorists have disagreed and still radically disagree about the nature of the good life and what moral goals men and women ought to seek. In politics antagonism seems to be a feature of contemporary public life, reaching a near-religious pitch of emotional intensity. Even in the world of science strong and persistent controversy obtains.

Thus it would seem that religion is not alone in its diversity of viewpoint on matters of great importance. Yet, unlike the sphere of religion, in the realms of philosophy, politics and science, compromise seems possible, nuance in the articulation of viewpoint is more often than not tolerated, and even where differences remain, people in these realms find it possible to live relatively amicably with each other.

Yet, while religion understandably harbors the same right to differ in its beliefs and practices as is allowed by the other disciplines, something more is involved here, and that is what appears to be zealotry's endemic character.

Conservatism

Some of this intensity of difference can be explained simply as conservatism. A person gets used to a particular way of thinking and doing things and dislikes change. This may apply from sitting in a favorite pew in a house of worship to dwelling on a favorite idea of God. Much of the attraction of one way of worship over another is simply this at-home feeling that attaches to the familiar pattern; and a significant part of religious loyalty is the love of familiar buildings, symbols, leaders, fellow religionists, and patterns of devotion.

The Distinctive for Itself

The particular or distinctive is cherished for itself—in religion and other spheres of life. It would be inspiring to think of religion as universally practiced by all men everywhere and in the same ways, and of belonging to a fellowship of faith in thorough uniformity that girdles the globe Alas, that is not the way living and breathing human beings function; people need what William Ernest Hocking has called the "grit of the particular" —*our* particular building for worship, *our* special hymns, *our* edition of the Bible, *our* formulated ideological principles, *our* form of organization that nurtures *our* way of thinking and action, *our* way of doing things suited to *our* personal needs and inclinations.

Religion Linked to a Natural Grouping

Religious particularity, especially where the religious group becomes closely identified with some natural grouping—be it biological, political or social—is a factor. The Jewish faith early became identified with a particular group of people with common traits and historical background. The dominant interpretation of the faith tied it up closely with the preservation of the group itself; to be religious was to be Jewish, and to be Jewish was to be religious. Thus group pride, self-consciousness and preservation strengthened religious exclusiveness. This mindset was contained in Mahatma Gandhi's reaction to those who were seeking to convert him to Christianity. He said, "Hinduism is the faith of my fathers and of my people. Why should I change from it to a foreign faith—especially when that faith is the one professed by those who rule India oppressively and illegally?"

Religion and Moral Idealism

There is yet more to this. Religion calls forth moral idealism and devotion. Morality has always appeared in a religious context and remains part of religious concern. While moral standards of the past may well not be accepted in later ages, the moral impulse, whether or not appropriately articulated or its details actually practiced, is stimulated by religion. Thus a considerable part of the enthusiasm that is religious consists of moral conviction. One thinks of the tremendous force of the idealism and devotion aroused by such concepts as righteousness, justice and love. And when these notions are woven into the fabric of religion—as they usually are by being attributed to God and prescribed by that Divinity, their force is incalculable.

The Core Reason

Religion and Man's Deepest Concerns

This may well be the definitive root cause of the fanatical devotion that religion as such arouses in its devotees. Religion deals with the area of man's deepest concerns, with *his attempt at relating himself to the most ultimate reality he can find*, i.e., God, the Transcendent, the Divine, the Ultimate Power of the universe— however, the believer may choose to express this yearning. Thus, *everything attached to that relationship partakes of great seriousness. This is religion's vital nerve; whatever touches it touches religion at the core of its being*; it is instantly alert to any threat in this area. This is what religion signifies by marking off certain things with the mark of "holiness" or "sacredness." It is saying of such things, "These have to do with the most vital concerns known to man; beware how you handle them!"

This is where the passion for details enters the picture. Since religion's rituals and techniques, its institutions and theological principles are *methodologies to achieve bonding with God*, these are matters of supreme importance; one cannot afford to jeopardize this supremely important goal by neglecting, changing or belittling any part of the process no matter how minute.

Thus, for example, the inappropriate inclusion or the omission of certain prescribed prayers or words in the *Amida* prayer invalidate the entire *Amida*; and the Jew is then required to repeat it in its entirety. In an African ritual dance one wrong word or gesture may invalidate the whole. One who utters a single phrase disparaging Muhammad could be subject to the death penalty. Christians battled intensely over the inclusion or exclusion of the letter "i" in a Greek word in a religious statement, and Catholics once fought bitterly over the legitimacy of the language of the Mass: should it remain in Latin or changed to the vernacular? The issue hinged on the validity of the entire prayer process, which could be vitiated by use of the incorrect language.

I've often thought of this phenomenon in this way: picture a ladder reaching from the ground upward toward heaven; if one single rung of the ladder is missing, the whole climb upward [to God] would be thwarted!

Is There a Way to Temper Religious Zealotry?

As delineated, religion's zealotry appears to be one of its basic characteristics. This condition leads us to ask: are there ways to temperance in the articulation of a faith's doctrines? Is there a measure of caution called for on religion's heavy emphasis on the firm validity of its particular religious practices? To buttress such stances, it might be well to heed the wise Kohelet of scripture who advised, *al t'hee tzadik harbay*, "do not be overly righteous (for it has been observed); there is no man on earth always in the right who (always) does the proper thing and never errs."[11]

A new perspective on religious doctrine and practice encapsulated in the phrase "Abiding Principles in Changing Categories" might help point in the direction of religious temperance.

Religious zealotry (of the negative kind detailed in this essay) is often rooted in a fundamentalist approach to faith's beliefs and practices. Both biblical and post-biblical dicta and observance as formulated in the texts themselves or as an elaborated on by recognized sages are authoritative and partake of permanent and binding authority. Such is the fundamentalist stance.

It is here where a different approach to this way of thinking is called for. This perspective makes distinctions between basic beliefs and practices and categories in which they are formulated. The categories change with time but not the essential validity of the principles they encase. For full explication of this perspective which might well lead to temperance of religious zealotry, see Essay Nine, "Abiding Principles in Changing Categories" which follows.

---

11. Ecclesiastes 7:16, 20.

– Nine –

ABIDING PRINCIPLES IN CHANGING CATEGORIES

The faithful modernist affirms the permanent, continually valid principles of religious teaching while recognizing the varied ways the principles have been articulated and applied in accordance with changing times and climes. The categories of articulation and application have constantly changed from age to age—but not the essential teachings.

Permanent Truth in Transient Phrasing

Few books have had a more abiding influence on my thinking, both as a modern Jew and practicing non-Orthodox rabbi, as has Harry Emerson Fosdick's *The Modern Use of the Bible*. What this work has taught me is to recognize the permanent experiences, the continually valid teachings of Scripture in their changing contexts. In the past these teachings have been encased in mental categories by authors who formulated them in terms of their own times. *The categories have constantly changed from age to age—but not the essential teachings.* Thus, for example:

The notion of immortality, that is, the persistence of one's persona after death, is an abiding and vital matter of faith. In the past, the notion has been expressed in the category of resurrection, the very body of a human being coming back to life. Such a notion of physicality defies rationality. However, the mind of a person of faith does not summarily jettison an affirmation of the continuity of the soul. People ought not assert that "if the setting went, the jewel would be lost."[1]

The belief in the reality of evil and misery in the world has always been a fact of life, phenomena that men and women have needed to confront and overcome. In the past, this condition has been depicted in the category of demons or evil spirits. These are the sources for the manifold evils in the world: for melancholy, hysteria, disorders of the brain. It is the source of bad dreams, witchcraft and all manner of superstition. Obviously modern men and women cannot and have not embraced such a category of thought. However, an abiding experience is encased in this thought-line which is a transient phrasing of the phenomenon. The age-old eclipse of a man's life in sin and misery is as much a fact and as terrible a fact as it ever was. Indeed, nothing that devils and evil spirits ever stood for has as yet gone out of human life: personal temptation, disease and the result of a polluted environment, addiction to drugs that scramble the mind and hobble normal activity; the ever-present mystery of human suffering and death—all of this and more are still with us.[2]

The belief in a God who cares for and protects His people is a fundamental conviction of religious man throughout the ages. In the past it has been articulated via a complex, active presence of angels. These were beings who bestow all manner of positive things on the world of human beings. They form an innumerable host; they serve men by causing useful dreams; they strengthen the spirit in the face of temptation; they open prison doors by giving peace and power in times of stress.

This way of articulating God's blessings muffled their perceived reality. By way of contrast, the experience of and conviction about God's beneficence resonates for modern men and women but is expressed in different, and for them, compelling, categories of thought. When, for example, the Jew on Friday

---

1. Fosdick, Harry Emerson. "Abiding Experiences in Changing Categories." *The Modern Use of the Bible.* Macmillan, 1961; Lecture IV, p. 96.
2. Ibid., p. 98.

evening welcomes the Sabbath by singing *Shalom Alekhem mala-chay hasharayt malakhay elyon,* "Greetings, angels of service, angels on high," he is not welcoming angelic beings into his midst; rather, he sees them as symbols of the joy and contentment that God is bringing into his Shabbat observance. Indeed, he is affirming a vital truth, an essential principle of religion: the presence, providence, directing care and constant availability of that unseen friendship whose source is in God.

This fundamental notion is applicable to numerous areas where modern religionists encounter religious fundamentalists. I much appreciate Fosdick's succinct summary of it:

> Nothing in human history seems so changeable as mental categories. They are transient phrasings of permanent convictions and experiences. They rise and fall and pass away. To bind our minds to the perpetual use of ancient matrices of thought just because they were employed in setting forth the eternal principles of Scripture seems intellectual suicide. *What is permanent in religion is not mental frameworks but abiding principles* that phrase and rephrase themselves in successive generations' ways of thinking and that grow in assured certainty and in richness of content.[3]

Rabbi Akiba Articulates Moses' Principles

This perspective is articulated in rabbinic sources in different ways. The sages sought to emphasize that human beings in their own time play a significant role in formulating authoritative religious idea and practice based on initial teaching.

The story begins with a statement by Rabbi Judah (an early third century Babylonian scholar). He says that when Moses ascended on high, he found the Holy One, blessed be He, sitting and weaving crowns on the letters of the Torah. Moses asked God for the meaning of these crowns. God replied that at the end

---

3. Ibid., p. 104.

of many generations there would arise a man, Akiba ben Joseph by name, who would expound upon each of the crowns "heaps and heaps" of laws. "Lord of the universe," declared Moses, "Permit me to see that man," to which God responded, "Turn around," and Moses suddenly found himself behind eight rows of students in Rabbi Akiba's house of study.

Unable to follow the discussion and failing to understand Rabbi Akiba's formulations of the biblical teachings at hand, Moses became ill at ease. However, when one of the students asked Akiba, "How do you know this is so?" the sage replied, "It is a law given to Moses at Sinai." Whereupon Moses was comforted.

When Moses returned to God, he said to Him, "Lord of the universe, You have such a man as this Rabbi Akiba and You give the Torah through me!" To which God said to Moses, *Shtok, kach ala b'machshava l'fany* "Be silent, such are My thoughts." Which is to say that this is a part of God's greater plan to which Moses was not privy.[4]

The point of this story? Louis Jacobs summarizes what I believe to be its essential meaning. He says that the Torah Akiba was teaching was so different from the one given to Moses—because the social and economic, political and religious conditions were so different in Akiba's day—that, at first, Moses could not recognize his Torah from that which was taught by the sage. But he was reassured when he realized that Akiba's Torah *was implicit* in his Torah, was, indeed, an attempt to make his teachings relevant to the spiritual needs of Jews in the age of Akiba. To do this effectively, the sage articulated Moses' principles in categories of thought reflective of his own time.[5]

In a striking article, "Kabbalah and Modern Judaism," Ariel Mayse writes about the exegetical creativity of the traditional scholars including Hasidic leaders. Here, too, their work seeks to reveal what is implicit in the work of their predecessors:

4. Talmud, *Menakhot* 29b.
5. Jacobs, Louis. *A Jewish Theology*. Behrman House, 1973; p. 207.

Hasidic leaders as well as classical rabbinic sages, have extraordinary freedom in interpreting the Bible. In fact, it is this exegesis that completes the Torah in a manner befitting any particular time and place. Many sources even extend this mandate for spiritual renewal into the realm of legal creativity, for *halakhah* must also be reinterpreted and reformulated in keeping with the call of the hour. And Hasidic sources also refer to biblical exegesis as a moment akin to the theophany at Sinai. These ideas of exegetical creativity and continuous revelation remain a part of contemporary Hasidism as well, visible in the works of thinkers like R. Judah Leib Alter of Ger (d. 1905) and Menachem Mendel Schneerson (1902-1994).[6]

As I have often cited elsewhere, Jonathan Sacks has articulated this perspective in striking fashion:

> In the earliest stages of an embryo, when a fetus is still no more than a bundle of cells, already it contains the genome, the long string of DNA, from which the child and eventually the adult will emerge. The genetic structure that will shape the person it becomes is there from the beginning. So it is with Judaism. "Bible, Mishna, Talmud and Aggada, even what a senior disciple is destined to teach in the presence of his master, was already stated to Moses at Sinai.[7]

"My Sons Have Defeated Me. My Sons Have Defeated Me."

Rabbi Eliezer's position on an *halachic* matter was disputed by his colleagues, and so he argued that if he was right, let the heavens prove it to be so. Whereupon a heavenly voice proclaimed

6. *Encyclopedia of the Bible and its Reception.* Vol 14; p. 1178.
7. Sacks, Jonathan. *Koren Rosh Hashana Mahkzor.* Koren Publishers Jerusalem, 2011; p. XII. For the rabbinic passage quoted, see Talmud Yerushalmi Pe-ah 2:4.

that the rulings of Rabbi Eliezer were to be followed. Rabbi Joshua stood up and emphasized, No! *Lo ba-sha-myim he,* "The Torah is not in heaven," quoting Deuteronomy 30:12. And Rabbi Jeremiah followed this up saying that the sages do not rely on a voice from heaven, but rather, as Scripture in Exodus 23:2 states, *acharay rabim l'hatot,* "after the majority you must incline." This means that the law must be decided by a majority of human judges and no appeal to a heavenly voice is valid and determinative.

The story concludes that when Rabbi Nathan met Elijah the prophet, he asked him: "What did the Holy One, blessed be He, do at that hour?" The reply: *ka cha-yaych, v'amar: nitzchunee ba-ny, nitzchunee ba-ny,* "He smiled and said, 'My sons have defeated Me. My sons have defeated Me.'" Which is to say that the decisions in a given generation were to be made by God's human progeny—and not God Himself.[8]

The point of this passage: the rabbis conceived of God's will for mankind in dynamic rather than static terms. For them, "revelation" was seen as an encounter between the Divine and people, in that there is an active human role in the formulation of god's will. Indeed, His teachings as to how humanity is to live are revealed through human beings. And it is their task to translate principle rooted in Divine source into the concrete settings of new times and climes.

Prayer Then—and Now

When the book of Leviticus ordains in great detail the content and methodology of the sacrificial system to be employed in the Temple, it is clearly depicting the mode of worship of the Israelites after having settled in the Promised Land. Indeed, the Temple built by King Solomon (ca. 920 BCE) took place well over three hundred years after the period of Moses (ca. 1300 BCE). Yet the Bible in Leviticus asserts that the various specific details about the sacrificial system were ordained by Moses himself,

---

8. Talmud. *Baba Metzia* 59b.

which was, as noted, centuries before the Temple was in existence and the Israelite settlement in the land. Such a claim can be, and is in religious fundamentalist circles, justified by a faith assertion to wit: Moses could depict specific rules and regulations via prophecy, in this case meaning the capacity to predict events and regulations centuries into the future.

A faithful modernist, wedded as he is to rational thinking, cannot but eschew such a claim. He embraces the view of Abraham Ibn Ezra (1089-1167), the Spanish Bible commentator, who wrote, "He who believes in something that contradicts the *sechel* (i.e., logic, reason) abuses the finest gift God has given him."

What Moses did was to establish a basic principle: "you shall love the Lord your God with all your heart and soul and might[9]—*ul'ovdo,* and *worship* the Lord with all your heart and soul."[10] This basic principle—the obligation to worship—was to be implemented by the stated priests in Israel; they were to use the category of the sacrificial system which was the prevailing mode of worship of their own time. The authority of this system was that it was implicit in Moses' teaching at Sinai. So, too, in the period following the defunct sacrificial system, the mode of worship reflecting the love of and reverence for God, was morphed by later generations into worship via prayer in the synagogue and elsewhere.

Indeed, the modern religionist uses the principle of abiding, religious obligation as his mantra which is articulated in categories of thought and action reflecting the period in which he lives.

---

9. Deuteronomy 6:5.
10. Deuteronomy 11:3.

– Ten –

THE BIBLE COMMENTARY OF
ABRAHAM IBN EZRA
The Developmental Process in Nascent Form

There is no house of study without a hidush, *new insight.*

—Hagiga 3a

In my book, *The Idea of Monotheism: The Evolution of a Foundational Concept*, I sought to depict the evolutionary process involved in the development of biblical ideas. The writers of the Bible, it was and is contended, penned their work from the perspective of their own time and clime. The basis for this approach was early pointed to by Benedict Spinoza in the seventeenth century and brought into full view by modern biblical scholarship. The latter has documented the multiple strata of Scripture developed over time. This has enabled arrangement of the biblical documents in their approximate chronological order. Thus an important result of seeing the biblical writings in sequence is the ability to study the development of biblical ideas—some written early in the biblical era by one particular writer, and some later by a different author.

What this process has brought about (among many things) is the capacity to view various striking biblical passages heretofore unexplored from the developmental point of view. Thus, for example, the prominent Bible commentator, Abraham Ibn Ezra (1092–1167) has pointed to six specific scriptural passages that appear to be clearly non-Mosaic. These have been amplified by

Ibn Ezra's authoritative super commentator Yosef ben Eliezer Bonfils (ca. 1375). These are:

1. Deuteronomy 34:1-12: The final twelve verses of the Pentateuch
2. Genesis 12:6: "The Canaanites were then in the land"
3. Deuteronomy 31:9: "Moses wrote down this Torah"
4. Genesis 22:14: "Whence the present saying"
5. Deuteronomy 3:11: "Now in Rabbah of the Ammonites"
6. Genesis 36:31-39: "Before any King reigned over Israelites"

What follows examines the first two above passages…and does so in the spirit of the following story related in the Talmud (Hagiga 3a): Rabbis Yochanan and Elazar once visited their mentor, Rabbi Joshua, who asked them what *hidush*, what new interpretation, had they learned in the house of study today. They responded: none, since their mentor (Rabbi Joshua) was not present and it was from him they learned. To this Rabbi Joshua averred: "despite my absence, *ee efshar l'bayt hamidrash b'lo hidush, there is no house of study without a* hidush, *new insight."*

Deuteronomy 34:1-12: Final Twelve Verses of Pentateuch[1]

The opening verses of chapter 34 reads: "Moses went up from the steppes of Moab to Mount Nebo, to the summit of Pisgah opposite Jericho and the Lord showed him the whole land…"

---

1. What follows is taken from the following sources:
   - Abraham Ibn Ezra's commentary on each of the passages in Deuteronomy and Exodus cited above.
   - Bonfils, Yoseph. *Tzafnas Panayakh*. Ed: David Herzog. Berlin, 1930, p. 65.
   - Sarna, Nahum. *Studies in Biblical Interpretations*, "Abraham Ibn Ezra as Exegete." Jewish Publication Society; 2000.
   - Heschel, Abraham Joshua. *Heavenly Torah: As Refracted Through the Generations.* Continuum, 2005; p. 610-617, 633-638.

Ibn Ezra comments: "Moses went up"—in my opinion from this verse on Joshua was the author, for after Moses went up he was no longer writing. And Joshua wrote the passage through prophecy.

Bonfils comments: Ibn Ezra explains there that after Moses went up to Mount Nebo, he did not come down from the mountain. Therefore it is necessary to explain that Joshua wrote this passage through prophesy. This is the simple *peshat* (understanding). Regarding the rabbis' suggestion that Moses indeed wrote this passage about himself "with tears," there is a debate in the Talmud: *Makkot 11a*, *Menakhot 30a* and *Baba Batra 15a*.

Sarna comments: The twelve final verses of the book of Deuteronomy speak of Moses in the third person unlike the body of the book which is couched in autobiographical style. This indicates that these verses were written by someone other than Moses.

This issue concerning the final section of Deuteronomy as having been written by someone other than Moses (i.e. Joshua, his immediate successor, or, according to others, the scribe Ezra) had long since been dealt with—as early as the third century CE. Thus the Sifré on Deuteronomy: "'So Moses died there'—is it possible that Moses died and then wrote 'Moses died there'? Rather Moses wrote up to that point, and from there onward Joshua wrote."[2] The Midrash continues to tell us that reason leads us to such a position "for how shall one say that Moses wrote something after he died? Is it possible that Moses *was alive* and wrote 'Moses died'? If so, this would indicate that he wrote something that was not true."

The Talmud itself records, "Our Rabbis taught that Moses wrote his book, the episode about Balaam and the book of Job (!) and Joshua wrote his book and the eight verses of the Torah."[3] Similarly, Rabbi Judah holds that Joshua wrote the last verses—

---

2. Sifré. *Vezot Habrakha* 357.
3. Bava Batra 14b.

though Rabbi Simeon disagreed, saying that these verses were written by Moses "in tears" (i.e. while weeping, his being close to death).[4]

Further, there is extensive discussion in rabbinic literature concerning the doubtful halakhic and liturgical status of Deuteronomy's final twelve verses which alludes to "suspicion" concerning them.[5]

Genesis 12:6: "The Canaanites Were *Then* in the Land"

The verse reads: Abram passed through the land as far as the site of Shechem, at the terebinth of Moreh. The Canaanites were *then* (Hebrew UZ) in the land.

Ibn Ezra comments: It would seem that the Canaanites took the land of Canaan from a different group, but if this is not correct, then *yesh lo sod*, there is a secret here, *V'hamaskil yidom*, and the wise would best remain silent.

Bonfils comments: Ibn Ezra writes on the verse, "the Canaanites were then in the land": "How can he say 'then," implying that they were in the land then but are now there no longer? When Moses wrote the Torah, were not the Canaanites still in the land? So it is unlikely that Moses wrote "then," for reason dictates that the word "then" was written at a time when the Canaanites were not in the land. We know that the Canaanites did not leave until after Moses' death, when Joshua conquered the land. Therefore it appears that Moses did not write this word here, but rather Joshua or another of the prophets."[6]

Bonfils continues: Now since we are bound to believe the

---

4. Bava Batra 15a; Menahkhot 20a.
5. Heschel, Abraham Joseph. *Heavenly Torah: As Refracted Through the Generations*. Continuum, 2005; p. 613-617
6. Bonfils, Yoseph. *Tzafnas Panayakh*. Ed: David Herzog. Berlin, 1930, p. 91-93.

words of tradition that Moses himself wrote the entire Pentateuch which Ibn Ezra apparently contradicts: "What difference does it make if some other prophet wrote this verse, since all the words are true and divinely inspired?"[7]

Sarna comments: Clearly this passage about the location of the Canaanites reflects the work of a late biblical writer in whose era the Canaanites were not in the land, having been decimated (presumably?) by Joshua. The writer of this passage is looking back, as it were, into the earlier Mosaic period—centuries before his century—when indeed the Canaanites were in the land. Hence, as E. A. Spenser has averred, Bonfils, as does Ibn Ezra, is telling us here that Moses could not have authored the *then* statement, and notes Ibn Ezra's cryptic suggestive concluding remark: *yesh lo sod, V'hamaskil yidom*, "There is a mystery here and the wise had best keep silent."

It was not only Ibn Ezra and Bonfils who took on this view. R. Moses ben Judah, in his supercommentary, *Tappuhei Zahav*, commented on Ibn Ezra's view that Moses did not write this verse: "Even though we do not agree with him, since it is incumbent on us to believe that Moses our Master wrote from the first verse of Genesis to the last verse of Deuteronomy, without missing a single letter, I have thought to write in his defense. For he points out that simply because a future or present sensory fact has escaped a prophet's attention, does not detract from his perfection as a prophet."[8]

R. Moses Almosnino also solved Ibn Ezra's riddle, pointing out that in Moses' day the land "was still in the hands of the Canaanites, but this verse was presumably written by Joshua or Ezra. This is the secret, that Moses our Master did not write this."[9]

---

7. Ibid.
8. Friedlander, M. *Essays on the Writings of Abraham Ibn Ezra*. 1963, p. 239.
9. R.N. Ben Menhem. *Moses Almosnino Commentary on Ibn Ezra*. Sinai 10; 1946, p. 153.

The Thrust of this Analysis

A telling question which Joseph Bonfils poses in the context of his analysis of the "Canaanites were then in the land" passage points to the essential point we are seeking to make in this essay. He writes: "Now, since we are bound to believe the words of tradition that Moses himself wrote the entire Pentateuch (which Ibn Ezra apparently contradicts), *what difference does it make if some other prophet wrote this verse, since all the words are true and divinely inspired.*"

The implication of Bonfils question is clear enough. Faith in the word and presence of God does not depend on whether Moses himself in his own time was Scripture's exclusive author. Many others extended and amplified the basics Moses posited, and the Jewish tradition has understood these as God's intent.

Jeffrey Tigray in his foreword to Nahum Sarna's *Studies in Biblical Interpretation* (JPS, 2000, p. xii), points to Sarna's affirmation of modern critical studies which have uncovered multiple sources in biblical texts. "In its general outlines," Sarna has written, "the non-unitary origin of the Pentateuch has survived as one of the finalities of biblical scholarship." Nor does Sarna, Tigay continues, see this as a problem for religious faith and adds significantly Sarna's words: "God can work through four documents as effectively as through one, unfolding His revelation in successive stages as well as in a single moment in time."

I repeat here what I have written elsewhere about his perspective:

> Faith and basic traditional affirmations are often enhanced by modern critical thinking. When, for example, a contemporary Bible researcher detects multiple strata in the texts of the Pentateuch that reveal the hands of different writers and different eras in biblical life, we cannot conclude that the Pentateuchal texts are the product of a single hand and their provenance in but one period of time and clime. However, for the faithful modernist, what these researchers do show is that *the Divine speaks*

*to humanity in all eras of Jewish life and to the many faithful
in their own period and place who are attuned to God's will.*
Indeed, genuine faith and basic traditional affirmations
about the Divine role in human life are thereby enhanced
rather than diminished.[10]

The Role of "Reason" in Religious Exploration

Indeed, facets of the rabbinic tradition itself, along with Ibn Ezra
and Josef Bonfils and other committed religionists, accepted in
nascent form the modern critical notion of the biblical writers
having penned their work from the perspectives of their own
times and historical conditions. This approach cannot be cavalierly dismissed in the name of traditional faith, hallowed and
longstanding as it is. Faith is not allowed to be jettisoned by non-
awareness of the findings of the critical mind guided as it is by
"reason," as Yosef Bonfils put it in his analysis of Ibn Ezra, and
as is evident in much of the rabbinical literature and modern biblical scholarship. Critical thinking is one of God's marvelous endowments on His human children, as Ibn Ezra himself emphasized in the introduction to of his commentary to the book of
Genesis. A guiding principle he employs in interpreting Scripture was that the human intellect is a *malakh hashem*, "the mind,
an angel of God," and he further emphasized that he who believes in something that contradicts the *sekhel* (that is, common
sense, logic, reason) abuses the finest gift God has given him.[11]

Yet more: Ibn Ezra echoed his famous Muslim predecessor,
theologian and jurist Abu Hamid al-Ghazali (1058–1111), who
emphasized that *lo barah Hashem b'riah yotair nikhbedet min hasekhel*, "God has created nothing more honored/distinguished than
reason" (translated from the Arabic into Hebrew by Rabbi Avraham ben Hasdai [ca. 1230], an enthusiastic scholarly partisan
of Moses Maimonides, who was a champion of rational thought

---

10. See essay #7, "The Faithful Modernist: The Synthesis Between Tradition
   and Modernity."
11. Ibn Ezra's introduction to his commentary on the book of Genesis.

in the pursuit of religious studies). So, too, Thomas Aquinas (1224-1274), the preeminent spokesman of the Catholic tradition who saw reason in harmony with faith. The critical mind, Aquinas emphasized, was a divine gift highly to be cherished (Aquinas' notion, for example, of a Prime Mover/Causeless Cause demonstrated his reasoned thinking about the existence of God).

In a word, tradition cannot prevent us from considering valid what reason urges upon us.

– Eleven –

JUDAISM AND THE PROTESTANT ETHIC: PARALLELS

According to Scripture:

Man is to work for six days of the week. This is the will of God and thus a way to come into His graces.

According to the Puritans:

Man needs to work diligently in his world as the monks did in their monasteries. This is the way to come into God's graces.

Question:

What is the relationship between Judaism and the Protestant ethic with regard to work in the world of the here and now?

Judaism and Work

The Bible, rabbinic teachings and longstanding Jewish tradition have stressed the positive character of work in the world of the here and now. Indeed, it is as much a religious duty as is prayer and ritual observance. Man is enjoined to labor in and on this earth—to change it, to improve it, to get it to yield its many advantages for human benefit. The Messianic age is a this-worldly notion that calls for humans to work to make their world a better place in which to live. In the Jewish view this all is ultimately rooted in the will of God: to work is to follow His dictates and thus to come into His good graces.

The creation story[1] tells us of God's "work" as it were. He *fashioned* light from darkness; He *created* heaven and earth; He *brought into being* vegetation, seed-bearing plants and fruit trees; He *created* the sun and the moon and the stars; He *fashioned* birds that fly and fish that swim; He *brought into being* all manner of animals; and to cap all this off, He *created* human beings—Adam and Eve.[2]

When God created human beings, He did so by creating them "in His image;"[3] they were thus to function in the world with the same divine characteristics. Thus even as God worked in creation of the world, so is man to work: "Six days *shall you work*," they were told, "and on the seventh day shall you rest." When Adam and Eve were placed in the Garden of Eden, they were told *l'avda ul'ashamra*, "to work it and take care of it."[4] God created the plants and all else that exists, as well as all that walks and crawls and flies in the world, and man is to cultivate the soil, he is to fashion all that God has fashioned, and do so for mankind's benefit.

Subsequent Scripture, rabbinic teaching and Jewish tradition morphed these primary ideological notions about the affirmation of work into the arena of practical living. Thus when the Israelites in the desert were given the manna, they were told, "The people shall go out and gather (the food)."[5] They were to get up early in the morning and get their provisions. Moses was not to appoint surrogates whose duty it would be to gather the food and distribute it to the people. Rather, all who wanted food had to go out and find it themselves. There was to be no idle class dependent on the exertion of others, we are told here, as was

---

1. Genesis 1.
2. Ibid., 1:27; 2:7; 2:22.
3. Ibid., 1:27.
4. Genesis 2:15.
5. Exodus 16:4.

Israel's experience in Egypt where the privileged class lived in idleness and luxury via the labor of their slaves.

One of Benjamin Franklin's dicta about labor, drilled into his head by his Calvinist father who had fully imbibed the contents and spirit of the Hebrew Bible's book of Proverbs: "See a man diligent in his work—he shall stand before kings; he shall not stand before obscure men." [6] Franklin knew that a diligent worker would attain to a position of high status in the world, and this was a good and legitimate aspiration. The rabbis reinforced this ethic about work, pointing to the assertion in Proverbs 22:21: "Sleepiness will robe a man in rags."[7] Indeed, life is complex and competitive and those who do not put forth the necessary effort are left behind, destined to failure.

Human Dignity is Enhanced When One Sustains Oneself By One's Own Efforts

In a Talmudic passage the Babylonian teacher Rav urged his disciple, Rav Kahana, "Rather do difficult work for a fee than be supported by charity. Do not say, 'I am a scholar' as if to say that such work is beneath your dignity."[8] When Adam is told that he had to toil for his daily bread he came to realize,[9] the rabbis tell us, this was reassurance that his dignity was not being compromised by his incessant quest for sustenance because the human spirit remains discontented unless a man earns his keep. This is part of what the rabbis refer to when they speak of a man as "a partner with God in the work of creation."[10]

In the Jewish tradition, a person's work is seen in positive terms because it is an opportunity to secure the future for his fellow humans. Well known is the Talmudic tale of the man who saw an old man planting trees. "Why do you plant these trees

---

6. Proverbs 22:29.
7. Genesis Rabbah 17:6.
8. Pesakhim 113a.
9. Genesis 3:17-19.
10. Shabbat 119b.

since you will never enjoy the fruit?," he was asked. The old man answered, "I found trees planted by my ancestors from which I enjoyed the fruit. Surely, it is my duty to plant trees that those who come after me might enjoy their fruit."[11]

In our own time, A.D. Gordon's "religion of labor" has had a great influence on the kibbutz movement in Israel. At the age of 48, Gordon settled in Palestine to till the soil with his own hands and to teach that modern man can rediscover God by working close to nature in the fields. There one experiences more vividly the miracle of vegetable and fruit emerging from the earth prompted by small seeds showered by the waters. There one experiences more directly the gift of animal life which nourishes men and women. There one experiences more impressively the brightness of the sun and moon and stars, and the drama of the changing seasons.

And so, Judaism teaches that one must not only work in the world of the here-and-now but do so diligently and conscientiously if he is to exercise his duty to himself, to society—and to his God.

How this consciousness about the role of work in the business of life has manifested itself in the modern world is embedded in the discussion to follow as we seek to show the relationship between Judaism and the Protestant work ethic.

The Protestant Ethic and Work

The Judaic work ethic—the obligation to labor diligently and conscientiously—is closely related to the famous premise of Max Weber in his *The Protestant Ethic and the Spirit of Capitalism* which posited the notion that the Protestant ethos about work was the source for the spirit and rise of capitalism in the modern world.[12]

---

11. Taanit 23a.
12. Weber, Max. *The Protestant Ethic and the Spirit of Capitalism: A Classic Study of the Fundamental Relationships between Religion and the Economic and Social Life in Modern Culture.* Scribner, 1958.

Weber's epic work contained the seminal formulation of this idea. He noted the clearly greater economic prosperity amongst Protestants in Europe as opposed to the economic poverty of Catholics. He then proceeds to explain this disparity in the context of Puritan theology as formulated by John Calvin. Certain unintended but real psychological consequences were created by the Puritan notions of predestination and the calling—notions that Calvin and his followers pressed with great logical severity.

The doctrine of predestination asserted with heavy emphasis that only a certain few—the monks by virtue of their diligent and focused acts of piety and their wholehearted asceticism—were destined for salvation. The rest of the people were destined for damnation and there was little they could do about it. This was God's will; He was omnipotent and omniscient. Moreover, it was beyond human understanding to discern why it was that only the monks in monasteries were the destined elect.

This doctrine created great psychological insecurity for Calvin's followers; they could not hope to come into God's graces; they could not aspire to salvation, to a life in the world to come. To be stern believers in hellfire was a burden too heavy to bear.

And so, they began to look for loopholes, other avenues, that would indicate the direction of divine will. They would be the "monks" in the outside world. *They would be like the elect monks in the monasteries; they would function as did the monks—work diligently and conscientiously and unceasingly in their world and thereby come into God's graces and have hope for salvation.* The result of this was development of fervent commitment to one's worldly calling and any lapse would indicate that one's state of grace was in doubt. Another crucial result was the common man's monk-like abstinence from enjoyment of the profits reaped from such labors. This accounted for the rapid accumulation of wealth and development of a prosperous society. Thus, according to Weber, whereas heretofore the accumulation of money was considered by religionists as decadent, this perspective enabled people to conceive of wealth in an affirmative way; nay more: a sign of God's affirmation. Herein lies the source of legitimate modern capitalism.

The practical fallout of this mode of thought projected by Calvin and his Puritan followers was what Weber dubbed The Protestant Ethic which is characterized by:

- Hard work
- Diligence
- Punctuality
- Good organization
- Orderliness

- No wasting of time
- Frugality
- Rational thinking
- Careful calculation

Why these rules of conduct? Because they were the means by which one accumulated wealth and became successful in life — a condition that represented the will of God and the means of coming into His graces.[13]

The Link to Judaism and the Jews

It is manifest that the work ethic as formulated by Max Weber concerning Calvinist ideology and that of Judaism stem from different motivational sources — Weber: Calvinist predestination and Jewish: ideology and practice. The practical fallout of both views of the work ethic, however, is strikingly similar as depicted in our earlier pages.

Because of this striking similarity, Weber could not, and chose not to, avoid the tantalizing view of their commonality and the apparent possibility of the Protestant ethic having been significantly influenced by Judaism and the Jews. Some examples:

Weber notes "the sense of inner relationship to Judaism which is expressed even in the well-known work of August

---

13. Robert Bellah's revealing book, *Tokugowa Religion: The Cultural Roots of Modern Japan*, does for Japan what Max Weber's *Protestant Ethic* did for the West. Bellah uses Weber's sociological frame of reference to demonstrate the influence of certain Buddhist, Confucian and Shinto religious value orientations and native doctrines which helped form the matrix for the prodigious and vigorous later economic and political developments in Japan into a major industrial nation.

Kohler who found it widespread among the Puritan peasants of Holland." However, Weber is quick to note Puritanism's differences from Hebrew ethics in practical affairs.[14]

According to Weber, "As far as Talmudic Judaism is concerned, some fundamental traits of Puritan morality are certainly related to it." Weber examples the Judaic ethical principle of "loveless fulfillment of duty" which Puritan ethics would essentially accept. Here again, Weber caveats that as Hebrew ethics apply to practical capitalism, the English Puritans, with disdain, consider "Jewish capitalism speculative pariah capitalism, while for the Puritan it was bourgeois organization of labor."[15]

In the context of discussing the role of the Hebrew Scripture in connection with the Protestant ethic, Weber writes this: "The whole power of the God of the Old Testament who rewards the people in this life necessarily exercised a similar influence on the Puritan who, following Baxter's[16] advice, compared his own state of grace with that of the heroes of the Bible...Jacob, a plain man, dwelling in tents who represents the man of grace. And in the process interpreted the statements of Scripture as articles of a book of statutes.[17]

And then this: "Old Testament morality was able to give a powerful impetus to that spirit of self-righteous and sober legality which was so characteristic of the worldly asceticism of this form of Protestantism. Thus when authors, as was the case with several contemporaries as well as later writers, characterize the basic ethical tendency of Puritanism, especially in England, as English Hebraism, they are correctly understood, not wrong." The Weber caveat: this applies only to those natural laws that

---

14. Weber, Max. *The Protestant Ethic and the Spirit of Capitalism: A Classic Study of the Fundamental Relationships between Religion and the Economic and Social Life in Modern Culture*. Scribner, 1958; p. 269.
15. Ibid., p. 270-271.
16. Richard Baxter, an influential English Puritan church leader and theologian.
17. Ibid., p. 126, 269.

apply to all people, not just the Jews.[18]

Further, says Weber, the Puritans believed themselves to be God's Chosen People, as were the Jews of old, which notion played its part in developing that formalistic, hard, correct character which was peculiar to the men of that heroic age of capitalism.[19]

Weber's references to Benjamin Franklin's view of labor depicted above as being drilled in him by his Calvinist father might well capture the essence of the connection of Hebraism to the Protestant ethic. Franklin's father had fully imbibed the contents and spirit of the Hebrew Bible as did the Puritans at the time.[20]

Werner Sombart

Max Weber's friend and colleague, Werner Sombart, often differed with Weber in his own trenchant analysis of the root causes of the capitalist spirit. However, in many essentials he, in fact, supplemented Weber. He, too, pointed to the convergence of the Protestant ethic with the Jewish work ethic embedded in Scripture and reinforced by Jewish historical experience.

Thus in Sombart's 1911 book, *Die Juden und das Wirtschaftsleben (The Jews and Modern Capitalism)*, he described the Jews as the ones who had caused economic progress wherever and whenever they had appeared, and had caused economic downfall wherever and whenever they had disappeared. The Jews had moved across Europe like the sun: where they arrived, new life had blossomed; when they left, whatever had been in bloom had fallen in decay.[21]

Sombert set out to explain in detail the role of the Jews for modern economic development and the special qualifications of

---

18. Ibid., p. 165.
19. Ibid., p. 166.
20. Proverbs 22:29.
21. Sombart, Werner. *Die Juden Und Das Wirtschaftsleben*. Dunker Und Homblot, 1911, V1; p. 15.

the Jews for capitalistic enterprise. He believed to have observed the almost total agreement between Puritan and Jewish views with regard to the rise of capitalism as discussed by Weber and himself: the preponderance of religious interest; the idea of spiritual uncertainty; the merging of religious ideas and financial interest; the attempt to calculate matters of sin and salvation. And then Sombert concluded, "Puritanism is, means, represents Judaism." On the basis of his own and Weber's work, it was possible, Sombert continued, to establish the spiritual linkage, even the spiritual conformity, between Puritanism and Judaism.[22]

Addendum

The following trenchant analysis by Cecil Roth might well help us understand some of the external factors which prompted the conclusions of Sombert about the role and effect of the Jewish people on the economic and other characteristics of the Western world:

Not allowed to be a citizen in any land, the Jew became perforce a citizen of the world, and as a citizen of the world he performed an irreplaceable service. For one of his greatest and most characteristic functions throughout history has been his part as an intermediary—not only intellectual, but economic, social, and political as well.

In addition to his role as the Eternal Protestant, he was also the "International Jew"—a title properly of pride not of obloquy. He always had the advantage of standing astride more than one civilization. He had personal connections and interests not hemmed in by political borders. He had a realization of lands and cultures lying far distant from those of his own

---

22. Ibid., p. 292-293. This summary of Sombart's writing is taken from Lehmann, Hartmut. "The Rise of Capitalism: Weber versus Sombart." *Weber's Protestant Ethic: Origins, Evidence, Contexts.* Cambridge University Press, 1993; p. 199-200.

environment. He had access to foreign languages. His kinsfolk were scattered in many lands, so that in every country there was some coreligionist who could act as his correspondent or his agent, or give him hospitality, or extend him credit. Hebrew could carry him, in a pinch, from one end of the world to another, and lay open to him the intellectual treasures of every age and every land.[23]

---

23. Roth, Cecil et al. *Great Ages and Ideas of the Jewish People.* Random House, 1956.

– Twelve –

THE BELIEF IN THE HEREAFTER
This World, the Messianic Age, the World to Come, and the Meaning of "Soul"

אֵין כְּעֶרְכְּךָ, יהוה אֱלֹהֵינוּ, בָּעוֹלָם הַזֶּה
וְאֵין זוּלָתְךָ מַלְכֵּנוּ, לְחַיֵּי הָעוֹלָם הַבָּא
אֶפֶס בִּלְתְּךָ, גּוֹאֲלֵנוּ, לִימוֹת הַמָּשִׁיחַ
וְאֵין דּוֹמֶה לְךָ, מוֹשִׁיעֵנוּ, לִתְחִיַּת הַמֵּתִים

None can be compared to You,
Lord our God — in this world.
There is none besides You, our King —
in the life of the World to Come.
There is none but You, our Redeemer —
In the days of the Messiah.
There is none like You, our Savior —
At the resurrection of the dead.

—The Shabbat morning service

For many years I taught a course at the University of Judaism on the subject of "The Hereafter." The experience revealed that many Jews remain mired in the mistaken idea that Judaism is unconcerned with the notion of a world beyond this earthly life. The claim is made that it is Christianity that is preoccupied with the idea, whereas Judaism focuses on living fully and well in this world with scant concern about a world beyond.

I stressed then to the students, and did so before and since, that such a sharp distinction between the two faiths is much too facile. Judaism, indeed, engages with the notion of a Hereafter: this world, the Messianic Age and the World to Come. A careful reading of the normative, authoritative Jewish religious texts clearly demonstrates that such is the case. What can be said about the difference between Christianity and Judaism on the subject is that, while Judaism clearly embraces the belief in a life beyond the present, it is less preoccupied with it than is Christianity for which the notion is primary. What follows seeks to depict the Jewish view of the subject.

We begin with the reasons for the notion of continuity of personhood beyond the grave, why it is so vital to persons of faith. We then limn the traditional view and proceed with the depiction of what we call the "Faithful Modernist" who affirms the notion of the soul alone as having continuity in the beyond. We then conclude with an effort to define what we mean by the term "soul."

Why is the Belief in the Hereafter So Vital to a Person of Faith?

At the outset, it must be stressed that the notion of the continuity of people after their demise is, of course, a matter of faith, beyond human capacity to reason into being. It cannot be proven or demonstrated by the subtlest of argumentation. According to the sages, however, the notion is a fundamental in Jewish faith, and they signaled its centrality by including numerous references to it throughout the Jewish liturgy.[1] How it will be we do not know, but that it will be is what Judaism affirms. Death is not the end. Loss is not final.

The best we can do in this circumstance is to seek to explain

---

1. One example, among numerous others, is the opening of the standard Amida where a basic aspect of the notion is repeated four times: "You, O Lord, are mighty and You revive the dead" and "You revive the dead with great mercy" and "You order death and restore life," and finally, "Blessed are You, O Lord, who revives the dead." This Amida prayer is recited at every religious service—weekday, Sabbath and holiday.

why the believer affirms the notion and make an effort to understand his/her thinking about it.

The Meaning and Purpose of Life

To be immortal means that there is something about the human being that has continuity beyond the grave; to believe this is of great consequence because it responds to the most important questions in life. The meaning and purpose of man's existence have always been looked upon as vital: Who am I? Why am I? Where am I going? These questions have been uppermost in the minds of men and women at all times. The doctrine of the Hereafter speaks to these questions. When a person affirms that a facet of his self lives on after his demise, life takes on deeper meaning. People see themselves as destined to a positive tomorrow if they've lived a life of goodness and compassion. The sorrows and disappointments of life—there are many in the lot of every man and woman—no longer are unbearable, but are borne with patience and fortitude in the hope of positive reward in the morrow. On the other hand, a life lived as a reprobate will, in the beyond, experience negative consequences. Thus, whether pleasant or unpleasant, the belief in the Hereafter gives meaning to life in the present.

Justice Affirmed

A primary reason for the tenacious hold of the belief in the hereafter is articulated in the following midrash:

רַב יוֹסֵף בְּרֵיהּ דְּרַב יְהוֹשֻׁעַ חָלַשׁ וְאִתְנַגִּיד.
כִּי הָדַר, אָמַר לֵיהּ אֲבוּהּ: מַאי חֲזֵיתָ?
אָמַר לֵיהּ: עוֹלָם הָפוּךְ רָאִיתִי, עֶלְיוֹנִים לְמַטָּה
וְתַחְתּוֹנִים לְמַעְלָה. אָמַר לוֹ: בְּנִי עוֹלָם בָּרוּר רָאִיתָ

Rabbi Joseph, the son of Rabbi Joshua ben Levi, became ill and fell into a coma. (Now, the ancients believed that a person in a coma experienced the other world, so that) when Rabbi Joseph recovered, his father, Rabbi Joshua, asked him, "What did you see in that other world?"

> *The son replied: "I saw an upside-down world: those who were on the top of this world (that is, those who prospered but were not good people) are at the bottom there (in the other world)…and those who were at the bottom of this world (that is, who were poverty-stricken but good people) are at the top there (in the other world)."*
>
> *To which the father said: "My son, you saw a clear—or corrected—world." (Justice has been done.)*[2]

Rabbi Jonathan Sacks cites an indicator for this notion of justice. It can be found in the mirror-image symmetry in the Torah. Many of its passages are constructed in the form of symmetry where the second half of a verse reverses the order of the first half. Thus, the six-word commandment that forms the central element of the Noahide Covenant:[3]

"(A) who sheds (B) the blood (C) of man (C) by man (B) shall his blood (A) be shed."[4]

This is more than a stylistic device. It is the expression of one of the Torah's most profound beliefs—the reciprocal nature of justice. Those who do good are blessed with good. Those who do evil suffer evil. What happens to us is a mirror image of what we do. Thus, form, as in this passage, mirrors substance: Mirror-image symmetry is the *literary equivalent of a just world.*

This, then, is a fundamental rationale for the strongly held doctrine of a world beyond this world: to right the injustices that pervade our lives in the here and now. A good God will not allow injustice to permanently prevail. Good people will ultimately be rewarded and those who practice evil will ultimately "pay the price." When once this notion was established, that this life extended to a life in the Hereafter, theodicy (defense of God in view of the existence of evil) needed no longer harass faith.

---

2. Pesakhim 50a.
3. Genesis 9:6.
4. *Koren Siddur*, p. XXIII.

The Traditional Notion of the Hereafter

The following depiction of the traditional Jewish notion of the hereafter follows closely George Foot Moore in his landmark study *Judaism: In the First Centuries of the Christian Era: Volume II*, "Eschatology," and Louis Jacobs in his authoritative, *A Jewish Theology*, Chapter 25, "The Hereafter."

Three Stages of The Hereafter

The various elements of the Hereafter doctrine were separately formulated over the years and were subsequently established in the classical rabbinic period. At that point the Rabbis systematized them into an integrated scheme. What they did was to impose a sequence to the various elements, forging a clear framework that became the normative Judaic notion of the Hereafter that prevailed at the time of the rise of Christianity. It is at this juncture that Christianity altered the notion it inherited from Judaism with the inclusion of Jesus into the picture (e.g. the nature of the messianic leader). It was at this point that Judaism clung to the normative rabbinic notion on into the future.

*This World…*When a person dies after having lived in the world of the here and now, the soul of the righteous person is separated from the body and proceeds to a blessed abode known as Heaven (*Gan Eden*). The soul of the reprobate is also separated from the body and proceeds to a cursed abode known as Hell (*Gehinom*). This is the first stage of reward and punishment. The bodies of both the righteous and the sinners remain in an amorphous abode called "Sheol" in which there is no judgment.

*The Messianic Age…*In the initial period of the Messianic Age (*Yemot Hamashiach*), the deceased bodies will emerge from Sheol resurrected; they come back physically and there, in the concrete, this-worldly Messianic era, the bodies will be rejoined by their respective souls and these now whole persons as they lived in this world of the here and now (*Olam Hazeh*), will answer to God for their character and conduct: the righteous person will enjoy the blessedness of the Messianic Age and the reprobate will suffer (for a maximum of twelve months) in the Messianic Age after which he will be eligible for final judgment—as will the righteous person. This all takes place in the early Messianic Age, and is the second stage of reward and punishment.

The World to Come… At the end of the Messianic Age, which endures only until the World to Come (*Olam Habah*) is apprehended, the whole person which consists of both body and soul, both the righteous and the reprobate, stand before God for final judgment: in this World to Come the individual righteous person experiences blessedness forever and the reprobate experiences permanent negation. This is the third and final stage of reward and punishment.

The Hereafter for the "Faithful Modernist"

The faithful modernist affirms the basic notion about the continuity of the person beyond the grave while eschewing the intricate details depicted above. However, he affirms faith in the continuity of the soul rather than of the body. The terms: immortality of the soul rather than the physical resurrection of the dead. One can understand the point about the whole personality surviving into the beyond but a modern who is a believer cannot accept the biological details of an actual recomposition of a physical body. However, he is prepared to affirm as a matter of faith a notion that does not require him to abdicate his mind, which knows well physical reality. And that is affirmation of the continuity of that intangible yet very real soul that was his during his sojourn on this earth. That soul, he believes, lives on.

What Do We Mean by "Soul"?

There are phenomena about the human being that exist independently of his/her physicality. Indeed, there is reality to the immaterial:

Ask someone to touch your body and thereby to feel your love. The person does so and discovers that love is very real, yet quite beyond the tangible.

To help grasp the reality of the unseen, that immaterial element in the world that creates and determines what happens in a purposive way, note the following passage in a Hindu work, *The Chandogya Upanishad*:

> "Bring me a fruit from that tree." "Here it is, venerable Sir." "Cut it open." "It is cut open, venerable Sir." "What seest thou in it?" "Very small seeds, venerable Sir." "Cut open one of them." "It is cut open, venerable Sir." "What seest thou in it?" "Nothing, venerable Sir." Then spake he, "That hidden thing which thou seest not, O gentle youth, from that hidden thing verily has this mighty tree grown."

In speaking about an intangible yet very real element of the human being, Isadore Epstein writes this:

> What imparts to the mind personality is not the hands, the eyes, the brain, but the power to organize, direct and unify the various component parts of the body into a purpose and goal. Personality is mind become autonomous, mind become emancipated from bondage to the body.[5]

Soul is that which animates the life of the body. It makes a person think, feel, love, hate, envy, evaluate and aspire. Winston King puts it this way:

> There are in general two ways in which religions describe the duality they find in man. One of these is the prevalent body-soul division. This is partly the result of empirical observation of the obvious duality of man's being—his physical and apparently more-than-physical characteristics. Now the term soul is religion's designation for the more-than-physical part of man, and is usually intended to include intelligence, force of will, moral character, and the generally spiritual or immaterial part of man. It or its equivalent term is used almost universally in the world's

---

5. Epstein, Isadore. *The Faith of Judaism*. Bloch Publishing Company, 1954; p. 145.

sacred literature.[6]

King proceeds to explicate what is meant by soul in the context of religion. Another form of the dualism of the human being is the distinction between the "higher" and "lower" selves. The former is the seat of his spiritual and moral desires and powers, the latter the source of his negative physical appetites. Further, says King, the soul is what the human being uniquely is, his character as a person. The soul or the self is the knower, the feeler, behind and beyond the physical acts that characterize the observable man. This is the human subject or personality that calls itself "I" and is more than its states of mind or their contents. It is the "I-ness" of all a human being's acts, the doer of all his deeds, and thinker of all his thoughts.

Robert Gordis has articulated what is meant by "soul" in this way:

> Man possesses a physical constitution with a basic instinc-
> tual heritage, geared to life on the animal level here and
> now. But man is endowed also with a "plus," for which
> terms "spirit" and "soul" come to mind. Whether we em-
> ploy these terms or not, it is undeniable that man pos-
> sesses aspirations and hopes beyond the limitations of
> time and space by which he is physically bound. The
> yearning for the ideal, the panting after the infinite, the
> perpetual dissatisfaction with the world as it is because of
> a vision of the world as it can be—all these are specifically
> human aspects of man's personality.[7]

It is this very real yet immaterial element in the human being that the faithful modernist can and does affirm. The standard Jewish prayerbook contains the early morning prayer recited when one rises in the morning:

---

6. King, Winston L. *Introduction to Religion: A Phenomenological Approach*. Harper & Row, 1968; p. 420-421.

7. Gordis, Robert. *A Faith for Moderns*. Bloch, 1961; p. 238.

אֱלֹהַי, נְשָׁמָה שֶׁנָּתַתָּ בִּי טְהוֹרָה הִיא.
אַתָּה בְרָאתָהּ אַתָּה יְצַרְתָּהּ אַתָּה נְפַחְתָּהּ
בִּי וְאַתָּה מְשַׁמְּרָהּ בְּקִרְבִּי וְאַתָּה עָתִיד
לִטְּלָהּ מִמֶּנִּי וּלְהַחֲזִירָהּ בִּי לֶעָתִיד לָבֹא

*God, the soul You have given me is pure. You created it, You
formed it and You breathed it into me. You preserve it within
me, and You will take it from me and restore it to me in the
Hereafter.*

The source of this prayer is in Scripture, where the doctrine
of the immortality of the soul is affirmed:

וְיָשֹׁב הֶעָפָר עַל הָאָרֶץ כְּשֶׁהָיָה וְהָרוּחַ תָּשׁוּב
אֶל הָאֱלֹהִים אֲשֶׁר נְתָנָהּ

*The dust (i.e., the body of man) will return, to the dust as it
was (i.e., from which it came), but the spirit (i.e., the soul) will
return to God who gave it.*[8]

The point of this is that the soul is independent of a person's
body. It emanated from the very breath of God who breathed in
man "the soul of life,"[9] and returns to its Source (God) when,
upon death, it separated from the body. More: Scripture proclaims "the candle of the Lord is the soul of man;"[10] this
lamp/light is a metaphor for the Divine. And so, since God is
permanent, the soul which verily is something of the Divine
within man is permanent.

It is this immaterial reality—the soul of a human being—
which the faithful modernist can and does affirm as having continuity in the beyond.

Precedents for the Modern View

This view is not an original one on the part of moderns. It is

---

8. Ecclesiastes 12:7.
9. Genesis 2:7.
10. Proverbs 20:27.

found in the work of Philo of Alexandria, the first-century CE Jewish philosopher, as well as in the writings of the great authority on Jewish law and seminal philosopher, Moses Maimonides (1185-1204).

Philo wrote in Greek and used for his biblical comments the Greek translation of the Bible, the Septuagint. His main endeavor was to reconcile the Platonic philosophy, popular in his day and place, with Judaism. Thus he adopts the Greek view that the body is the tomb of the soul. Only that soul is immortal which refuses to become trapped in bodily desires. Such a soul returns to its source at the death of the body. Philo quotes the Greek philosopher Heraclitus, who says, "We live their death, and are dead to their life," meaning that during earthly life, the soul is entombed in the body as in a sepulcher, but at the death of the body the soul lives its proper life, released from the corpse to which it was bound.[11]

This view is found in rabbinic literature as well, though it does not represent the normative view at the time, nor for that matter, for the unyielding traditionalist in modern times. Louis Jacobs points to adumbration of this perspective in Maimonides.[12] The latter based his view about the subject of the World to Come on a saying of the third-century CE Babylonian teacher Rav:

> Not like this world is the World to Come. In the World to Come there is neither eating nor drinking, no procreation or business transactions, nor envy or hatred or rivalry; but the righteous sit enthroned, their crowns on their heads, and bask in the radiance of the Shekhina.[13]

Maimonides elaborates on Rav's statement and focuses on the soul as that which endures in the beyond:

---

11. For Philo's views about the soul, see Wolfson, Harry, *Philo*, Volume I, Harvard University Press, 1948; p. 389-395.
12. Jacobs, Louis. *The Jewish Religion: A Companion.* Oxford University Press, 1995; p. 228-230.
13. Berakhot 17a.

For the World to Come there is no bodily form, but the souls only of the righteous without a body. Since there are not bodies in it, there can likewise be neither eating or drinking nor any of the other things which the bodies of men need in this world. Nor can any of the incidents to which bodies are subject in this world, such as sitting, standing, sleep, death, pain, laughter, and so on, occur there...To compare the "bliss" of the soul in the World to Come with the happiness of the body in this world by means of eating and drinking is quite incorrect. Nothing can compare or be likened to the world beyond.

And then, this, which summarizes the view of moderns who believe:

Death cannot be and is not the end of life. Man transcends death which occurs in altogether naturalistic fashion. He may be immortal biologically through his children via the survival of his memory: in influence by virtue of the continuance of his personality as a force among those who come after him, and, ideally, through his identification with the timeless things of the spirit. [14]

When Judaism speaks of immortality it has in mind this primary meaning: man contains something independent of the flesh which survives it: his consciousness and moral capacity; his essential personality; a soul.[15]

---

14. *Mishne Torah*, Hilkhot Teshuva (Laws of Repentance), Chapter 3:8.
15. Steinberg, Milton. *Basic Judaism*. J. Aronson, 1987; p. 78.

– Thirteen –

THE PASSION FOR LEARNING AND ITS UNDERLYING MOTIVE

He who possesses both learning and faith is like a crafts-man with the tools of his craft in hand.

—Yohanan ben Zakkai
Avot de Rav Nathan, 22

Be sure to ask your teacher for his reasons and sources.

—Rashi, Commentary
Bava Metzia, 33b

From early biblical and rabbinic times and into the present, the study of Scripture, the vast corpus of rabbinic literature, and all manner of learned literary output has been a supreme personal, communal and *religious* obligation. The fruits of this strong emphasis have been manifest in many ways. For many contemporary Jews one of these ways has seen the phenomenon take on a life of its own, to wit: the learning emphasis persists detached from the initial underlying motive which caused it to be. Thus for many, the intense drive for education for young and old, for higher education, for deep respect for scholars, for reverence for books—Jewish and general—the stark prominence of highly educated Jews in the academic world and the "secular" domain despite the very small portion of Jews in the general population and more.[1]

What follows seeks to depict something of the learning phenomenon in Judaism as such, and proceeds to explore the often unrealized underlying motive for it.

The Learning Phenomenon

In medieval Europe, when nearly all Christian and Muslim men, and certainly women, were illiterate, nearly all Jews could read and write, and many achieved high levels of knowledge. A twelfth-century monk, a student of the great Catholic theologian Peter Abelard, reported that "a Jew, however poor, if he has ten sons, would put them all to letters, and not only his sons but his daughters."

In the *beit midrash*, the house of study, the sacred books were greatly respected. Nobody would sit on a bench if there was a book anywhere on it. A book that fell to the ground was picked up and kissed. To put other things on top of a valued book was a sin. When a book was so badly torn that it could not be used, the caretaker took it to the cemetery and buried it. Even the smallest scrap of paper must not be left lying around on the floor if it had Hebrew characters printed on it, letters that spell out a sacred text.

In his ethical will, Rabbi Judah ibn Tibbon of the twelfth century reminds his son that he traveled far and wide to find teachers for him in science and other secular subjects. He adds: "My son, make your books your companions. Let your shelves be your treasure grounds and gardens. If you are weary, change from garden to garden. Your desire will renew itself, and your soul will be filled with delight…. Arrange your library in fair order so as not to weary yourself in your search for the book you need. Never refuse to lend books to anyone who can be trusted to return them. Honor your teachers. Treat them with respect in

---

1. For amplification of this phenomenon, see essay #7, "The Faithful Modernist: The Synthesis Between Traditional and Modernity."

all places and under all circumstances."

This penchant was manifest not only for the young but for the adult as well. At the YIVO Institute in New York, an organization which commemorates Jewish life in pre-World War II Eastern Europe, there is a volume of the Mishna saved from the Nazis and brought to the United States. On the front page of the book is stamped "The Society of Woodchoppers for the Study of Mishna in Berditchev." That the men who chopped wood in Berditchev, a job that had no status and required no education, met regularly to study Mishna shows the pervasiveness of study in the Jewish community. It also helps explain the avidity for education among the grandsons and granddaughters of these woodchoppers wherever Jews reside today.

Why This Emphasis on Education?

Abraham J. Heschel has articulated what has always been the basic underlying motive for the heavy emphasis on learning, and he does this with special reference to the contemporary world. Writing in the context of the Nazi regime in Germany in the 1930s, Heschel stressed that in an age of rampant disregard for human values, education must refocus on honing the sensibilities of the inner person. People in our time can read and write, make music and draw, describe nature and practice crafts. They possess a sense of order and duty, a talent for organization, a gift for public speaking and more of the "promise of potential." However, at the very same time...

> ...the inner life of the modern person is so chaotic....In the witch's cauldron of a person's drives, resentments and complexes whatever insights and understanding he has gained and digested can become the ingredients for a devil's meal.[2]

This is why Heschel stresses that education in our time, as in

---

2. Heschel, Abraham Joshua. *In This Hour: Heschel's Writings in Nazi Germany and London Exile.* The Jewish Publication Society, 2019; p. 10-11.

the past, must focus laser-like on the honing of moral and ethical and sacred sensibility in response to the will of God, what he designates as "Spirit." Men and women, Heschel stresses, must learn, relearn and internalize knowledge of that which is good and that which is evil, what is just and what is unjust, what is true and what is false, what is sacred and what is profane, why One God is different from many gods. And, he/she needs to use his/her acquired knowledge ("information"), his/her advanced literacy and thinking capacity, pen and paintbrush, refined speech and elegant demeanor and the rest of his/her many talents toward realization of these quintessentially important ends.

This has been the basic motive for the thirst for education in the Jewish way. Scripture tells us that Joshua, Moses' successor, was told to "keep this book of the Torah always on your lips and meditate on it day and night."[3] Similarly, the very first Psalm declares, "The teaching of the Lord is a (man's) delight and he studies that teaching day and night."[4] Why such study? The Deuteronomist sums it up well when he explained that even a king in Israel was commanded to write his own Torah scroll and keep it with him and read it all his life, *so that he may learn to revere the Lord his God, to observe faithfully the words of its teaching as well as its laws.*[5]

So, too, with regard to Talmudic study. The rabbis state that the "things which have no fixed measure (i.e., are of limitless obligation) are deeds of loving kindness and the study of the Torah (Talmud Torah).[6] And Rabbi Yosi stresses, "let your house be a meeting place for the wise; sit amidst the dust of their feet, and drink in their words thirstily."[7] Why such fervent study? The appropriation of knowledge was not for its own sake. *One learned lessons because of one's interest in the substance of religion and*

---

3. Joshua 1:8.
4. Psalms 1:2.
5. Deuteronomy 17:18-19.
6. Peah 1a.
7. *Ethics of the Fathers* 1:4.

religiosity. One studied because God commanded man to have knowledge and reverence for Him. After all, Talmudic texts, more often than not, have scant to do with the concerns of a contemporary student. It deals with arcane matters of a distant past. It is complex, elusive. Its text regularly moves suddenly from one topic to an unrelated topic. It consists of many a speculative discussion. Indeed, it is difficult material for study.

And yet, we may ask, is it not paradoxical that a significant part of Jewish religiosity was spent on such intellectual activity? Heschel explains:

> The Jew treasured the feeling of being close to the revealed holy words. To be present in the sphere of truth and purity meant to stand in the radiant field of metaphysical light. This experience was made possible by the participation of the entire person. Not only reason but also the soul participated in study. And the soul was also pulled in by the power of the music, by the Talmud—*niggun.* With its sweetness and forcefulness it captured one's feelings in an infinite net and introduced the student of Talmud, when he gave himself entirely to its thinking, into a beautifully noble world.[8]

And so, thinking about Torah and Talmud was experienced by the Jew as thinking with God. Learning is thinking in God's presence. This phenomenon may well seem strange to many. But that's how it was, and still is today, and needs to be in the morrow. It is the capacity to experience learning as prayer. The task of Jewish education is to nurture attachment to the transcendent, to the faith of Israel, and to its way of life.

Learning that Took on a Life of Its Own

As pointed out above, in our time, more often than not, the original motives for this passion for learning—recapturing

---

8. Heschel, Abraham Joshua. *In This Hour: Heschel's Writings in Nazi Germany and London Exile.* The Jewish Publication Society, 2019; p. 11

community and its values, deepening religious thought and practice—are forgotten, yet the drive for learning itself remains operative. This phenomenon frequently manifests itself in interesting and unintended ways. Such is the case with many highly educated Jews in the so-called "secular" world. Here I cite two examples taken from the non-Jewish world.

Rene Rodriguez

I was en route from the parking lot to Office Depot to replenish some of my home office supplies. A swarthy, dark-eyed man approached me thinking I looked like someone he knew. Though not the case, he insisted on talking to me.

We entered the store together. I don't know why, but he asked me if I was Jewish. Yes, I was. And that unleashed a torrent of talk. His name was Rene Rodriguez. He was a native of Puerto Rico and came to the United States at age eight. His father had left home and his mother died from neck cancer. He was brought to Manhattan in New York by an aunt to live with her, his grandmother and the aunt's two daughters. They all lived in a cold, sparsely furnished, two-bedroom apartment. It was a hard life living as they did from hand to mouth.

Things looked up for Rene in elementary school primarily because of his Jewish teachers. One such teacher, Mr. Goldstein, gave him extra sandwiches during lunch periods because he saw the lad didn't have enough to eat. Another teacher, Mrs. Cohen, encouraged and urged him to study hard, to master reading and writing, to be different from the other Puerto Rican kids who were more indolent than he was and were looked down upon by the other students. Mrs. Cohen often stayed with him after school hours to help him with his homework. Periodically, too, she invited him to her home on weekends so that he would feel comfortable and imbibe its atmosphere for study. These experiences stayed with him all his life. How grateful he was to the Jewish people for all that.

But there was more. When he was in junior high school, his

science teacher, Mr. Schwartz, saw that he wore tattered shirts and sweaters during the freezing winter. With tears in his eyes, Rene said his teacher bought him his first warm brown coat, the thought of which keeps him warm to this day.

With palpable passion, Rene said that because of these Jewish teachers who loved him, who cared for his needs, who consistently urged him to get a good education so that he would one day be a successful "somebody," he persisted in that direction. He continued his studies and graduated high school which few of the other Puerto Rican kids did. He went on to a technical school to study mechanics. He then joined the U.S. Air Force and studied for a pilot's license, which he got. When he came out of the air force, he studied in college on the G.I. bill and got a degree in aeronautics technology. Now Rene has been in his own business selling, repairing and supplying copiers, printers and fax machines using the skills he acquired during his studies. That's how I met him at Office Depot; he was on one of his stops throughout Southern California doing business, doing quite well, he said, and able to take good care of his family.

When he finished his narrative, I told him how impressed I was, and that as a Jew and a rabbi I understood this great emphasis of the Jewish people on education. When I mentioned "rabbi," he waxed lyrical, saying how eternally grateful he was to the Jewish people "who made me who I am today."

The conversation was not yet over. Rene told me about a local Jewish-owned electronics store which had been vandalized. He was enraged and spoke in protest at a town meeting. He was then asked to appear on a local television program during which he told of Jewish benevolence, emphasis on learning and all the rest, and that such behavior at a Jewish store—any such store—was intolerable. Whereupon a group of skinheads sought him out and smashed the windows of his car and his house, as well as calling him and threatening him on the phone. To which Rene said to me, "There's no way these guys intimidated me. I am from Puerto Rico!"

Finally, the encounter was over. Rene Rodriguez gave me his business card. I gave him my card. We embraced. He proceeded to his business with the Office Depot manager. I went out of the store musing about Jewish compassion and the passion for learning, and the difference it can make in a person's life.

Wanda Austin

Years after I wrote the preceding vignette, I came across the following item on the front page of the *Los Angeles Times*, dated March 4, 2019. Shades of Rene Rodriguez's Mrs. Cohen, Mr. Goldstein and Mr. Schwartz!

How Wanda Austin Blazed a Trail from Public Housing to a Perch as USC's President

In the Bronx, Wanda Pompey occupied two worlds: the tenements and public housing projects where she lived and the white schools her mother pushed her to attend.

Teachers paid scant attention to her and the few other black students. But one day in seventh grade, her math teacher, Mr. Cohen, had the class do a difficult algebra problem.

When he handed back the papers, he said, loud enough for the class to hear, "Hey you're good at math. Don't let anyone tell you you're not." His praise inspired her. She doubled down on math, skipped eighth grade and was accepted into the elite Bronx High School of Science.

Her brilliance at math—and later engineering—drove her through exclusive schools in New York and Pennsylvania to male-dominated defense giants in Southern California.

After she married, Wanda Austin joined the Aerospace Corp. in El Segundo in 1979 and thrived. In the final eight years of her career, she ran the $950-million company—a nonprofit brain trust tasked with developing and overseeing the nation's missiles and satellite systems.

Her reputation as a highly educated, clear-headed, empathetic leader pulled her out of retirement last year for a new challenge: Austin, 64, was appointed president of the University of Southern California—the first woman to lead this great university and the first person of color. [9]

9. Mozingo, Joe. "How Wanda Austin Blazed a Trail from Public Housing to a Perch as USC's President." *Los Angeles Times*, 4 Mar. 2019.

SACRED ACTION

You have heard that in Egypt the waters of the Nile, overflowing its banks, take the place of rain; and that these fructifying waters are led by various channels into the remote fields to irrigate them. Now, the Nile with its precious floods would be of no benefit to the fields without these channels.

Thus it is with the Torah and its principles. These constitute the mighty stream of spirituality, flowing since ancient times through Israel. It would have caused no useful fruits to grow, and would have produced no spiritual progress, no moral advancement, had the mitzvah not been there to lead its Divine floods into the homes, the hearts, and the minds of the individual members of the people, by connecting practical life in all its variety and its activities with the spiritual truths of religion.

It is a mistake to assume that people are capable of living in a world of ideas only, and can dispense with symbols that should embody these ideas and give them tangibility and visible form.

—Leo Jung, The Jewish Library

"Know Him in all Your Ways"

Ideals and values are, of course, the vital basics of religion. However, they are enduring when enacted and put to the test in everyday life. Without this perspective, the ideals are but a cluster of speculative abstractions and of conceptual worth at best. Thought and life go hand in hand. Affirmations about divinity need integration with human physicality. A life of piety needs to be fashioned from worldly elements. God needs "dwelling" in man, as it were.

The prophet Isaiah 43:12 says, "You are my witness, says the Lord, and I am God." The Rabbis understood this as "*When* you are my witnesses, I am God; but *if you are not* my witnesses, *then I am not God*." God is a reality in human life whenever and wherever human beings attest to His presence through their personal and collective character and the specific ways with which they conduct their lives.

How can we humans embrace such principle? The author of Proverbs (3:6) helps: *bekhol derakhekha da-ayhuh*, know God in all your ways. This means that one needs to seek to train oneself to see God in all the ways we conduct our lives and to mobilize all the resources of one's heart, mind and hands in our effort to embrace the life of the spirit.

What follows is our focus on various domains of Jewish religious practice and seeks to show how Judaism has sought to translate idea into practice.

Fourteen

THE "AMEN SPECIALIST" AND THE FOURTEEN MORNING BLESSINGS
Contemporary Versions

הָיָה רַבִּי מֵאִיר אוֹמֵר:
חַיָּיב אָדָם לְבָרֵךְ מֵאָה בְּרָכוֹת בְּכָל יוֹם
וְעַתָּה יִשְׂרָאֵל, מָה ה' אֱלֹהֶיךָ שׁוֹאֵל
מֵעִמָּךְ כִּי אִם לְיִרְאָה אֶת ה' אֱלֹהֶיךָ

Rabbi Meir used to say: a person is obligated to recite a hundred blessings every day, for it is stated in Deuteronomy 10:18 "and now, O Israel, what (maw)* does the Lord your God require of you? Only this, to revere the Lord your God."

—Menakhot 43b

On 100 Blessings: A Creative Approach

Reverence is expressed via blessings, words of thanksgiving, and, according to Rabbi Meir, an exercise to be repeated one hundred times every day. In an apparent effort to ease somewhat such a burdensome obligation, the rabbis instituted a clever practice. One could meet the one-hundred-blessing obligation by listening to one or more others recite the blessing after which the listener would say *Amen*. In what might be considered an interpretive "stretch," they justified the practice by citing a passage

---

* The number 100 is here derived from reading the Hebrew word *maw* (what) as *may-aw* (100).

in *Berakhot* 9b in which David, the presumed author of the book of Psalms, recited the "haleluyah" at the conclusion of the more than one-hundred psalms he was said to have composed.

Abraham Joshua Heschel urges us to focus on the essential character of the blessing phenomenon:

> The sense of the "miracles which are daily with us," the sense for the "continual marvels," is the source of prayer. We are trained in maintaining our sense of wonder by uttering a prayer before the enjoyment of food. Each time we are about to drink a glass of water, we remind ourselves of the eternal mystery of creation, "Blessed be Thou…by Whose word all things come into being." On eating bread or fruit; or enjoying a pleasant fragrance or a cup of wine; on tasting fruit in season for the first time; on seeing a rainbow, or the ocean; on noticing trees when they blossom; on meeting a sage in Torah or in secular learning; on hearing good or bad tidings—we are taught to invoke His great name and our awareness of Him.[1]

Coming to Synagogue Early

As a youth in the fervently traditional synagogue in Brooklyn, New York where I grew up, I was required by my grandfather to arrive for Shabbat morning services some fifteen to twenty minutes before the scheduled starting time.

During this early lull, an old, bearded, pious Jew practiced his "specialty." He would get hold of anyone he could, have him stand next to himself and require him to recite each of the fourteen *Berakhot* (blessings) of the preliminary service. This afforded the old man the opportunity to recite *Amen* after each of the blessings. I was one of the man's regular "customers."

Over the years, I have thought of this old-timer as "The Amen Specialist." I calculated that he averaged six "customers" each Shabbat morning, which gave him some one hundred and eight

1. Heschel, Abraham Joshua. Man's Quest for God. Aurora Press; 1998.

Amens—not a bad quota for one day's religious work. I also surmised that since, according to tradition, one is required to recite one hundred blessings each day, the man figured he had it made by reciting *Amen* after other people's blessings, and these, added to his own blessings, enabled him to fulfill his religious obligation by a good margin.

Every time I recite these morning blessings, I think of that old-timer of my youth and what he was up to as he corralled me and his other customers. I must confess that as a youngster I was vaguely aware of what the old-timer had in mind when he recited all his *Amens*. Nor did I grasp the full import of the meaning of the blessings themselves. As time went on, however, I began to delve more deeply into their meaning and to understand better what was going on in the synagogue of my youth on Shabbat morning—and what was on the mind of the old-timer. His zealous practice sought to inculcate a genuine sense of gratitude to God for the marvelous world bequeathed us, and an appreciation for the manifold blessings a person receives in his daily life—this in addition to the obligation he felt to meet the one-hundred *Berakhot* requirement.

These blessings are brief expressions of thanks for the great benefits that are a person's upon rising in the morning after a night's sleep. Each blessing focuses on a specific gift. Eric Hoffer once said that "the hardest arithmetic to master is that which enables us to count our blessings." And so, I felt these blessings needed amplification in contemporary terms, unpacking their implications for modern men and women. Hence I composed supplementary prayer-meditations for each of the blessings toward those ends. Here they are:

בָּרוּךְ אַתָּה ה' אֱלֹהֵינוּ מֶלֶךְ הָעוֹלָם אֲשֶׁר נָתַן לַשֶּׂכְוִי בִינָה לְהַבְחִין בֵּין יוֹם וּבֵין לַיְלָה

Blessed are You, Lord our God, King of the Universe, who has given to the mind understanding (i.e., the capacity) to distinguish between day and night.

Now that I've awakened in the morning, I thank You, God, for restoring in me full consciousness so that I can tell the difference between day and night. I'm grateful for the unfailing human instinct that rouses me in the morning so that I can continue living. I appreciate that I can experience a new day with eyes now open so that I can see and with a mind now clear so that I can think. *Amen.*

בָּרוּךְ אַתָּה ה׳ אֱלֹהֵינוּ מֶלֶךְ הָעוֹלָם שֶׁעָשַׂנִי בְּצַלְמוֹ

Blessed are You, Lord our God, King of the Universe, who has fashioned me in His image.

I realize, God, that you have embedded in me some of your very own characteristics: love and compassion, justice and mercy, discernment and creativity—and for these I am grateful. How appreciative I am, too, that I find in myself the yearning to realize these human qualities in my life which I believe to have come from You. *Amen.*

בָּרוּךְ אַתָּה ה׳ אֱלֹהֵינוּ מֶלֶךְ הָעוֹלָם שֶׁעָשַׂנִי בֶּן/בַּת חוֹרִין

Blessed are You, Lord our God, King of the Universe, who has made me a free man/woman.

How fortunate I am to have been fashioned by You, God, free to choose right or wrong; in addition, you have endowed me with an innate passion for freedom—a yearning which will not be smothered. I am grateful to be living in a country where my personality as a Jew is respected, and where I am free from oppression and discrimination. *Amen.*

בָּרוּךְ אַתָּה ה׳ אֱלֹהֵינוּ מֶלֶךְ הָעוֹלָם שֶׁעָשַׂנִי יִשְׂרָאֵל

Blessed are You, Lord our God, King of the Universe, who has made me a Jew.

God, I deeply appreciate being an integral part of the faith and people of Israel, to share in the joy of our way of life and to value its passion for learning. I realize, too, that to be able to participate in my people's destiny as a "light" to others, I must first be true to myself as a Jew. How valuable it is to have self-respect, to know who I am and where I come from. *Amen.*

בָּרוּךְ אַתָּה ה' אֱלֹהֵינוּ מֶלֶךְ הָעוֹלָם פּוֹקֵחַ עִוְרִים

Blessed are You, Lord our God, King of the Universe, who opens the eyes of the blind.

I savor the ability to see—the marvel of the blue sky, the towering mountains, the verdant foliage, the budding flowers; these and the myriad other glories of nature have their source in your beneficence, God. I'm grateful for this capacity to resonate to these natural wonders and for the faith that You have fashioned all this. *Amen.*

בָּרוּךְ אַתָּה ה' אֱלֹהֵינוּ מֶלֶךְ הָעוֹלָם מַלְבִּישׁ עֲרֻמִּים

Blessed are You, Lord our God, King of the Universe, who clothes the naked.

How valuable it is to have the clothes that keep me warm, the raiment for Shabbat and Holy Day, suit and dress for my children, shoes which allow me and my family and so many others to go about our daily rounds safely and comfortably. I feel good about these blessings—but I also feel discomfort when I think of so many others who don't have what I have. Help me to share what I have with those in need. *Amen.*

בָּרוּךְ אַתָּה ה' אֱלֹהֵינוּ מֶלֶךְ הָעוֹלָם מַתִּיר אֲסוּרִים

Blessed are You, Lord our God, King of the Universe, who sets free those who are bound.

How glad I am to be able to free myself from the bonds of evil thoughts about others, bad dreams and dishonest schemes. Help me, God, to continue to break the shackles that imprison my heart, that I may be free from jealousy and selfishness and thus enabled to reveal the nobler virtues within me. Please, God, free me from the chains of negativity. *Amen.*

בָּרוּךְ אַתָּה ה' אֱלֹהֵינוּ מֶלֶךְ הָעוֹלָם זוֹקֵף כְּפוּפִים

Blessed are You, Lord our God, King of the Universe, who raises up those who are bowed down.

Because of the wondrous way you have designed the human body, I can uncoil a bending spine, lift up slumping shoulders and drooping neck. Yes, I can straighten myself out physically — and mentally — so that I can go about my life proudly and confidently. How good and satisfied I feel about myself when I add my own earnest effort to your design. Thank you, God, for giving hope to the oppressed, the downcast, those who are bent over in spirit. *Amen.*

בָּרוּךְ אַתָּה ה' אֱלֹהֵינוּ מֶלֶךְ הָעוֹלָם רוֹקַע הָאָרֶץ עַל הַמָּיִם

Blessed are You, Lord our God, King of the Universe, who spreads the earth over the waters.

You, God, are, indeed, "King of the Universe," for you created and continually sustain our magnificent world — the earth and seas, the sky and the galaxies, the whole of nature with its extraordinary system and order. As I ponder Your world, I cannot help but see Your hand in the brushstrokes of creation. Thank You for all this. Thank You. *Amen.*

בָּרוּךְ אַתָּה ה' אֱלֹהֵינוּ מֶלֶךְ הָעוֹלָם שֶׁעָשָׂה לִי כָּל צָרְכִּי

Blessed are You, Lord our God, King of the Universe, who provides for all my needs.

God, I realize that if I partner with You, I will prosper and have what I need for daily living, for You provide the basic stuff from which I myself hew out the resources that sustain me. Without what You provide, I can have nothing. Thank You for helping me grasp the dictum, "Man is a partner with God in the creation of the world." *Amen.*

בָּרוּךְ אַתָּה ה' אֱלֹהֵינוּ מֶלֶךְ הָעוֹלָם אֲשֶׁר הֵכִין מִצְעֲדֵי גָבֶר

Blessed are You, Lord our God, King of the Universe, who makes firm the steps of a person.

Thank You, God, for planting within me the capacity to choose my goals in life, to set these goals today and then be able to muster the conscious purpose to go forward and reach them on the morrow. How confident can one be in one's choices when one's goals are clearly set. Thank you, again, for this. Amen.

בָּרוּךְ אַתָּה ה' אֱלֹהֵינוּ מֶלֶךְ הָעוֹלָם אוֹזֵר יִשְׂרָאֵל בִּגְבוּרָה

Blessed are You, Lord our God, King of the Universe, girds Israel with strength.

Thank you for giving my people the strength to endure the slings of an outrageous fortune over the centuries, and to come through with our faith intact. And thanks for the grit in us which continues to maintain our religion and peoplehood today even without hostile outside pressure. I appreciate that the faith of Israel has the innate power and truth that are the source of this endurance. Amen.

בָּרוּךְ אַתָּה ה' אֱלֹהֵינוּ מֶלֶךְ הָעוֹלָם עוֹטֵר יִשְׂרָאֵל בְּתִפְאָרָה

Blessed are You, Lord our God, King of the Universe, who crowns Israel with glory.

I recognize that when I act honestly, justly, charitably, I bring honor to my faith and people. And when I act immorally, I bring dishonor to my faith and people. I try to realize that every Jew holds the honor of Israel in his/her hands. Yes, You, God, work through human agents so that "glory" for the Jew depends upon me and my fellows. Amen.

בָּרוּךְ אַתָּה ה' אֱלֹהֵינוּ מֶלֶךְ הָעוֹלָם הַנּוֹתֵן לַיָּעֵף כֹּחַ

Blessed are You, Lord our God, King of the Universe, who gives strength to the weary.

When I am tired from daily toil, weary from frustrations in my family, depressed about alienation from friends, upset about the state of my faith and people, I believe You give me the fortitude to confront my turmoil and alleviate my distress. I know that life inevitably brings with it problems, but faith in a Power which animates us from within helps us overcome. Thank You. Amen.

Addendum

This all seems to be asking for a lot of blessings for a good deal, either already experienced or hope to be experienced…which leads me to this story:

> Once, when Rabbi Moshe of Kobrin was young, he spent Purim with his teacher Rabbi Mordechai of Lechovitz. In the middle of the meal, Rabbi Mordechai exclaimed, "This is a time for gifts. Reach out your hands and I will give you whatever gifts of spirit you crave!" The other disciples present asked for a variety of spiritual gifts and received them, but Moshe was silent.
>
> Finally, the rabbi inquired, "Well, Moshe, and what do you want?"
>
> He replied, "The only thing I want is to serve until I deserve what I get."

When something painful happens to us, we usually ask, "What have I done to deserve this?" We might also ask, "What have I done to deserve all the good that happens to me, or the good that I hope happens to me?"

– Fifteen –

RECAPTURING STRENGTH AND CREATIVITY, AND A "NEW" HIGH HOLY DAY PRAYERBOOK

הַיּוֹם הֲרַת עוֹלָם

Today is the birthday of the world.

–High Holy Day Liturgy

The Holy Days Retain Their Grip: Why? How?

Despite the widespread indifference of many Jews to the life of practicing religion, Rosh Hashana and Yom Kippur have retained strong hold on the Jewish imagination. They remain days on which even those who are absent from the synagogue for most of the year flock to it in record numbers. This has been a phenomenon that has always puzzled me; yet, upon reflection, it harbors compelling elements that might well explain the phenomenon.

Two eminent thinkers help us understand the matter: the pioneering anthropologist, Mircae Eliade, from the anthropological perspective, and the former Chief Rabbi of the British Commonwealth, Jonathan Sacks, from the religious.

In his famous work in comparative religion, Eliade understands man's New Year observance as an attempt to recapture the spirit of the original act of creation on the part of the divinity. Man seeks to make present that initial creative act. Most all religions conceived the world (the cosmos) as a living entity that is born, develops and dies on the last day of the year—*to be reborn* on New Year's Day. This is a rebirth because at every New Year, time begins anew; it recovers the original sanctity which it possessed when it came from the Creator's hands:

> The meaning of this yearly turning back to the as yet unsullied world was this:
>
> ...All the sins of the year, everything that time has soiled and worn, was annihilated. By symbolically participating in the re-creation of the world, man, too, was created anew; he was reborn, for he began a new life. With each New Year, man felt more free and more pure, for he was delivered from the burden of his sins and failings. He had reintegrated the fabulous time of Creation, hence a sacred and strong time—sacred because transfigured by the presence of the god, strong because it was the time that belonged to the most gigantic Creation ever accomplished, that of the universe. Symbolically, man became contemporary, present with the creation of the world.

Eliade continues: this all helps us understand why the memory of that marvelous time has haunted man (whether consciously or unconsciously "religious") and why periodically he determines to return to it. By doing so, he seeks to recapture for himself in the year ahead renewed strength, abundance and creativity.[1]

According to Jonathan Sacks, one has but to point to the Rosh Hashana liturgy where, following the sounding of the shofar, the congregation proclaims: *Hayom Harat Olam*, "today is the birthday of the world," to see the relevance of Eliade's analysis to the Jewish New Year. Sacks explains the renewal phenomenon at High Holy Day time:

---

1. Eliade, Mircea. *The Sacred and the Profane: The Nature of Religion*, Harcourt Grace, 1959; p. 79-80.

It is as if the world has become a courtroom. God Himself is the Judge. The shofar announces that the court is in session, and we are on trial, giving an account of our lives. Properly entered into, this is a potentially life-changing experience. It forces us to ask the most fateful questions we will ever ask:

Who am I? Why am I here? How shall I live? How have I lived until now? How have I used God's greatest gift: time? Who have I wronged and how can I put it right? Where have I failed, and how shall I overcome my failures? What is broken in my life and needs mending? What chapter will I write in the book of life in the year ahead? No one who has genuinely experienced Rosh Hashana and Yom Kippur lives an unexamined life.[2]

And we might add to Sacks' moving comment that via this intense process of introspection and self-examination, the worshipper on these great days of transition from past year to future year yearns for forgiveness for past error, for a new start, for re-charge of heart and mind, for, as Eliade put it, "renewed strength, abundance and creativity."

Here then are factors which seem to account for the phenomenon of fulsome worship on the High Holy Days. When one supplements these factors with contemporary initiatives in the worship process, the phenomenon might well be further understood. For an example of one such initiative, read on:

A "New" Prayerbook

Some years ago, the Conservative Movement published a "new" prayerbook (*Makhzor*) for the High Holy Days. It was an exciting development at the time because it represented a much-needed and anticipated liturgical work after a generation of eager waiting. It reflected the ongoing effort of renewing the ways prayer

---

2. Sacks, Jonathan. *The Koren Yom Kippur Makhzor*. Koren Publishers Jerusalem; 2011, Introduction, p X.

was to be structured and its spiritual meaning articulated in both traditional and modern fashion—a characteristic stance of the Conservative Movement in contemporary Jewish life. This is what I wrote at the time in the congregation's bulletin:

The Makhzor's Virtues

B'nai Israel is a congregation in which innovation has become a tradition. It is in this spirit that I am proud to inform you that our Board of Directors has approved the introduction of a new High Holiday prayerbook to be launched during the forthcoming New year. The "Makhzor for Rosh Hashonah and Yom Kippur" issued by the Rabbinical Assembly, is now the official book of High Holy Day prayer for Conservative Judaism in America. It is our fervent hope that the use of this new liturgical work will mark a significant religious and spiritual advance in the life of our congregation.

I should like to point out some of the distinguishing characteristics of this new book of prayer.

In the *first place*, it accurately reflects the fundamental approach to Judaism which has always characterized the Conservative Movement, i.e. change within the context of tradition, modern yet reverent of the Jewish past. The new Makhzor is a "traditional" prayerbook in the best sense of the word. The basic structure and content of the classical liturgy has been faithfully transmitted, the historic continuity with past Jewish prayer has been lovingly preserved, and the fundamental requirement of Hebrew fully provided for.

At the same time, and this is its *second* distinguishing characteristic, on matters not affecting the core of the classic liturgy, the book is flexible—adding, omitting, abbreviating and adapting the text throughout, in full awareness of the contemporary Jew's desire for greater brevity in prayer as well as his yearning for relevance to modern concerns. It is, therefore, also a very modern prayerbook in that it clearly reflects the mind-set of the Jew of today. It contains much new and sensitive prose and poetry and readings from the pens of great writers, poets and thinkers of our time. These concern, for example, the Holocaust, Israel reborn, the ambivalence of faith, and much else of concern to a twenty-first century Jew in America. This, I might add, is in keeping with an observation by one of my master teachers at the Jewish Theological Seminary, Professor Shalom Spiegel who wrote:

> The standard prayers, the oldest nucleus of the liturgy, always and everywhere became the center of Jewish worship, a bond of union despite geographical dispersal and a bridge across the ages linking the present with the past. At the same time, each period and place was left free, if not encouraged, to speak its own mind in new compositions added to or inserted within the ancient prayers.[3]

A *third* characteristic of the new Makhzor is its educational value. There are brief notes throughout which serve as guideposts for those who are less familiar with the structure of the traditional service. These explanatory notes clarify the themes of the various prayers and enlighten the worshipper about the motifs of the different services.

Fourthly, the English translation is completely new. It is a felicitous rendering of the Hebrew text, faithful to its content yet expressive of the heart and mind of the modern American Jew. This is an English that can be prayed. It avoids archaisms, and yet manages to be the language of the sanctuary, rather than that of the marketplace. The Torah readings and Haftarot, as well, are newly translated and also edited with the contemporary congregant in mind.

The new prayerbook's *fifth* distinguishing characteristic is its attractive physical format. This is in the spirit of the teaching of Rabbi Ishmael ben Elisha in the midrash (*the Mekhilta to Exodus*

---

3. Spiegel, Shalom in Finkelstein, Louis (ed). *The Jews: Their History, Culture, and Religion*. Jewish Publication Society of America; 1949.

15:2), who said, "I will be beautiful before Him and I will prepare beautiful ritual objects before my God." More: a lover of books once said this: "Read only beautifully written and handsomely bound books in a tastefully furnished room. Let your eye rest on graceful objects. Beauty must be everywhere."

Indeed, our freshly minted book of prayer has aesthetic appeal. It is a fine example of the bookmaker's art. The pages are beautifully printed in terms of layout, typeface, spacing, sharpness and clarity, and in two colors. It is user friendly. And we will be worshipping with this volume in the majestic sanctuary of our congregation—a beautiful place marked by its striking tapestry, imaginative modern stained-glass windows, glistening chandeliers and arresting ritual objects.

Yes, B'nai Israel is a congregation where innovation has become a tradition. This prayerbook, in my view, is a constructive and responsible innovation because it takes place within the context of a great tradition—the sacred heritage of the people of Israel. We are grateful to the leadership of the Conservative Movement for producing the new High Holiday prayerbook, for it will help us immeasurably, please God, to fulfill our spiritual mandate as a congregation.

Above all, we earnestly pray that this Makhzor will evoke in each of our hearts renewed hope, new zeal, rekindled love for the faith of Israel, for the life of the spirit which makes life worth living.

– Sixteen –

BEFORE GOD FORGIVES, MAN MUST FORGIVE

The Hebrew word Teshuva *is derived from the root* shuv *which means "turning" or "turning back." There are those who do not only return to assess bygone incidents, but also to return to their better selves. What is involved is a self-critique (the Hebrew word* l'hitpalel, *"to pray," means to judge oneself). It is to resolve to act in accord with the dictates of one's conscience which is the presence of a spark of divinity within. This presence prompts a person to reflect on times when one failed to be at one's best. However, the forgiveness process is not complete until the one who has been aggrieved forgives when asked.*

Two Types of Atonement

Jews associate the repentance/forgiveness process with the High Holy Days—Rosh Hashana and Yom Kippur. Many misunderstand the nature of this process which is embedded in their faith's religious way. Even when one enters the synagogue with sincere regret about one's misdeeds, one does not realize that repentance is felt to win forgiveness only for offenses committed against God (e.g. no prayer, no Shabbat observances, etc.). For offenses committed against fellow man (e.g. slander, business deception, etc.), only the one who has been offended can forgive; until that happens—prior to Yom Kippur when the offender sincerely asks for forgiveness for what he has done to hurt his fellow—does Yom Kippur itself "work," as it were, does God forgive. The Mishna is clear about this:

עֲבֵרוֹת שֶׁבֵּין אָדָם לַמָּקוֹם - יוֹם הַכִּפּוּרִים
מְכַפֵּר: עֲבֵרוֹת שֶׁבֵּין אָדָם לַחֲבֵרוֹ - אֵין יוֹם הַכִּפּוּרִים מְכַפֵּר,
עַד שֶׁיְּרַצֶּה אֶת חֲבֵרוֹ.

The Day of Atonement atones for sins against God, not for sins against man, unless the injured party has been appeased.[1]

What is the reasoning which undergirds this perspective? Rabbi Jonathan Sacks, in an insightful exploration of this subject, helps on this score.[2] He cites a midrash which deals with the issue of man's deeds and God's reaction to them:

Rabbi Yannai said: from the beginning of creation God foresaw the deeds of the righteous and wicked. *The earth was void*—this refers to the deeds of the wicked. *And God said, Let there be light*—this refers to the deeds of the righteous. *And God separated the light from the darkness*—this means the deeds of the righteous from the deeds of the wicked. *God called the light "day"*—this refers to the deeds of the righteous. *The darkness He called night*—this refers to the deeds of the wicked. *And there was evening*—the deeds of the wicked. *And there was morning*—the deeds of the righteous. *One day*—this means that God gave them [both] a single day. Which was it? Yom Kippur.[3]

Sacks understands the midrash's use of the words "one day" to mean the singular, unique day of days which, in Jewish terms, means Yom Kippur. What the midrash is asserting here is that *divine forgiveness preceded the creation of the first humans.* However, God did not exercise His power to forgive immediately after humans were created: He did not forgive Adam and Eve; He mitigated Cain's punishment but did not forgive him; He did not

---

1. Mishna Yoma 8:9.
2. Sacks, Jonathan. *The Koren Yom Kippur Makhzor*. Koren Publishers Jerusalem; 2011, p. xvi-xxv.
3. Beresheet Rabbah 3:8.

forgive the generation of the Flood nor the sinful people of Sodom. Why? Because He waited for the period of Yom Kippur—*the time during which mankind could exercise the* freedom *God gave her to choose the paths of her life*—good, bad or otherwise. This was the mechanism provided by her creator to do *teshuva*, to repent of her misdeeds, to recognize that she did wrong, to express remorse for the past and learn from it, to resolve not to repeat the wrongs—and to seek forgiveness from the ones offended. *It was only then—at that Yom Kippur time—that God would exercise His pre-existing power of forgiveness.*

Without such a mechanism for repentance, guilt would accumulate. There would be no way to mend the past and move forward from it. Human beings would be weighted down by the heavy burden of remorse, and worse, liberated from the inner voice of conscience, and thus become like the beasts of earth and sea.

Good enough. However, even if one repented and sought forgiveness from the one he has offended, our text still sees God as withholding His forgiveness. For, again, if He created pardon before He made man, why does it play no part in the stories of Genesis from Adam and Eve to the Patriarchs? Some element of the exoneration process was still missing. Jonathan Sacks avers that response to that question suggests itself overwhelmingly: *God does not forgive human beings until they learn to forgive one another. Thus, when a wrongdoer asks for exoneration from the persona he has wronged, the response of the latter must be: "you are forgiven."*

Indeed, Jewish law offers guidelines for the victim of wrongdoing. He must first be convinced that the person who has wronged him is sincere in asking for forgiveness; when such is the case, *he is required to grant the forgiveness asked for.* If he refuses, the offender must ask again. If he refuses a third time, it is considered cruel and, in itself, a sin. Consider the alternative, writes Sacks:

> What would happen if God forgave but humans did not? Then history would be an endless story of retaliation,

vendetta, vindictiveness and rancor, violence begetting violence, and evil engendering new evil—in short, the world from before the Flood, the world that still exists today in the form of tribal warfare and ethnic conflict, the world of Bosnia, Rwanda, Kosovo and Darfur, a world of victims seeking vengeance thereby creating new victims and new vengeance in a process that, without forgiveness, never ends.[4]

The first act of forgiveness in the Torah is when Joseph forgave his brothers to teach that only when we pardon one another does God pardon. It was only after Joseph's brothers asked for exoneration for having sold him into slavery did Joseph, now prominent in Egypt, exonerate his siblings. It is only when the book of Genesis reaches this instance of forgiveness and reconciliation did God on Yom Kippur invoke His pre-existent power to forgive.

Easier Said Than Done

Such magnanimous forgiveness is, of course, easier said than done. There are times, when grievous hurt inflicted understandably resists pardon. Yet, there is the rabbinic statement, "The world depends on three things: Torah, *Avoda* (service of God) and *Gemilat Hasadim* (acts of kindness)."[5] The latter virtue denotes a special sort of kindness—*Hesed*—such as clothing the poor, providing a dowry for an indigent woman, burying the dead. These are deeds that go beyond the normal requirement of the law. *Hesed* is also the gift of forgiveness as much as humanly possible. Scripture commands, "Do not take revenge and do not bear a grudge."[6] Such actions only prolong a wound inflicted and are "payback." *Hesed* intervenes here and attempts a new beginning or renewal or, at least, an attempt to grasp something humane in another even though that person overlooked the

---

4. Sacks, Jonathan. *The Koren Yom Kippur Makhzor*. Koren Publishers Jerusalem; 2011, p. xxv.
5. *Ethics of the Fathers*, 1:2.
6. Leviticus 19:18.

humanity of the other. In this way, Hesed seeks to keep the principle of kindness alive. The world depends on it.[7]

A True Story About One Who Repented and One Who Forgave

At my congregation B'nai Israel in Pittsburgh, I was ever eager to maintain a decorous service and atmosphere; this included limiting the already rather lengthy traditional Conservative service. Part of the effort was my determination to keep the number of *aliyot* at the standard seven. For the most part, the system worked, but not without rumbles, especially when some could not get a coveted aliya with its accompanying *mi-she-bayrakh* (prayer for the sick or happy occasion), or when a prominent congregant was involved.

Dr. Laben Melnick, an especially sensitive spirit, was president of the congregation when one such rumble" occurred. An important congregant demanded an *aliya* we could not offer. Whereupon Dr. Melnick, who sat on the *bimah*, rose from his chair and approached me and rather emphatically insisted that I allow the aliya. I stood my ground; *he then repeated his demand, this time not realizing the microphone was on and had caught his unusually disrespectful tone.* I prevailed and that was the end of it.

Twenty-five years later in Los Angeles, where we had moved to work at The University of Judaism, I received a call from Laben Melnick. It was two weeks before Yom Kippur. He told me rather sheepishly that he regretted having spoken to me disrespectfully during that long-ago incident concerning the refused *aliya*. At the direction of his then rabbi, he was calling to ask for *mechila* (forgiveness) for only the sins committed against fellow men can be forgiven by the aggrieved. Also, his rabbi cited for

---

7. Fishbane, Michael. *Sacred Attunement: A Jewish Theology.* University of Chicago Press, 2010; p. 152-153.

him the passage in the Midrash (*Lamentations Rabbah 3*) that "the gates of repentance are always open." He was especially regretful, he emphasized, because the whole congregation had heard his disrespectful tone.

My response: "Of course, Laben, I forgive you."

"Rabbi, please put it in writing; this is very important to me," Laben asserted.

"I will, Laben," but I did not get to write him the forgiveness note immediately.

A week later, I got another call from Laben. "Rabbi, please, I beg you to send me the written *mechila*." The urgent, pleading sound of his voice prompted me to immediately pen and dispatch the note of forgiveness.

Seventeen

BLESSING THE NEW MONTH
Articulating Values and Aspirations

מִתּוֹךְ בִּרְכוֹתָיו אַתָּה יוֹדֵעַ מַחְשַׁבְתּוֹ

From his prayer-blessings you can know his thoughts.

–Numbers Rabbah 20

Prayer clarifies our hopes and intentions. It helps us discover our true aspirations, the pangs we ignore, the longings we forget. It is an act of self-purification. It teaches us what to aspire to, implants in us the ideals we ought to cherish.

–Abraham Joshua Heschel

A Prayer for a New Month

Why this special prayer at the end of one month and the beginning of another, the appearance of a "new moon"?

The moon is a body which waxes, wanes, disappears and reappears. For three nights the starry sky is without a moon, but this "death" is followed by a rebirth—the "new moon." It has thus long since represented for the religiously inclined the process of birth, demise and rebirth and the various stages of human experience in between. This perpetual process, the ever recurring cycle, makes the moon for human beings the heavenly body concerned with man's rhythms of life.[1]

---

1. Eliade, Mircea. *Patterns in Comparative Religion*. World Publishing Co., 1963; p. 154, 176.

Since, for religious man, all the world is, by definition, "sacred" because God created it, this element of creation—the moon—and its characteristics are sacred. Thus humans have always resonated to the moon's "behavior,"' if you like, and have developed rituals and prayers to express its implications for their life on earth. And so, the Rosh Hodesh prayer which looks to the future, of life "becoming," of new life, of renewed life. The prayer proceeds to be specific about the things the worshipper hopes for in the month ahead. Read on.

THE PRAYER

יְהִי רָצוֹן מִלְּפָנֶיךָ, ה' אֱלֹהֵינוּ וֵאלֹהֵי אֲבוֹתֵנוּ,
שֶׁתְּחַדֵּשׁ עָלֵינוּ אֶת הַחֹדֶשׁ הַזֶּה לְטוֹבָה וְלִבְרָכָה.
וְתִתֶּן לָנוּ חַיִּים אֲרוּכִים, חַיִּים שֶׁל שָׁלוֹם, חַיִּים שֶׁל
טוֹבָה, חַיִּים שֶׁל בְּרָכָה, חַיִּים שֶׁל פַּרְנָסָה, חַיִּים שֶׁל
חִלּוּץ עֲצָמוֹת, חַיִּים שֶׁיֵּשׁ בָּהֶם יִרְאַת שָׁמַיִם וְיִרְאַת
חֵטְא, חַיִּים שֶׁאֵין בָּהֶם בּוּשָׁה וּכְלִמָּה, חַיִּים שֶׁל עשֶׁר
וְכָבוֹד, חַיִּים שֶׁתְּהֵא בָנוּ אַהֲבַת תּוֹרָה וְיִרְאַת שָׁמַיִם,
חַיִּים שֶׁיִּמָּלְאוּ מִשְׁאֲלוֹת לִבֵּנוּ לְטוֹבָה, אָמֵן [סֶלָה].

מִי שֶׁעָשָׂה נִסִּים לַאֲבוֹתֵנוּ וְגָאַל אוֹתָם מֵעַבְדוּת לְחֵרוּת,
הוּא יִגְאַל אוֹתָנוּ בְּקָרוֹב וִיקַבֵּץ נִדָּחֵינוּ מֵאַרְבַּע כַּנְפוֹת הָאָרֶץ
חֲבֵרִים כָּל יִשְׂרָאֵל. וְנֹאמַר אָמֵן.

May it be Your will, Lord our God and God of our fathers, to renew for us this coming month for good and blessing. Grant us long life, a life of peace, a life of goodness, a life of sustenance, a life of physical health, a life marked by reverence for heaven and dread of sin, a life without shame or disgrace, a life of wealth and honor, a life in which we have love for the Torah and reverence for heaven, a life in which our hearts' desires are fulfilled for good. Amen, Selah.

May He who performed miracles for our ancestors and redeemed them from slavery to freedom, redeem us soon, and gather in our dispersed people from the four quarters of the earth, so that all Israel may be united in friendship, and let us say: Amen.

Following his recital of the Amida prayer, Rav, the third century CE Babylonian Amora (rabbinic sage), composed this prayer after he had concluded the prescribed blessings. Rav and his counterpart in Talmudic discourse, Samuel, were among the leading scholars of their time. Rav settled in the town of Sura and Samuel in Nehardea, both centers of learning.[2]

1) We Pray for Collective Well-being

Note the repeated use of the words *us, we* and *our* in this prayer. It is yearning in plural terms. Our hope for true well-being is grounded in the well-being of the community of which we are a part. Further, when we pray for freedom, for ingathering exiles, it too is *us* we have in mind; it is *all Israel* (that) may be *united* in friendship.

Yet more: originally the time of the onset of the New Moon (Rosh Hodesh) and its religious observance was established by the Sanhedrin (supreme legislative body and court) in Jerusalem. Because it was to be observed collectively by all Jews, including those in the diaspora, messengers were sent from Jerusalem to officially establish the observance by Jews wherever they lived. And so, the welcoming of the New Moon in Jewish life along with aspirations expressed in the above prayer-text, constitute a *collective* matter—publicly announced and publicly observed— to be shared by the entire community of Israel.

2) We Pray for Physical and Material Well-being

Note the terms *long life, physical health, sustenance* and *wealth*. Judaism has always stressed the importance and decided legitimacy of the material things of life. The rabbis tell us that when we arrive in the next world, we will be asked if we enjoyed all the legitimate material aspects of life the world fashioned by God offered human beings.[3] Moreover, taking good care of one's own physical self was a dictum of the sage Hillel because it was

---

2. Rav's prayer for the new month is found in the tractate Berakhot 16b.
3. *Jerusalem Talmud*, Kiddushin 4:2 end.

seen as an act of reverence for the body's creator.[4] The Jewish mystics added another reason for this dictum: the human physical structure is precious because it harbors a "spark" of Divinity and thus must be treated with the utmost respect.[5] Then, too, longevity, physical health and fiscal resources not only make possible the good life, but also provide one with the capacity to do good for others.

Yet more, we recognize that God is the ultimate source of the things which constitute our material well-being, but do so in this sense: God gives us the resources—the soil; the seed, the rain— which make life possible, the things that man must use, must cultivate with his God-given capacities to think, create and transform, so that he/she may live, and live well.

3) We Pray for Spiritual Well-being

Note the term *reverence for heaven*. This speaks to our aspiration to be aware of the awesome Power in the universe—a Force— non-human—that pervades our world and our lives. Indeed, this means that when we behold our wondrous universe, its astonishing order and system and reliability, when we are conscious of the extraordinary structure and mechanism of the human body, we see the hand of God—their Fashioner, their Mind, their Designer, and thus are provoked to profound reverence. Indeed, this reverential sensibility is at the core of spiritual well-being.

4) We Pray for Psychological Well-being

The yearning for *a life of peace*, a life *without shame or disgrace* and d*read of sin*. Often people are seized with internal anxiety causing sleepless nights. The prayer for peace here seeks to ease this condition.

The Hebrew word *shalom*, peace, means more than amicable relationships with others—personal and communal. The Bible

---

4. *Leviticus Rabbah* 24:3.
5. See Shechter, Jack, *The Idea of Monotheism*, Hamilton Books, 2018; p. 133–34.

tells about Jacob's sons who had traveled from Canaan to Egypt for provisions. On the way back home they discovered that the money they thought they had paid for the provisions was found in the sacks of their donkeys. The brothers were full of anxiety. Maybe one of them *did* take their money back! Perhaps this incident would come to haunt them because of the nefarious deed they perpetrated on their brother Joseph in selling him as chattel to travelers en route to Egypt! They were conflicted because they felt guilty; yet they needed the provisions to survive and provide for their families. What was to happen to them when they had to return to Egypt for additional provisions?

> When they returned, Pharaoh's steward responded to their worries this way: *Shalom lahkem — Peace be to you* [that is, rest assured], do not be afraid; your God and the God of your fathers must have put treasure [that is, your money] in your sacks for you; I had received your money."[6]

In order to reassure them, the steward apparently manufactured the idea that "God," i.e., some unknown figure, put that money in their sacks; he had already received the money they had legitimately paid for their provisions.

When the steward responded to the brothers with *shalom lakhem*, "peace be to you," he was telling them not to worry, not to be anxious; they were innocent about the money — in a word, that they have peace of mind and heart.

The root meaning etymologically would seem to confirm this understanding of the word *shalom*. The word derives from the Akkadian *salāmu*, which means "complete," "whole," "healthy." While, for the nation or family peace consists of prosperity, safety and security, peace for the individual means not only physical health and well-being, but also psychological health, i.e., *an integration and harmony of thought and deed, of body and spirit. Thus a person at peace is not haunted by inner conflicts, by*

---

6. Genesis 43:23.

warring emotions, by unresolved issues that pull him in different directions. Indeed, he possesses peace of heart and mind. As the Amida prayer has it, he has *nachat ruach,* a "serene spirit."

The rabbis formulate this perspective in imaginative fashion. Peace is not a mere absence of strife, but a positive, harmonizing principle in which inner opposites are reconciled. The verse, "He makes peace in His high places"[7] by combining the aspects of both Michael and Gabriel—mercy and justice.[8]

ADDENDUM: BLESSING OF THE NEW MOON
In Hebrew: Birkat Levanah or Kiddush Levanah

This is a ceremony whose purpose coincides with the Rosh Hodesh prayer depicted. It was initially designed to express praise of God for the renewal of the moon which indicates the wonder of creation. The Talmud (*Sanhedrin* 42a) conceived of this blessing over the New Moon as a public ceremony and added a comparison between the notion of Israel and the moon.

וְלַלְּבָנָה אָמַר שֶׁתִּתְחַדֵּשׁ, עֲטֶרֶת תִּפְאֶרֶת לַעֲמוּסֵי בָטֶן, שֶׁהֵם
עֲתִידִים לְהִתְחַדֵּשׁ כְּמוֹתָהּ וּלְפָאֵר לְיוֹצְרָם עַל שֵׁם כְּבוֹד מַלְכוּתוֹ.

To the moon He said that it should renew itself as a crown of beauty for those He carried from the womb (Israel), for they are destined to be renewed like it, and to praise their Creator for the sake of the glorious majesty.

The sages who instituted the moon blessing ceremony thus conceived the cycle of the moon as a symbol for the people of Israel who, in exile, become diminished, but in the time of redemption, will be renewed. This perspective resulted in the ceremony becoming a group rite during which congregants go out at night, focus intently on the moon which appears to be growing

---

7. Job 25:2.
8. *Deuteronomy Rabbah* 5:13.

in size and recite the following prayer:

Blessed are You, Lord our God, King of the universe, who by

בָּרוּךְ אַתָּה ה' אֱלֹהֵינוּ מֶלֶךְ הָעוֹלָם, אֲשֶׁר בְּמַאֲמָרוֹ בָּרָא שְׁחָקִים
וּבְרוּחַ פִּיו כָּל צְבָאָם, חֹק וּזְמַן נָתַל לֶהֶם שֶׁלֹא יְשַׁנוּ אֶת תַּפְקִידָם.
שָׂשִׂים וּשְׂמֵחִים לַעֲשׂוֹת רְצוֹן קוֹנָם, פּוֹעֵל אֱמֶת שֶׁפְּעֻלָתוֹ אֱמֶת.
וְלַלְבָנָה אָמַר שֶׁתִּתְחַדֵּשׁ, עֲטֶרֶת תִּפְאֶרֶת לַעֲמוּסֵי בָטֶן, שֶׁהֵם
עֲתִידִים לְהִתְחַדֵּשׁ כְּמוֹתָהּ וּלְפָאֵר לְיוֹצְרָם עַל שֵׁם כְּבוֹד מַלְכוּתוֹ.
בָּרוּךְ אַתָּה ה' מְחַדֵּשׁ חֳדָשִׁים.

His word created the heavens, and by His breath all their host.
He set for them laws and times, so that they should not deviate
from their appointed task. They are joyous and glad to perform
the will of their Owner, the Worker of truth whose work is
truth. To the moon He said that it should renew itself as a
crown of beauty for those He carried from the womb [Israel],
for they are destined to be renewed like it, and to praise their
Creator for the sake of His glorious majesty. Blessed are You,
Lord, who renews the months.

It would appear inevitable that the rabbinic authorities in our time would link the Blessing of the New Moon ceremony to *Yom Ha-atzmaut,* Israel Independence Day. For the rite reflects the Jewish people's recognition of its renewal with the return to Zion, the establishment of a Jewish State, and new life for Jews everywhere.

Eighteen

ON A HASIDIC WEEKEND AT A CONSERVATIVE SYNAGOGUE... A THEOLOGY...AND A PERSONAL LETTER FROM THE LUBAVITCHER REBBE

The essence or substance of the soul is divine spirit, as truth vouched for by Moses especially, who in his story of the creation says that God breathed a breath of life upon the first man[1] the founder of our race, into the Lordliest part of the body, the face, where the senses are stationed like bodyguards to the great king, the mind. And clearly what was then thus breathed was ethereal spirit, even an effulgence of the blessed, thrice blessed nature of the Godhead.

–Philo of Alexandria[2]

A Theology

The Chabad movement in contemporary Jewish life harbors a vital yet, for most, little-known idea. Actually, it is really not much of a secret for those who are familiar with its ideology, or, in this case, to use a more accurate term, its "theology." The *Tanya*, the basic sourcebook of the movement, tells us that a "Divine Spark"

---

1. Genesis 2:7.
2. Philo. *On the Special Laws.* Translated by F. H. Colson. Loeb Classical Library. Harvard University Press; 1937 Vol. 8, p. 85.

is to be found in every human being. Shneur Zalman of Liadi, the founder of this Hasidic group, echoes the Philo of long ago:

> The soul in Israel is an actual portion of God from above (*haylek Eloha mi-maal mammesh*), as it is said, "And He (God) breathed into his (man's) nostrils the soul (*neshama*) of life and man became a living being.[3] As the Zohar comments, "When one blows, it is from himself that he blows," that is to say, from his most inward essence, for man ejects his most inward vitality when he blows powerfully.
>
> In the same way the souls of Israel "ascended in God's thought" (i.e., were fashioned by God), as it is written "Israel is my son, my first born"[4] and "You are the children of The Lord your God."[5] This means that as the child derives from the "brain" (i.e. the semen) of the father so, as it were, the soul of every Jew is derived from God's thought and wisdom. *D'ihu hahim*, "For God is wise," and *Hu v'hahmato ehad*, "He and His wisdom are one," as Maimonides says: *Hu Hamada v'hu Hayodaya*, "He is the knowledge and the knower."[6]

Now, the *Tanya* takes Maimonides' comment to mean that "wisdom" and "God" are one and the same. Thus when Shneur Zalman asserts that the soul stems from "wisdom," he is asserting that the soul of man stems from God Himself. This is confirmed by Shneur Zalman's previous reference to the biblical statement that God breathed of his very own breath into man making him a living being. And so, according to Chabad's founder, there is an actual portion of Divinity in the human being, what he terms elsewhere a *nitzutz*, a "spark" in every person who God himself created.

I do believe that it is accurate to say that this basic notion has

---

3. Genesis 2:7.
4. Exodus 4:22.
5. Deuteronomy 14:1.
6. Shneur Zalman. *The Tanya.* Kehot Publication Society, Ch. 2.

been internalized by Chabad followers and that, in fact, *it is a determining operational notion motoring the work of the movement's leaders to this day still.* Let me explain.

What Are the Implications of This Theological Thought-line?

The implications of this perspective are, indeed, of profound significance in terms of people's attitude toward their fellows and their concrete relationship to them. Thus, if a person is aware that Divinity abides within the human being as such—within *all* human beings—that it is a fundamental aspect of his nature, it follows that he must treat with honor and respect the Divinity that both he and others harbor. Why? Because he is obliged to so honor and respect Divinity (God) as such—a basic and utterly compelling obligation of a man of faith. Thus the principle: man must treat fellow man with deep reverence.

This attitude and posture toward one's fellow must persist even when the other practices Judaism in non-traditional fashion, even when he does not believe in the principles of the faith, even when he does not practice or identify with Judaism altogether. Why? Because even if a single "spark" is believed to inhere in every single person who lives, that person partakes of Divinity and must be treated with unflagging care and respect, concern and compassion, honor and reverence. Judaism has long since taught that how one relates to the other is equivalent to how one relates to God. As the Book of Proverbs has it, "He who withholds what is due to the poor affronts his *Maker*. He who shows pity for the needy honors *Him*.[7] And for the religious man this is his ultimate obligation."[8]

This is how the Lubavitcher Rebbe in our own time put it at a *Farbregen,* an assembly with his followers in Brooklyn, New York. He was laying out his approach to Jewish outreach. What follows is an excerpt from his Yiddish discourse recorded on a

7. Ibid 14:31.
8. See also Genesis Rabbah 24:7 and Mekhilta to Exodus 20:16.

video (currently on YouTube) which contained English subtitles produced by Chabad personnel:

> When you have an opportunity to approach a fellow Jew, you need to do so with love even though the fellow might not share your spiritual outlook, and you seem to have nothing in common that binds you. Yet, given that he is your fellow Jew who the Torah describes as a child of the same God, a descendent of Abraham, Isaac and Jacob, it means that despite any lapses you see, he is still a Jew....We cannot give up on or write off—God forbid—any Jew regardless of the life he leads. He is your fellow who you must love like your own self. And because you cannot and must not write off a single Jew, you must make every Jew your business. [For the entire discourse, see Addendum II below.]

Read now and see how a staunchly orthodox Chabad group related to an equally staunch non-orthodox (Conservative) synagogue, member of a movement at major variance with Chabad both in thought and practice.

A Hasidic Weekend at a Conservative Synagogue

Some two dozen Chabad Hasidim had been invited to Congregation B'nai Israel in Pittsburgh for a weekend of prayer, study, song and dance, fellowship and one-on-one interchange. The program was sponsored by the synagogue's United Synagogue Youth (USY) organization. What follows is a description of the event by Mr. Spitz, B'nai Israel's educational director, followed by my own reflections about it, both published in the Synagogue's bulletin.

Mr. Spitz:

"It was a very enriching experience and I got a lot out of it. It made me see a different part of Judaism which I never saw before....When I first got here I was a little apprehensive, but afterward, I found that the Hasidim were regular people....It was a unique experience."

These were just a few of the reactions of our young people to the Hasidic weekend sponsored by B'nai Israel USY, Friday through Sunday, January 19 through 21.

The activities took place in our new Youth Lounge that Rabbi Shechter persuaded the Perilsteins to build and furnish when he first came to our congregation. The lounge was set up as an orthodox *shul,* with a *mechitza* (divider) separating the males from the females. Other activities took place in the social halls, chapel and classrooms. Twenty-four young men—clearly talented and carefully chosen—came from Pittsburgh itself, New York and Boston. Ninety of our teens along with some one hundred adults met with them in fellowship and prayer, study and discussion, singing and dancing throughout the weekend.

The conclave opened with *Kabbalat Shabbat* services enlivened by lusty singing of the prayers. As prelude to the festive meal that followed, all washed their hands in the traditional fashion accompanied by the appropriate blessings. The ample food was spiced with *z'mirot* (table songs) and the full grace after meals.

The keynote speaker following dinner was Professor Avraham Hasofer, chairman of the Department of Statistics and head of the School of Mathematics at the University of New South Wales in Sydney, Australia, and currently an exchange professor at M.I.T. in Boston. Dr. Hasofer set the theme of the weekend by explaining aspects of the teaching of the Baal Shem Tov, founder of the Hasidic movement: love of the Jewish people, love of the Torah, and love of God. It was a lucid and passionate presentation. A lively confrontation between Mrs. Hasofer, a clinical psychologist, and members of the audience about "women's lib" ensued. The differences of opinion on the role of women in Jewish and religious life were apparent.

Rabbi and Mrs. Shechter told me about their experience with some fifteen of the young men who spent Friday and Saturday as guests in their home. They slept in the basement on cots; however, not much sleeping took place. Far into both nights, until about 3:00 a.m., they kept them and their three sons engrossed in their storytelling. Especially riveting were their enthusiastic descriptions of the Lubavitcher Rebbe's "miraculous" deeds, his uncanny intuition, his towering stature, his vast authority, and his visions of the future. Rabbi Shechter indicated that aspects of this storytelling were taken by him with a "grain of salt." However, it was these young people's passion in the telling that was gripping.

Shabbat morning services, predominantly in Hebrew and highlighted by vigorous song and chant, featured the sermon of Rabbi Ephraim Rosenblum, one of Pittsburgh's charismatic Hasidic leaders. He stressed that we Jews are "slaves" to our environment and that we should seek freedom from it and be true to our inner selves as Jews. Then Shabbat luncheon, limited to the young people, was followed by group discussion, with the participants divided into various subgroups that dealt with specific topics of contemporary concern.

Exploration of Jewish ideas, singing and dancing, fellowship and one-on-one interchange with the leaders—and amongst the participants themselves—took place throughout the afternoon. Our young people were particularly intrigued by the Hasidic precepts transmitted through the medium of popular catchy tunes, led by Yossi Baumgarten and Yisrael Shusterman, Yeshiva students from New York. They explained with characteristic verve the various prayer customs and sections of the services.

Some two hundred teenagers and adults attended the *mincha*, *shalosh seudot* (third meal), *maariv* and *havdalah* services. A *Melaveh Malka event* ("escorting the Queen" out of Shabbat) on Saturday evening followed with stories, singing and dancing to the accompaniment of one of our USYers on his guitar. The evening culminated with a basketball game in the B'nai Israel gymnasium, which had been reactivated at Rabbi Shechter's urging, with the young men and the USYers the players.

On Sunday morning our visitors met with hundreds of our youngsters attending Sunday school explaining religious ideas through animated storytelling and discussion and again through song and dance.

While the younger visitors met with the children, Dr. and Mrs. Hasofer addressed the B'nai Israel Men's Club Sunday breakfast convened for the occasion. The meeting, which stretched into lunchtime, featured a vigorous interchange about the spiritual underpinnings and purposes of Jewish observances. It also focused on the need for a gradual and incremental approach to Jewish observance, but that the ultimate goal of Jewish living must ever be kept in mind. It was an illuminating session and, as Rabbi Shechter has often observed, the incremental methodologies of the Chabad and Conservative Movements have more in common than meets the eye.

The success of this weekend experience for our young people can best be summed up via the reaction of one of our USYers, who said, "The singing and dancing made everyone happy because the Hasidim were happy. They taught us a lot about being good Jews. They put a lot of enthusiasm into everything. I liked the whole thing very much. When are they coming back?"

The reaction of the adults was more tempered. Clearly they were enamored by the visitors' warmth and enthusiasm. They were less compelled by some of the intellectual substance presented. They did not appreciate the *mechitza* and what some considered the absence of "dignity" in some of the activities. Nonetheless, the adult consensus was that the weekend was stimulating and provocative, and a creative and instructive undertaking.

Rabbi Shechter:

Mr. Spitz's report above details the extraordinary weekend experience we at B'nai Israel had with the followers of the Lubavitcher/Chabad movement. Here I want to add some personal observations and indicate what I believe we need to learn from the experience as it applies to us as principled non-orthodox Conservative Jews.

When I initiated this undertaking, I did so as a long-confirmed "fellow traveler" of the Hasidic movement in America. From earliest childhood through high school, I knew few other synagogues but a little Hasidic "*Shtiebel*" in Brooklyn, New York. This synagogue in the Brownsville section was appropriately called "Reyim Ahuvim" ("Beloved Friends") and was well known at the time even in Europe as a vigorous center of religious life in America.

In this synagogue setting I learned the Hasidic *nusach* (melodic prayer modes). I witnessed prayer with genuine *kavanah* (focus, sincerity). I saw fervent piety in Mr. Groner, a Chabad follower, whose talit-covered head, swaying body and outstretched hands made me think that his heart beckoned heaven itself to respond to his earnest pleas. I grew up in that synagogue alongside Mr. Groner's son, Label, who later became the secretary to the Lubavitcher Rebbe himself. I paid many a visit to Crown Heights, the Brooklyn neighborhood that houses the Chabad headquarters. And then there was the *Yeshiva* (elementary school) and the *Mesivta* (high school) I attended, both infused with the spirit of Hasidim.

This intensive religious environment of my youth demonstrated to me that Judaism was a warm and enriching way of life, that religious expression was not primarily somber, sober and sad, but full of joy and enthusiasm, suffused with vigor and excitement, replete with spontaneity and informality. I learned that Judaism was not only for the mind, but for the heart and soul as well, that it was not an ascetic abstraction but a vigorous affirmation of life in all its manifestations. I learned that the Jewish way of life was not a "sometime thing" but an everyday thing and that to gain the fullest measure of inner satisfaction, all of a person's senses must be brought into use. And I learned that the synagogue, next to the home, was the setting in which this spiritual beauty was to come to fruition.

I have, of course, since moved out and away from the orthodox Hasidic realm into that of the Conservative Movement and have done so with strong commitment to its non-fundamentalist ideology and practice. I've long since become aware that many of the movement forms—its garb, its rigid ritualism, its avoidance of "secular" education (almost all "emissaries" do not attend college) are neither appropriate nor workable in the modern American milieu. And yet, I am convinced that the essential spirit of that "old time religion" remains relevant, that its message of love and joy is as vital to the Jew today as it was to the Jew of my youth. As a matter of fact, Conservative Jews—young and old—sense that something vital is missing from their lives, and thirst for full-hearted and genuine religious conviction and expression. The warm and positive response of our people to our Hasidic friends over the January weekend testifies to that yearning.

For us, the essential lesson and challenge which I believe has emerged from this weekend is this: how can we contemporary Jews, within the necessary and indispensable context of the Conservative Movement, incorporate the spirit of Hasidism in our midst? To use Martin Buber's distinction between spirit and form in the religious enterprise: how can we incorporate the "religiosity" (i.e., spirit) of the "religion" (i.e., forms) of our Hasidic brethren into our lives? I believe we need to come up with an answer to that question, along with a pattern of action, lest we modern, staid and "sophisticated" Jews wither on the vine from spiritual apathy and sheer boredom.

ADDENDUM I
A Letter from the Lubavitcher Rebbe

After this edition of our bulletin appeared with Mr. Spitz's report and my observations about the weekend, I sent the bulletin to the Lubavitcher Rebbe in New York with a letter of thanks and with commendation of his wonderful followers who had spent the weekend with us.

The Rebbe, a busy man as the worldwide leader of the Chabad movement, wrote back to me personally and at length. The letter was carefully typed, written with characteristic passion, though, from my perspective, with a somewhat "fundamentalist" caste. He insisted that the "forms" I claimed were outmoded were necessary as distinctively Jewish ones and that they encase and nourish the "spirit" of which I spoke. They were needed, he insisted, in order to get the Jewish way to work in our day as they did in the past. Thus, for example, to appear in public in distinctive Hasidic garb demonstrates "here is a Jew."

I rest my case, as the Rebbe undoubtedly rested his.

Incidentally, I had told my Pittsburgh Chabad friends about the Lubavitcher Rebbe's personal letter to me. As fervent followers of their leader, they urged me to show them his letter, for to receive a letter from the Rebbe and especially about their activity was somewhat of a "happening" for them. I had misplaced the letter. They kept urging me to locate it. Try as I might, I couldn't and, alas, I never recovered it. I had to repeatedly "swear" to the Chabadnicks that I really received that letter. Truly I did. I always hoped they believed me.

ADDENDUM II
The Lubavitcher Rebbe Lays out His Approach to Jewish Outreach

This is a translation of a discourse in Yiddish delivered by the Lubvitcher Rebbe at a Farbrengen (an assembly) with his followers at the Chabad headquarters in Brooklyn, New York. The translation is taken literally from the screen of the live video and is that of the Chabad translator.

At first glance it appears that we need to reconcile an apparent paradox. On the one hand, Torah and Judaism need to spread in every place according to its particular context. On the other hand, Torah is eternal; it is unchanging and applies equally everywhere and at all times.

The explanation: making any changes to Torah and Judaism means that to strengthen Jewish observance in a given place one needs to take into account its particular circumstances and will need to consider the context, the character and milieu of the specific place and time. When you have an opportunity to approach a fellow Jew, you need to do so with love even though the fellow might not share your spiritual outlook, and you seem to have nothing in common that binds you. Yet, given that he is your fellow Jew who the Torah describes as a child of the same God, a descendent of Abraham, Isaac and Jacob, it means that despite any lapses you see, he is still a Jew. How much more so, when these lapses are no fault of his, but the result of being raised in a secular environment. You need to encourage him in his Judaism.

But there are various ways to inspire him. If you begin with a deep Chasidic discourse or with a Talmudic tractate, he won't understand you or gain an appreciation of the value of Torah study. It won't either bring him any closer to Judaism. Instead, you must begin from the *Alef-beis* of Torah and Judaism. Anything else is not what he needs.

You must, however, be cautious for him not to think that the Alef-beis is the entirety of Torah. That is false. Torah consists of various parts, all of which comprise one whole, and cannot be divided and separated. Except that a beginner, who is just starting to learn, cannot commence from the middle. One must educate "each youth according to his own way," to which he can relate. Only then will he come to a point at which he can appreciate the entire Torah as he grows old.

True Judaism contains no room for compromise; it does not look differently at one Jew than at another, nor does it apply in one place and not another. As far as the Torah is concerned, it was given by God, who does not change. So, too, there can be no change to the Torah He gave, nor to the tradition that He has given us.

Whenever trying to strengthen Judaism, in any city or country, one must first assess the best way to teach Torah there so that the local Jews will understand it and relate to it, such that it becomes their life. For Torah is "our life and the length of our days." This applies to every Jew, however he may affiliate. This is the point: there needs to be a resurgence of Judaism through the Torah first. Then, one should not be satisfied with working in his immediate environment, or be content staying where it is familiar, a place he likes. Rather, he must go wherever he can; wherever he has information that there might be other Jews. He cannot demand of them that immediately upon meeting them, they transform their lives to be like his, or anyone else's. Rather, he must reach out to them, and bring them closer to the Torah in a way which they can relate to. Then he will succeed in strengthening their Judaism.

To summarize: we cannot give up on or write off—God forbid—any Jew regardless of the life he leads. He is your fellow who you must love like your own self. And because you cannot and must not write off a single Jew, you must make every Jew your business. You must, in a way he can appreciate, tell him about the Torah which consists of 613 commandments and which are relevant to every Jew. Indeed, every Jew can fulfill them, and ultimately will fulfill them. Except that the way to reach them within their context is: for those who are unaware of *Alef*, begin by teaching them *Alef*. For those who already know *Alef*, begin with *Beis*, and so on, and continue until your student will no longer need you because he is able to stand on his own two feet.

ADDENDUM III
A "Polemical" Note

I have always felt that there is a remarkable similarity of the methodical approach to religious action between Chabad and the Conservative movement. That is to say, *the context of life in the present* and *the incremental methods* of both of them:

- "The need to take into account the particular circumstances"

- "The need to consider the context and milieu of the specific place and time"

- "If you begin with deep Chassidic discourse or a Talmudic tractate (translate profound contemporary Jewish theology or literature) he won't understand you, it won't bring him any closer to Judaism."

- "The way to teach them 'within the context' is: for those who are unaware of Alef, begin with Alef, proceed to Beis, and so on."

Note the following guiding principle for the Conservative Movement articulated by Rabbi Simon Greenberg, vice chancellor of the Jewish Theological Seminary, a seminal leader and authoritative spokesman of the Movement. The context of this statement is the approach the rabbi is to employ when dealing with congregants with minimal knowledge and practice of the Jewish way:

> I think it is good to remember that our duty in the Rabbinate is to bring others to a maximum observance of the Torah, and not merely to enable ourselves to save our own souls. Effective, democratic leadership, whose only weapon is persuasion, always entails a certain amount of compromise. The main difference between one democratic leader and another is the ability of one to keep is eye on the essentials, and compromise on the peripheral.[9]

Some contend that the difference between Chabad and the Conservative Movement is the former's eventual goal being a full Jewish religious life whereas the latter posits an eventual "watered-down" religious life. To this the Movement responds that, in fact, it posits a far more substantive religious life of thought and practice than when it starts with its constituents. It sees itself as commanded by God in this direction, but that it employs an incremental approach toward its realization, guided by "the context and milieu of the specific place and time," etc. This

---

9. In a personal letter to me and my wife, Leah, when I served as a chaplain in Fort Chaffee, Arkansas, 1958.

is precisely the Chabad practice with its characteristic acceptance of quite partial religious observance on the part of those with whom it deals. What else is compromise when Chabad worship locales everywhere allow, in effect, encourage, its followers to drive to their locales on Shabbat, Festival and High Holy Days for prayer? When it invites congregants who openly disregard Shabbat and holiday observance and/or kashrut in even minimal fashion, to be its congregation's Torah readers on Yom Kippur before hundreds of worshippers? Numerous examples of this tolerant, accepting, compromising methodology could be cited. This, by no means, is meant to be critical. Indeed, without this approach, the Chabad outreach enterprise could not begin to exist. Its incremental approach would simply not be possible.

An unbiased examination of the two movements will, indeed, show a remarkable similarity of the incremental approach to their constituencies, i.e. begin with the minimum and gradually proceed toward the maximum possible. The only significant difference between Chabad and Conservative in this context are the theoretical notions of what religious observance and ideology *ought to be*, in an ideal world, or as Chabad puts it, in the Messianic era. And this is a matter for discussion at another place and time.

Here, too, I rest my case.

– Nineteen –

ISHMAEL SOWA, PAGANISM AND LIVING RELIGION
A Message from Africa

מִכָּל־מְלַמְּדַי הִשְׂכַּלְתִּי

From all who taught me have I become enlightened.

−Psalm 119:99

On Pagan Religion

Ishmael Sowa was a native of Ghana, a small nation on the southwest coast of Africa. He was an ordained Presbyterian minister in America studying for a master's degree in biblical literature at the Pittsburgh Theological Seminary. He had already translated the New Testament into his native African tongue and, upon returning home, planned to translate the Old Testament.

My wife, Leah, a classmate of Ishmael at the Pittsburgh Seminary, had arranged a dinner at our home in order to introduce Ishmael to me, for relaxed conversation and perhaps to learn from each other something about our respective religious ideas and practices. We were the first Jews Ishmael had ever met and Ishmael was the first native African we had ever met. After telling him about some of the Jewish religious ways, I asked Ishmael to delineate for Leah and me the nature of native African religion and his reactions to it as a Christian. A warm, friendly and articulate man, he proceeded to do so.

Many Africans today are "pagans," Ishmael began. They literally worship rivers, stones, trees, bones. They offer animal sacrifices to these objects, accompanied by elaborate rituals and incantations. Instead of the Jewish-Christian-Muslim "Thou shalt" and "Thou shalt not," they have "taboos" that regulate and control family life and social relationships. These taboos, unlike the regulations of monotheists, partake of magic and superstition in that a specific prohibition against touching, saying or doing something is rooted in fear of immediate harm from a supernatural force. The Africans' belief in life after death is so strong that, like the ancient Egyptians, they bury food, water and eating utensils with their dead so that the deceased will continue to have nourishment during their life in the great beyond.

Ishmael told us that the day before his departure for America, his father took him to the river to pray to the river god for a safe journey. I later learned that what Ishmael was referring to was a widespread practice, when for example, the Masai of East Africa cross a stream, they throw a handful of grass into the water as an offering to the stream's "spirit." The grass, the source of life for their cattle, plays an important role in their tribe's superstition and ritual. Among the Baganda of Central Africa and the Ghanians in southern Africa, before a traveler forded any river, he would ask the spirit of the river to afford him a safe crossing and, as an inducement, throw a few coffee berries as an offering into the river. At certain spots on the rivers Nakiza and Sezibwa in Uganda, there was a heap of grass and sticks on either bank, and every person who crossed the river threw some grass or sticks on the one heap before crossing, and on the other heap after crossing: this was his offering to the spirit of the river for a safe passage through the water. From time to time, more costly offerings were made at these heaps; the worshipper would bring beer, or an animal, or a fowl or some bark-cloth, tie the offering to a heap, and leave it there after praying to the spirit. The worship at each of these rives was cared for by a priest.

This phenomenon recalls Mercai Eliade's description:

These spirits live and govern in the depths of the waters. Like the very elements in the waters, the divinities are at odds with each other and capricious; they do good and evil with equal carelessness, and like the sea, they generally do evil. More than any other gods they live outside time and history. Their life is perhaps less divine than that of the other gods, but it is more closely connected with the element they represent—the waters.[1]

It was these practices, Ishmael said, that prompted him and so many other Africans of his educated group, to adopt the religion of the western world.

Reaction to Ishmael's Description

We listened to Ishmael in astonishment. All this in the twentieth century! Literal paganism still alive in the life of millions of people! I felt transported back to ancient times when the Bible vigorously combated such primitive forms of religion and life.

Paganism surely was too primitive for the twentieth century. Yet something prompted me to ask: in what ways are Judaism, Christianity and Islam superior to this African paganism? Ishmael's response was rather diplomatic and nuanced, as well as frank and penetrating. In some ways, he said, these "higher" religions are superior to paganism; in other ways, they are not. This response was particularly interesting considering that Ishmael was a devout Christian devoted to converting his countrymen to Christianity—and yet, he could see merit in paganism. This is how he explained it:

It is quite true that paganism is inhibiting and based on fear. Pagans are nervous because they worship forces in nature that are themselves in conflict with each other. Once an African

---

1. Eliade, Mircea. *Patterns in Comparative Religion*. Sheed and Ward, 1958; p. 203-204. An aside: could the "angel" with whom Jacob wrestles when alone at the ford of Jabbok have been the ford's "spirit?" (Genesis 32:23-33)

breaks a taboo but experiences no negative consequences, he loses his faith completely and often goes "wild." The higher religions, on the other hand, are liberating and based on love, on discipline, on consistency. Hence an individual's monotheistic faith is more deeply rooted and more "civilizing."

But Ishmael cautioned against smug superiority. The higher religions are no match for the fervent faith and powerful conviction, the genuineness and naturalness of African religion. Paganism is rooted in the soil; it is part of the everyday life of the individual; it governs his every deed and thought; it seizes and holds his emotions and provides for their natural outlet. The pagans' beliefs are naïve, to be sure, but he believes in them with every fiber of his being.

On the other hand, major elements in Christianity have taken life out of religion; they've elevated it to an abstraction, converting it to an enterprise of rarified speculation. They have made faith pallid and weak, cold and obscure and irrelevant to lives of flesh and blood. African missionaries, Ishmael emphasized, want and need Christianity in Africa badly for its palpable beneficence, but they insist on combining it with the fervor and conviction of the native African way of life, for the strong connection with human beings and the concrete world. "Paganism, you see," concluded Ishmael, "is not all that bad."

As we parted from Ishmael that night, I knew that I had re-learned something very important. One naturally hesitates to draw lessons from pagan life (of all things!) for our highly sophisticated culture. But consider: Socrates, Plato, Aristotle, the Pythagoreans, Stoics and Epicureans were all pagans, yet they have taught men and women of all ages a great deal. Moreover, their being pagans did not inhibit some of the greatest minds in Jewish history—Philo, Saadia, Maimonides for example—from taking them seriously. Indeed, with careful discrimination, to be sure, they hewed out from their teachings what was relevant and applicable to Judaism and wove them into the fabric of Jewish life and thought. And so, I consider myself in good company when I seek to re-learn lessons for present day Judaism from elements of African paganism:

We modern Jews are inheritors of a great system of faith. Its nobility and influence are unmatched in history. Yet in our day, we tend to forget that the Jewish faith is not and never was a noble abstraction. It is coterminous with life itself, rooted in one's every deed; it can be spontaneous and warm; it is a thing of the body as well as of the mind; it is full of conviction, emotion, heartfelt faith.

Judaism expresses its lofty beliefs through all the senses—through the palate and hand, through song and dance, through laughter and tears, through sight and sound—from the Sabbath table to the "double-header" after the morning minyan, from the clapping of hands as people dance on a Synagogue pulpit (and on the street) on *Simchat Torah,* to reciting the *Shema* at night in pajamas, from the "holy and awesome" *Kol Nidre* to the *Purim* carnival, *hamantashen* and noisemakers. In short, our religion and our life (all of life) go together, are inseparable.

Thank you, Ishmael Sowa, for reminding us Jews what our Judaism, in its fullness, is according to our own tradition—and what if ought to be today.

Addendum

The above encounter with Ishmael Sowa took place some 35 years ago. Following Ishmael's stay in Pittsburgh, he returned to Ghana and proceeded to his work of translating the Hebrew Scriptures into his African language. I heard nothing about him since—until the year 2011—over three decades later.

Leah and I were at the Newark Airport beginning our trek back from New Jersey where we had spent the Sukkot holiday with our son Judah and his family. Because of her knee problem, Leah required a wheelchair at the airport to get her from place to place. A young Ghanaian woman worker at the airport met us and wheeled Leah. I struck up a conversation with the young lady, who was quite informed and articulate about life and religion in her native Ghana. She had graduated from college in

Ghana and was working at her present job to finance study in America to qualify for American accreditation.

I told her about Ishmael Sowa and our encounter with him in Pittsburgh. She proceeded to wax lyrical at the mention of the name *Ishmael Sowa*. He is famous all over the African continent, she exclaimed. He is an old man now; he lives in Accra, the Ghanaian capital; he has translated the New and Old Testaments into numerous native Ghanaian tongues; he is a great man whose work has helped to transform the pagan religion of much of Africa. She explained—much as Ishmael Sowa did for Leah and me 35 years ago—something of the nature of African religious practice and how Christianity has replaced it; this because of the work of Ishmael Sowa (and others in Ghana via its *Bible Translation Institute*).

The young Ghanaian woman was very impressed that we had known Ishmael Sowa personally.

– Twenty –

THE KADDISH
Prayer for the Deceased...
and for the Living

יִתְגַּדַּל וְיִתְקַדַּשׁ שְׁמֵהּ רַבָּא, בְּעָלְמָא דִּי בְרָא, כִּרְעוּתֵהּ,
וְיַמְלִיךְ מַלְכוּתֵהּ בְּחַיֵּיכוֹן וּבְיוֹמֵיכוֹן וּבְחַיֵּי דְכָל־בֵּית
יִשְׂרָאֵל, בַּעֲגָלָא וּבִזְמַן קָרִיב, וְאִמְרוּ אָמֵן:
יְהֵא שְׁמֵהּ רַבָּא מְבָרַךְ לְעָלַם וּלְעָלְמֵי עָלְמַיָּא:
יִתְבָּרַךְ וְיִשְׁתַּבַּח וְיִתְפָּאַר וְיִתְרוֹמַם וְיִתְנַשֵּׂא וְיִתְהַדָּר
וְיִתְעַלֶּה וְיִתְהַלָּל שְׁמֵהּ דְּקֻדְשָׁא, בְּרִיךְ הוּא לְעֵלָּא
מִן כָּל־בִּרְכָתָא וְשִׁירָתָא תֻּשְׁבְּחָתָא וְנֶחֱמָתָא דַּאֲמִירָן
בְּעָלְמָא, וְאִמְרוּ אָמֵן:
יְהֵא שְׁלָמָא רַבָּא מִן שְׁמַיָּא וְחַיִּים עָלֵינוּ וְעַל כָּל־יִשְׂרָאֵל,
וְאִמְרוּ אָמֵן:
עֹשֶׂה שָׁלוֹם בִּמְרוֹמָיו הוּא יַעֲשֶׂה שָׁלוֹם עָלֵינוּ וְעַל
כָּל־יִשְׂרָאֵל, וְאִמְרוּ אָמֵן:

May God's name be exalted and hallowed throughout the world that He created, as is God's wish. May God's sovereignty soon be accepted, during our life and the life of all Israel. And let us say: Amen.

May God's great name be praised throughout all time.

Glorified and celebrated, lauded and worshipped, exalted and honored, extolled and acclaimed may the Holy One be, praised beyond all song and psalm, beyond all tributes that mortals can utter. And let us say: Amen.

Let there be abundant peace from heaven, with life's goodness for us and for all Israel. And let us say: Amen.

May the One who brings peace to His universe bring peace to us and to all Israel. And let us say: Amen.

The kaddish speaks of neither life nor death, but rather of peace and of the future. We honor the dead by the way we live. We honor the past by the future we create.

−Jonathan Sacks

The Kaddish Persists

For some time I had not seen an acquaintance of mine at the recreation place we shared. I asked him where he had been. Sadly and quietly he said he had been preoccupied with his father's demise; just yesterday he had passed away and the funeral was scheduled for tomorrow. He was at our gym to get himself physically ready for the ordeal ahead. His father, he said, was ninety-three years old, a good man, Jewish but not particularly religious.

I asked my friend if a rabbi was scheduled to officiate at the funeral. He replied that the funeral was to be solely for the family, simple and graveside and that because the family had little religious feeling he had had no intention to have any clergy present. But then he got a call from the funeral parlor: a kindly Cantor asked if he might be present at the funeral and recite the *kaddish* for his father. Something inside of my friend tugged at him, he said, urging him to have the *kaddish* recited for his father. Yes, his family was Jewish, his father aware of his Jewishness though in quite peripheral fashion, yet something told the son it was the right thing to do He wasn't sure what that something was. But he said to the Cantor, "Okay, be there for my Dad."

Jews may have jettisoned much else of religious observance, but to the *kaddish* prayer, recited as a sacred act of reverence for a departed mother, father or other close kin, they remain anchored. At the funeral, at the unveiling of the tombstone, at the *Yahrzeit*, anniversary of the death, as well as at *Yizkor* time during the three pilgrimage Festivals and Yom Kippur, the *kaddish* is recited. For many still, for eleven months following the demise, the *kaddish* prayer is recited in the synagogue in the presence of a *minyan*, a quorum of ten adult worshippers. Jews throughout the world, young or old, rich or poor, well- educated or unlettered, recite these ancient words

There is a great power and poignancy embodied in the words of the *kaddish*. And yet it contains no references to death, to the hereafter, to immortality. Instead, it sings God's praises; it prays for God's Kingdom on earth; it yearns for peace for ourselves and for the house of Israel, and in its expanded form prays for the welfare of treasured teachers and students. Why, then, is the *kaddish* recited by the mourner? What does it do for those who have experienced profound loss? The answers reveal much about the Jewish faith.

A Brief History

The *kaddish* prayer was not originally part of the worship service. The Talmud records that it first served as a concluding prayer following a learned lecture in the House of Study.[1] The *rabbis' kaddish* testifies to that link; this is the basic prayer with a special passage inserted on behalf of the teachers and disciples engaged in Torah study because the sages felt "God's Kingdom" could be brought closer through diligent study of religious texts. Subsequently, the prayer became part of the prescribed liturgy in the synagogue, requiring the presence of a minyan, a quorum of ten persons; it was recited at key junctures of the service, and with the insertion concerning teachers and students following the citation of the selected rabbinic passages.

Later, in the house of mourning of a deceased scholar, periods of study in honor of the dead were instituted in the context of the minyan prayer service after which the usual *kaddish d'rabbanan*, "rabbi's kaddish," was recited. Subsequently, the feeling that all Jews, not only scholars, were equally deserving of such honor led to the study at every mourner's home followed by the *kaddish*. This became standard practice in the synagogue as well: *kaddish* for the mourner even without study. This all despite the

---

1. Sota 49a.

fact that the actual text does not deal with the subject of mourning.

Light Pierces the Darkness

The rabbis were not content to leave the actual *kaddish* texts unconnected to the phenomenon of death. Thus the above Talmudic (Sota) passage tells us also that after the destruction of the temple and the exile of Israel in 70 CE, the Jewish world was plunged in gloom; the painful loss was deeply felt and hope for the morrow seemed dim indeed for a mourning people. In the face of this condition, the Talmud proceeds to ask: עָלְמָה אֲמַאי קָא מְקַיְּימַ?, "if everything is deteriorating why does the Jewish people in truth continue to exist?" And they responded by citing the words of the *kaddish*:

Yitgadal v'yitkadash shmay Rabbah.

Magnified and sanctified may this great name be in the world created by His will. May He establish His Kingdom in our lifetime and in our days and in the lifetime of all the house of Israel, swiftly and soon—and say: AMEN.[2]

The *kaddish*, the sages were telling us, expressed great hope for the future of the Jewish people. God's Kingdom will be established. It will happen soon. Tomorrow we will experience new life, renewed life. And they went on by citing Job 10:23 about life's darkness, interpreting it to mean that via the *kaddish's* hopeful, optimistic emphases, the צַלְמָוֶת, the darkness of exile will be pierced by the light of eventual redemption. The message: the light projected by the *kaddish* pierces the darkness, of collective—and personal—loss, including the passing of a loved one. Read on.

An Affirmation of Faith

The rabbis in their comment on the "Women of Valor" passage in the Book of Proverbs tell this story:[3]

---

2. Ibid.
3.   Midrash Mishle 31:10.

Beruria   was the learned and compassionate wife of
Rabbi Meir. While Rabbi Meir was teaching on a Shabbat
afternoon, both of his sons died from the plague that was
affecting their city. When Rabbi Meir returned home, he
asked his wife, "Where are our sons?" She handed him
the cup for the *Havdalah* and he said the blessing. Again,
he asked, "Where are our sons?" She brought him food,
and he ate. When he finished eating, Beruria, said to her
husband, "My teacher, I have a question. A while ago, a
man came and deposited something precious in my
keeping. Now he has come back to claim what he left.
Shall I return it to him or not?" Meir responded, "Is not
one who holds a deposit required to return it to its
owner?" So she took his hand and led him to where their
two children lay. He began to weep, crying, "My sons,
my sons." She comforted him, "The Lord gave, the Lord
took. *Y'hei sh'mei rabah mevorach*. May the Name of the
Lord be blessed..."[4]

The *kaddish* is in the spirit of Job's (and Beruria's/Meir's)
words. During the period of mourning when one recites this
prayer in the presence of the congregation, one is sanctifying,
praising God fulsomely. In effect, one is saying: these are, indeed, dark and difficult days and though one cannot understand
all that God does, one also knows well that there is far more good
than bad in the world God has fashioned for His children: He
gives one the joy of a loved one who must return what has been
lent. You gave, You took back. We bless You.

Forging a Bond

Listen, my child, you must study diligently; you are

---

4. The translation of this Hebrew passage attributes the comforting statement to Beruria (presumably in keeping with the "Woman of Valor"
   context); here she adds the words of the *kaddish*, "May the Name of the
   Lord be blessed" to Job's (1:21), "The Lord gave and the Lord took."
   Actually the Hebrew text attributes only the Job passage to Rabbi Meir
   who, in his sorrow says only: the Lord gave, the Lord took."

fortunate that you are studying under your grandfather. It is written that "when grandfather and grandchild study the Torah together, the study of the divine Law will nevermore forsake the family, but will be handed down from generation to generation."

—Moses Hess' mother to him, based on Isaiah 59:21

The writer of this essay has been heavily influenced by his grandfather in terms of learning, religious observance and a quest for piety. Throughout the years, at his Yahrzeit and Yizkor time, I unfailingly recite the *kaddish* in his memory. At these times, I again gaze at the picture of Zayda that graces the wall of my home study and have this dialogue:

"Zayda, how am I doing?"

"Gut, but Yankel, did you study some Torah today?"

"Not really Zayda, I'm so busy with my administrative work."

"Yankel, no good. You must study every day some."

"Yes, Zayda, I'll try. I promise."

The next conversation would go like this:

"Zayda, I studied a good amount of *Chumash* (Pentateuch) today in preparation for my class."

"Gut Yankel, and did you daven (pray) today?"

"Yes, but hurriedly."

You should daven with *kavanah* (sincerity)."

"I tried, Zaydeh, it's not easy with so many things on my mind."

"Yankel, the *Ribono Shel Olam* (Master of the Universe) expects all His creatures to thank Him for all the good things in life we have. Daven every day and mean it."

"Yes, Zayda, I'll keep trying."

My grandfather has long since parted from this world but he remains very much alive to me as he continually speaks to me from that picture on my study wall. The late Chief Rabbi of the British Commonwealth, Joseph Hertz, wrote: "The kaddish prayer is the thread in Israel that binds the generations 'each to each in natural piety' and makes the hearts of parents and children beat in eternal unison."[5]

Linking to Community

Heinrich Heine, a leading German poet, renounced his Jewish faith as a way to advance in German and later French society. His apostasy did not bring him the expected advantages. Instead, he found himself outside both the Jewish and German/French camps. Heine articulated his painful alienation from his people:

> No Mass will be sung,
>
> No kaddish will be said;
>
> Nothing said and nothing sung
>
> On the anniversaries of my death.

For Henrietta Szold, the Zionist leader and founder of Hadassah, on the other hand, the *kaddish* expressed her kinship with her community. When her mother died and a male friend offered to say *kaddish* for her, Szold responded:

> The *kaddish* means to me that the survivor publicly and markedly manifests his wish and intention to assume the relation to the Jewish community which his parents had, so that the chain of tradition remains unbroken from generation to generation, each adding its own link. You can do that for the generations of your family. I must do

---

5. Hertz, Joseph (ed.). *The Daily Prayerbook*. Bloch Publishing Company, 1952; p. 268.

that for the generations of my family.[6]

For the Jewish family, the death of a loved one is a time for gathering within community. Relatives gravitate to the home of the deceased to be with their closest kin, participate in the rites, and offer comfort. Friends and neighbors visit during *shiva*, the seven days following the funeral, to express their sorrow and offer condolence. The synagogue helps arrange the needed *minyan* so the *kaddish* can be recited in community at the *shiva* home. At no other juncture in Jewish life is there a greater sense of family, of people bound together at a time of personal crisis to share in the loss and render solace.

Judaism strives to ensure that the mourner is not isolated. Recitation of the *kaddish* is required in the context of a *minyan* — a quorum of worshippers in the synagogue throughout the year. This inevitably brings together an assemblage of mourners who recognize that they are all in a common situation, that no one mourner has been singled out.

Thus, when others alongside ourselves rise to recite the *kaddish*, the feeling of having been individually victimized by our loss is blunted. We are not alone in our dark period. We see death in a larger context, as part of the mystery of human existence in which are interwoven the good and the bad, happiness and sorrow, life and death. Through the saying of the *kaddish*, we both honor the dead and help heal the living.

The *minyan* is a quorum of ten adult persons, which constitutes a "community"—the normative setting for Jewish prayer. Thus a person reciting *kaddish* does so in the fellowship of others. Why the need for ten?

The *ten* spies who brought back a negative report about the land were called an *edah*, a "congregation." Moreover, in response to Abraham's prayer about Sodom, God assured him that if it contained *ten* righteous individuals, their merit would save

---

6. From a letter to Hayyim Peretz. Sept. 16, 1916.

the city.[7] *Ten* is thus the minimum number to constitute a community. When the Temple stood, sacrifices were offered daily on behalf of the entire Jewish people. Since then, though Jews have been scattered and dispersed, whenever ten gather in prayer it is as if the whole Jewish people was present. The community is a microcosm of the nation. The person reciting *kaddish* is integral to and embraced by his/her people at his/her time of loss.

Indeed, the *kaddish* prayer is for the deceased—and for the living.

From Silence We Hear

A profound characteristic about the deceased is his/her absolute silence. Equally profound is the not so silent moment when one recites the *kaddish*, for it is then that the deceased is often heard with unusual clarity. Much is conveyed by the departed from the silence.

A bus was bumping along a back road. In one seat, an old man sat holding a bunch of fresh flowers. Across the aisle was a young girl whose eyes came back again and again to the man's flowers. The time came for the old man to get off the bus. Impulsively, he thrust the flowers into the girl's lap. "I can see you love the flowers," he explained, "and I think my wife would like for you to have them. I'll tell her I gave them to you." The girl accepted the flowers, then watched the old man get off the bus and walk through the gate of a small cemetery.

The old man knew that in the silence of the cemetery this is what his deceased wife would have wanted him to do. Indeed, it is in such silence that we still discern the goodness and wisdom of loved ones given so freely when they were alive.

Finding Inner Peace

"May He who makes peace in His high heavens make peace for us..." Here our prayer offers the reassurance that God can fulfill

---

7. Genesis 18:22-23.

one of the mourner's most pressing needs when confronted by the stark reality of death: peace of mind and spirit. The late Sidney Greenberg, a prominent member of the American rabbinate, wrote:

> Modern studies of the dynamics of grief indicate that in every situation there is present an element of guilt. No human relationship is so perfect that the survivor cannot berate himself for things done and said and things left undone and unsaid. The mourner needs peace from an accusing conscience. He needs the peace which comes from the faith that God who created imperfect creatures makes allowance for their imperfections.[8]

The death of a loved one, continues Rabbi Greenberg, often engenders anxiety and fear about one's own mortality. Resentments and guilt may follow in the wake of separation. Release from these feelings is implicit in the letter and spirit of the *kaddish* which offers the hope that peace may come to the mourner, dispelling the heavy overcast of grief.

Proclaiming Life's Meaning

The *kaddish* teaches something of a larger Jewish vision. It is connected with death though that was not its original intention. We begin the prayer by praising God for "the world He has created according to His will." The death of a loved one often leaves us perplexed and questioning whether life has meaning. In the face of these feelings, the *kaddish* prods us to affirm that there is a plan and purpose to the world which He made "according to His will."

There is order and harmony in the cosmos, a majestic regularity of the stars. All organic life is designed to sustain its own life. And there is the wondrous *human* capacity to think and to search for truth and beauty and goodness. These all point to a God who has a plan and a purpose for the world. The apparent

---

8. Greenberg, Sidney. *A Treasury of Comfort*. Hartmore House, 1966; p. 53.

absurdity of death is vitiated by the meaningfulness of God's world of which the destiny of man is a part.

The Not-So-Secret of Endurance

Earlier in this essay, reference was made to the Talmudic passage in Sota 49a to the effect that the optimistic outlook expressed in the *kaddish* prayer helps counter the sadness of loss. This positive attitude is also embedded in the following Talmudic passage and its expanded meaning by Rashi, that master commentator on both Scripture and Talmud.

The Jewish people were plunged into great gloom due to their exile from the land in 70 CE and the disaster of the Bar Kokhba rebellion in 125 CE. They were in despair about their very future as a people and as a faith. About this condition the Talmud asked that if things were so terrible, how was it that this people and its faith have survived intact through the centuries?

Their response: it is because of *akdusha d'sidra*, "the *kaddish* which is recited in the order of the prayer service." It is because the words of the *kaddish, yehay shmay rabba mevorakh*, "may this great Name be blessed," is recited following the study of Aggadah (rabbinic sacred text). It can, therefore, be inferred, says the Talmud, that when there are orders of prayer and study of sacred literature, both of which sanctify God's name, the people will be rejuvenated in the midst of darkness.

Rashi at this texts' location depicts in some detail this characteristic study phenomenon in the life of the Jew:

> The kaddish prayer was established in the context of all Israel being occupied with daily study of the Torah, even in small measure. The teachers read the text, translated it and explained its context and meaning. This constituted immersion in Torah and was the custom of all Israel, both for students and the *amay ha-aretz*, the laity alike. There is in this process both the sanctification of God's name and the mitzva of Torah study. The latter is very dear because it includes the words, *yehay shmay*

rabba mevorakh, "may His great Name be blessed." These constituted the kaddish's faithful affirmation recited following a Torah lesson by a *darshan*, a teacher in public every Shabbat when the people would gather to listen and learn since it was a non-working day. There is here Torah study and *Kiddush Hasham*, the sanctification of God's name.[9]

In the rabbinic mind what preserved the life and identity and religious way of the Jewish people through the ages in the face of persistent and endemic hostility was *immersion in the study of her classic rabbinic literature as a religious pursuit*. Such educational endeavor trained the people to think critically and creatively, how to strive to live a life by high moral and ethical standard, and most especially, to cling to the one and only God of all the world and all its human beings: the not-so-secret reason for the people's endurance.

---

9. Rashi's comment on the Talmudic passage, Sota 49a.

Twenty-One

THE RITE OF PASSAGE PHENOMENON
Managing the Ambiguous

כָּל הָעוֹלָם כֻּלוֹ גֶשֶׁר צַר מְאֹד
וְהָעִיקָר לֹא לְפַחֵד כְּלָל

The whole world is a very narrow ridge.
And the main thing is to not be afraid.

–Nakhman of Bratzlav

The "rites of passage" are ubiquitous in all cultures because they help negotiate the uncertain junctures that separate one stage of a person's life from the one to follow. These rituals are carefully observed by the consistent faithful, but also by many who are otherwise indifferent to religious observance. Some who observe do so without understanding the underlying purposes of these rituals. Here we seek some insight into these observances as we attempt to unpack in detail their root purposes and meaning for the contemporary religionist.

Another objective of this essay is to seek to demonstrate that the purposes of religious ritual extend beyond the mantra about religion being primarily for "moral" and "ethical" purposes (which, of course, they are in part). Human beings have additional needs—psychological ones, a sense of self, the need for personal self-confidence, for identity and community. These, too, are nourished by religious ritual.

Transition Periods in Individual and Group Life

The Role of Ritual

An elderly gentleman once came to me with an unusual request. His eighty-third birthday was drawing near and he wanted to arrange a special *Bar Mitzvah* ceremony in the synagogue to mark the occasion. I agreed. I understood what he had in mind. Seventy years in Jewish tradition is a person's full life allotment. The Bible, for example, tells us that King David, who had lived to age seventy, died *besayva tova*, "in a good old age."[1] Our elderly gentleman felt that, in a sense, his "second life" began at age seventy, so that his thirteen years beyond that deserved and required a *Bar Mitzvah*—a formal ceremony which would take him through another significant transition period in his life.

Transition periods in a person's life are crucially important to all of us. They need to be marked in special fashion because it is psychologically and in other significant ways helpful and necessary to do so—both for an individual personally and for the community. Let me explain.

Religion has always played a major role in preserving the structure and welfare of society. Arnold van Gennep, the French anthropologist, first coined the phrase "rite of passage." In describing this phenomenon, van Gennep used the metaphor of society as a house divided into rooms and corridors—the rooms being the clearly defined social positions, and the corridors as transition areas from one position of life to another. Every transition is marked by a blurring of social status and shifting roles and is characterized by tension, uncertainty and emotional stress.

These passageways are marginal social states, protected by ritual. The rituals surrounding the life transitions of birth, puberty, marriage and death, according to van Gennep, facilitate change by helping individuals through the difficulties of transition and by preparing society to accept their new roles.

---

1. I Chronicles 29:28.

These rituals are composed of three elements: *separation* when an individual is detached from an earlier time period in his or her life; the *liminal phase* which is the transition or "betwixt and between" period when the ritual removes barriers and eases movement to a new status; and *re-integration*, when the individual enters into a stable, defined state in society and is accepted as such within that society.

Victor Turner, another leading anthropologist, focuses on van Gennep's second element of the rite of passage, the liminal (literally "threshold"), the "betwixt and between," the actual transition phase. During this period, the individual is "not yet classified" and therefore represents the epitome of social ambiguity. The surroundings of this individual are complex, even "bizarre." The neophyte is "culturally dead" and such periods are "polluting" because of their ambiguity. This is a condition which the individual and society cannot abide. Hence the rite of passage that both expresses this ambiguity and provides the mechanism with which to assure the individual involved and keep the structure of society intact.

All societies have developed specific rituals that manage the ambiguity of this period. They've developed mechanisms that mark the transition stage in a person's life, a time crucial precisely because of its tension, uncertainty and emotional stresses. As Victor Turner has indicated, life's transitions need to be marked for calming psychological reasons.

Rites of passage are not confined to personal life transitions, but may accompany changes from one state of life of a group to another. When a people goes to war, or when a group celebrates a harvest festival attesting to the transition from scarcity to plenty, it marks these occasions with rites. Similarly, entry into a new achieved status, or entry into a new religious group, is also punctuated by ritual. All transitions interfere with the integrity of the structure of society and hence are surrounded by ritual and symbol.

An example of this in the context of Scripture: the ritual of the

first fruits, which is depicted in the biblical book of Deuteronomy may be seen as a rite marking passage from scarcity to
plenty, as well as marking, in the accompanying credo of the first
fruits ceremony, the passage of a rootless people to a landed people. Similarly, the Passover Seder ritual can be seen as marking
the passage from slavery to freedom.

Perhaps also the literary setting of the biblical book of Deuteronomy, which places Israel at the critical turning point between that of being a wandering people and a people about to
enter its promised land, is an indicator of a marginal and hence
danger-ridden state. It might also be the case, as Turner points
out, that liminality "may be considered as a realm of pure possibility whence newer configurations and ideas and relations may
arise." Thus the literary setting of Deuteronomy may be seen as
a deliberate technique using a "state of limbo" for the purpose of
pointing to new and enriching possibilities for the people Israel.

Peter Mattheissen puts it this way:

> Here lies the heart of ritual and even religion, manifested
> in the awe and care that accompany rites of passage. For
> these rites momentarily lift us from the petty confusions
> of existence and make us pay complete attention to the
> passages of our lives, complete attention to the human
> transformations that link and bind us all to other humans
> (as well as to the natural world), complete attention to
> the wonder of it all.

The Major Jewish Rites of Passage

Birth

Judaism provides a ritual to welcome a male child into the world
and integrate him into the community. These are occasions of
great joy mixed with some apprehension and solemnity. The ceremony is a *brit milah* at which the child is circumcised—literally
marked as a member of the Jewish community. It is, at the same
time, a mark of the covenant in the Jewish faith—the sign of
Abraham's pact with God that established for Hebrews then and

Jews in the morrow an enduring relationship. Genesis 17:11 says this: "You shall circumcise the flesh of your foreskin, and that shall be the sign of the covenant between Me and you." Circumcision, then, is an imprinting experience, imprinting boys with peoplehood and with indelible ties to God.

A fuller reading of this Genesis passage reveals the deeper connection between the circumcision rite and the pact forged by God with His people, and the people's role in the pact (the relevant terms are here noted and emphasized):

> This is my covenant with you: you shall be a father of a *multitude of nations*....I will make you exceedingly *fertile*...such shall be the covenant between Me and you and your *offspring* to follow which you shall keep: every male among you shall be circumcised. You shall circumcise the flesh of your foreskin and that shall be a sign of the covenant between Me and you.

Now, why specifically circumcision as the sign or mark of this pact with God? Surely there can be and there were other concrete signs/marks for this purpose such as a scar or tattoo on the body as among various African tribes.

Close reading of the above Genesis text seems to render a response. The covenant promises the continuity of the people of Israel; it envisions abundant progeny who will carry on the terms of the pact; it speaks of a "multitude of nations," of "fertility," of "offspring." The male organ which is the very source of such fruitful phenomena is thus the sign/mark, the concrete symbol of the covenant which makes these promises. Yet more: by removing a piece of the flesh from the organ and the appearance of the blood which thus appears, the human partner in the covenant demonstrates his concrete "sacrificial" contribution and commitment to the pact.

The Rite for Girls

While boys are named at the *brit milah* on the eighth day after birth, girls are traditionally named in the synagogue on the

Sabbath after their birth. Typically, the father is called to the Torah and recites a blessing in which the child is named. Another blessing prays for the healing of the mother. Most often, neither the child nor the mother is present. Naming, then, has none of the power of the *brit milah*; there is no connection to covenant or a messianic future, only the ceremonial conferring of a name on the (usually absent) child.

Thus, equivalent rituals appropriate for a female child have been developed in modern times. The essence of these rituals is their focus on the girl's entry into the covenant and the peoplehood of Israel, which is the core purpose of the *brit* for a boy. These *brit banot* (female covenant ceremonies) variously called *Simchat Lev* (Joy of the Heart) and *Simchat Bat* (Joy of a Daughter) include variations of the blessings at a male *brit*, the naming of the child which, presumably as much as circumcision transforms and "brands" a Jew. Some of those ceremonies take place on the eighth day after birth, others a month after birth when in the tradition a child is felt to be a *bar kayama*, a viable living being. Two symbols have become popular in *brit banot* ceremonies: moon/lunar celebrations whose liturgy is filled with images of renewal, regeneration and creation, and water/ritual bath immersion. The *Meiri*, a medieval commentator, suggests that when Abraham was circumcised, his wife Sarah underwent ritual immersion in order to enter the covenant.[2] Ritual immersion, then, is seen as the feminine physical equivalent of the male circumcision (the actual *cutting* at the *brit*) as a sign of the covenant. Further, both immersion in a mikva and, in the case of males, circumcision are required of converts to Judaism who embrace the covenant.

Adolescence

This period is the bridge between childhood and adulthood; it is a perilous passage. To become a full-fledged member of Jewish society, the adolescent must understand when childhood ends, when adulthood begins, and what the Jewish religion expects of

---

2. Talmud, Yevamot 46a.

him/her. Hence a Jewish boy acquires adult status in his religious community at age thirteen when he becomes a *Bar Mitzvah*, a "son of the commandment." He is now accountable for his actions and can be counted in the *minyan*, the quorum of adults for public prayer. At morning weekday prayer he needs now to don the *tefillin*, the small boxes containing scriptural verses placed on head and arm along with the straps around the arm which symbolize binding to the faith. Most important, he can now receive an *aliya* as adults do, be called up to the Torah and publicly bless and read from the Torah and the Haftorah. He proves he can now do what the adults do and thus becomes a full member in the Jewish community.

In modern times the *Bat Mitzvah* ceremony for the Jewish female has become widespread. This is the period of puberty and a time of transition from childhood to female maturity and entry into the adult community. At the adult synagogue service in the non-orthodox denominations, she receives an *aliya* (honor of reciting the blessings before and after the Torah is read) for the first time. She chants the Torah portion and Haftorah (prophetic reading) of the weekly cycle; she delivers a *Dvar Torah* (a homily); she leads sections of the liturgy. Through these actions the *Bat Mitzvah*, as in the case of the *Bar Mitzvah*, demonstrates in public her capacity to do what the adults do and thus are signs of her "official" entry as a full member of her Jewish community.

As members of the adult community, both the *Bar* and *Bat Mitzvah* assume new responsibilities. They now are counted for a *minyan*, the quorum of ten persons required for a worship service. They can now be counted for a *mezumin*, the quorum of three persons required for chanting the introductory portion of the Grace after meals. They are obligated now to fast on Yom Kippur. These responsibilities often might include non-ritual acts which, in admittedly small ways, demonstrate a measure of maturity. For example, at the *Bar/Bat Mitzvah* party, usually a festive occasion, the celebrant might visit each table of his/her guests and greet them and thank them for participating in his/her special occasion—this instead of just hovering around his/her peers throughout the party. Also, he/she might spend more time at a Shabbat service instead of scampering around as heretofore.

In light of the authentic significance of the *Bar/Bat Mitzvah* occasion as indicated, it would be well to ponder an inappropriate celebration of the event which is often practiced in our time. It would also help us understand what a "vulgar" observance is. Picture a *Bar Mitzvah* boy at a celebration on the Sunday after the Shabbat service. The celebration takes place in a commercial catering hall; to an accompanying musical flourish the boy is marching down an aisle draped in his talit, holding his talit bag in his two hands, proceeds to the head table, sits down after the applause dies down. His parents proceed to extol his athletic prowess and many other personal virtues. Two challot are uncovered, the motzi is made as the cameras continue to roll. Finally the huge assemblage proceeds to devour a sumptuous meal.

Dr. Abraham Heschel, my teacher at the Jewish Theological Seminary, once described such a scene as vulgar. Why? *Because elements of the event were paraded out of context.* The talit and talit bag the boy was carrying belonged in the synagogue at the Bar Mitzvah religious service; the two challot belonged to the Shabbat at the temple; the showering of effusive praise on the lad gave the impression that the assemblage was in the presence of a "finished product" already at the tender age of thirteen; the commercialization, glittering hall, sumptuous food and festive dress of the ebullient family and guests gave little clue about the religious significance of the rite of passage which is the Bar Mitzvah.

Changing Times

We remain attached to the traditional notion that age thirteen marks the period of transition from childhood to adulthood. This notion might need revision. Yes, age thirteen is the period of puberty and hence suggestive of maturity; however, in contemporary times this is hardly the time when youngsters reach adulthood in the psychological and functional sense. Indeed, the youngster remains dependent on parents, his/her education is still in its nascent stage, the body is still growing and developing, and experience with and about adulthood in modern society is scant. The teen years as a distinct period of life is, in fact, a modern construct. Even the college-age period is not an adult one if responsibility for one's own economic life is a criterion for genuine adulthood. Thus some have suggested that age twenty-two should be the time when one is deemed a genuine adult, for this is a time when a person either gets or is supposed to get a job, earns a living and is able to support a family.

With these observations in mind, we might consider the following:

- The *Bar/Bat Mitzvah* ceremony be moved to age sixteen when the teen gets a driver's license. Driving a car is an adult responsibility.

- The *Bar/Bat Mitzvah* ceremony be instituted when a young person reaches age 18 and/or 22 when he/she either graduates from high school or college and is now in a position to assume some gainful employment.

- The *Bar/Bat Mitzvah* ceremony take place at age twenty-six when the person gets and holds a job, and makes a living, gets married and has children.

In any case, in the Jewish religious scheme of things, ritual observances have always begun in childhood and not postponed until adulthood (e.g., grace after meals, prayer at various times). Picture, as well, a modern innovation in traditional circles: an eight-year-old girl independently lighting Shabbat candles alongside her mother—clearly a heretofore adult responsibility. In this construct, the *Bat Mitzvah* ceremony would not be linked to the obligation of ritual observance ("I do now what adults do"). Rather, it is a rite that prepares the youngster for later assuming responsibility for the health and welfare of the Jewish community along with the religious observances he/she has observed from childhood in increasing ways as maturity progressed.

Engagement

This is the first step toward marriage. In earlier times, Jewish marriages were conducted in two stages. The first stage is called *Erusin* or *Kiddushin*, "betrothal" or "engagement." During the months following, the woman was expected to assemble her trousseau and prepare for marriage, while the man readied himself financially and otherwise. The second stage, the marriage proper, which took place as much as a year later, is known as *Nisuin*, married state, wedlock. In the first stage, the wine was blessed, the bride received a ring, and a *ketubah* (marriage contract) was read. In the later second stage, a cup of wine was filled and seven blessings, called the *Sheva B'rakhot*, were recited by the rabbi or cantor at the conclusion of the ceremony. Only with the completion of this second step were the bride and groom officially married and permitted to live together as husband and wife.

Experience proved these two stages problematic because both the prospective bride and groom were in a state of limbo for a protracted period of time. As an engaged couple, what physical contact was permitted? Could they consort with others? It was a confusing and ambiguous time for them. And so in Germany and France during the twelfth century, the two ceremonies were combined and that is how the marriage ceremony is conducted to this day. It is actually both an engagement and marriage rite which marks the passage of a man and woman from single status to union with another in marriage.

Marriage

The transition from singlehood to union with another in matrimony is fraught with uncertainty—and opportunity. Originally an alliance between families, a way to reinforce kinship or improve the social or economic status of the families involved, marriage has long since emerged as a matter of personal happiness. Yet, more than family reinforcement, marriage seeks to encompass love, life-long commitment and secure attachment to the community as a whole. Hence, the extensive rituals that characterize a Jewish wedding ceremony.

Immediately prior to the wedding ceremony a number of important details are taken care of: the civil marriage license is signed by the officiating rabbi who will send it on to the appropriate courthouse which keeps the record. If one had been divorced, a *Get* (Jewish divorce document) is presented. The *ketubah*, the Jewish marriage document, is signed by the bride and groom and two witnesses along with the rabbi's signature. Then comes the *bedeken* ceremony during which the groom lifts the veil and sees the bride anew—not as a girlfriend or fiancée, but as the one woman he has chosen as a lifelong mate. The group present for these actions is now ready for entering into the locale in which the invited guests are waiting. The ceremony begins.

There is the wedding dress and veil that mark the present condition of the bride. There is the circling of the groom three or seven times by the bride, which symbolizes the *cordon sanitaire* that keeps away negative forces that might surround the bride. There is the *huppa*, the canopy under which bride and groom stand during the ceremony, which signifies "heaven," that is the Deity under whose providence the couple stand and to whom they will owe allegiance as a new family unit. There is the exchange of rings, which signifies their binding to each other via items of concrete worth. There is the chanting of the *Sheva Berachot*, the traditional seven blessings that articulate the joy and commitments of the occasion. There is the rabbi, the authoritative representative of the Jewish religious community, who officiates at the ceremony and speaks to the couple (and to the assemblage of relatives and friends present) of the vital nature of the occasion. There is the breaking of a glass by the groom, concluding the ceremony, which reminds all present that though the occasion is one of great joy, Jews must never forget (in this very setting) the unfortunate experiences that have befallen the Jewish people over the course of the centuries. There is the festive meal that follows, along with song and dance and toasts. There are the *Sheva Berachot* occasions during the seven days following the ceremony, at which relatives and friends toast the couple in different homes.

Divorce

The divorce ritual in traditional Judaism helps couples acknowledge the trauma of separation and to look toward the future. The man and woman appear before a *bet din*, rabbinical court. They witness a scribe drawing up the get, the formal divorce document, containing the terms of separation. The husband enacts the decision to divorce by transferring the get to the wife, who then places it under her arm and takes symbolic steps to show that she retains her dignity and now controls her own destiny. She keeps the get as tangible evidence of her former life and as sanction for the start of a new one. In the eyes of Jewish law, she has re-acquired the identity she relinquished as a bride.

Conversion

Transitioning from non-Jewish to Jewish status is a process fraught with concern—leaving a significant element of one's past behind, severing significantly from the traditions of one's family, accepting a new identity and way of life. The Jewish tradition provides a mechanism to constructively manage this process.

Jewish learning and experiences... The convert enters into a period of study which requires acquisition of a basic knowledge of Jewish history, thought and practice. He/she is expected to develop a knowledge of the Hebrew language so as to feel at home with the prayerbook and in the synagogue. He/she is required to experience something of Jewish life by mingling in the community of Jews, attending Jewish communal events, attending synagogue on Shabbat and Holy Days, partaking of Shabbat meals in observant Jewish homes, eating Jewish foods, learning Jewish songs, discussing specifically Jewish issues and general issues from a Jewish perspective. Thus through knowledge and practice, the prospective convert makes an effort to grasp the conceptual and experiential aspects of the heritage and way of life into which he/she is preparing to enter.

The Bet Din—Rabbinical Court... After prospective converts have prepared through study and experience for entry into the Jewish community and faith, and before circumcision or immersion in the Mikvah, they meet with a Rabbinical Court consisting of three rabbis. The court asks questions about their studies and acquisition of a basic body of Jewish knowledge and about their experience in the Jewish community. The rabbis want to know if they realize the full ramifications of what they are doing and that their action is being undertaken with sound mind and without coercion, that they understand the spiritual meaning of this transition. If the converts pass this "test," the Bet Din draws up the appropriate documents, *gives them a Hebrew name*, and the document is signed and presented.

Circumcision...If the male is already circumcised, a drop of blood is drawn from the penile area, known in Hebrew as *hatafat dam brit*, "drawing of blood as circumcision." If not, full circumcision is performed. This action introduces the convert into the religion of Judaism, circumcision being its bodily sign. It is thus a physical mark testifying that he becomes a participant in Abraham's covenant with God.

The Mikvah: Ritual Bath...Immersion in a body of water, which is the mikvah, for both male and female is required according to Jewish tradition. The convert is immersed three times and recites the appropriate blessings. When he/she comes out of the water for the third time, he/she emerges Jewish! In the case of the female, this immersion is the core physical act of the conversion rite. The mikvah has both the feel and function of a "womb" from which the convert emerges newly born as a Jew.

In sum, the conversion rite of passage gains for the convert a new faith, a new people, a new community, a new name and identity.

Death

When death separates us from a loved one, we experience a gamut of emotions: denial, anger, grief and, finally, acceptance (hopefully). To help make this transition, Judaism has evolved a comprehensive ritual. There is the wooden coffin in which the deceased lies, which indicates eventual disintegration in the grave and thus return to the dust from which a person originated, as the biblical book of Genesis posits. There is the eulogy by the rabbi, which points to a life beyond the grave for the deceased. There is the *levaya*, the escorting of the coffin to the burial site at the cemetery. There is the *shiva* (i.e., "seven" and "sitting"), the traditional week of mourning after the funeral.

Shiva begins with three days of ardent grief followed by four additional days. As specified in the Talmud, the family gathers at the home of the deceased or at the home of his or her children to mourn his or her passing. Children have cut their neckties or suit jacket lapel or dress to symbolize the tearing away of the dead from the living. Sons will not shave for a week or cut their hair for a month. The mirrors in the house are covered to avoid the normal vanity of life. Each day a *minyan*, a group of at least ten adult men (in nonorthodox circles women are included in this *minyan*) come to the house to recite the prayers. A candle remains lit all week. Friends bring food for the family and members of the Jewish community visit to express their condolences. The mourner's *kaddish* is recited by close kin for eleven months following the funeral, morning and evening, during religious services at the synagogue. *Yahrzeit*, the yearly anniversary of the demise, is observed by close kin through recitation of the *kaddish* at prayer services and the kindling of a candle at home which burns for twenty-four hours.

Morris Raphael Cohen characterizes all these rites of passage as acts "which celebrate the human need of trusting in the larger vision, according to which calamities come and go but the continuity of life and faith in its better possibilities survive." Thus a crucial transition period in the lives of grieving people is given meaning and purpose.

The "Minor" Rites of Passage in Jewish and Other Cultures
Starting School

When a Jewish youngster, age four or five, began school in Eastern

Europe, his teachers placed a dab of honey on his first primer. The child was told to lick the honey which was meant to convey that his studies from this first day forward would be "sweet." In the non-Jewish Ukrainian town of Odessa the first day of school was marked with pomp and circumstance. The children were dressed in their best finery, and with flowers and a parade of banners down the main street.

In the contemporary Jewish community, consecration services in religious schools are the order of the day. The ceremony, usually for children entering kindergarten, typically consists of a prayer, song and recitals which articulate the value of being a Jew through learning about the Jewish way of life. To mark the occasion, a miniature Torah is presented to each youngster along with a special certificate signed by the rabbi or school principal.

Starting College

The Norman Rockwell painting (on the Circle of Life heirloom in my home) graphically depicts the transition point in the life of a young man poised to break home ties and begin his college studies. Father and son sit on the running board of a battered auto beside the tracks of a rural railroad station. The son, dressed in his best suit, with a crisp white shirt and gaudy necktie, waits eagerly for the train that will carry him to college. The father, dressed in blue overalls, his face and hands weathered by work in the fields, stares off into space, presumably contemplating the passage of time. The family's collie rests its chin on the boy's knee. The boy holds lunch carefully wrapped by his mother, who—perhaps because of the sadness of the occasion—has not come to see him off. On the boy's satchel, plastered with a "State U" banner, sits a set of textbooks with markers in them, which tell us that, eager to continue his education, he has already begun his studies.

The boundary which Norman Rockwell's young man is crossing—from high school to college—brings with it a plethora of unknown situations which can be sources of apprehension: a new residence, new teachers, new subjects, new methods of inquiry, new roommates, new friends. In the midst of this swirling change and difference, the Jewish tradition that values roots, continuity and sacred teaching plays an important role. The Jewish campus community helps ease the transition through multiple points of entry: social gatherings, Israel action committees, Torah learning, religious services, Friday evening Shabbat meals in community, Jewish feminist study groups, associations of Jewish business, law and medical students. The programmatic sweep of an active Hillel addresses the head, body and spirit of the Jewish students. This all might be called "programs (rather than 'rites') of passage."

Graduation

High school and college graduates everywhere celebrate their new status in ceremonial garb such as caps and gowns and, in the case of military and civic academies, with uniforms. Despite changing fashions, the ritual dress tends to stay the same—a link to tradition. The young men and women have finished their course of study and are now "candidates" for their degree. The term is derived from the Latin *candidates*, "dressed in white," because the practice stretches back to Roman times. The black cap and gown, on the other hand, date from the thirteenth century when Christian monasteries were among the few centers of learning in Europe.

Some high schools feature a huge circle of graduates, which serves as a symbol of completion and unity in the process. It marks the end of their school days at this point in their lives and the last time they will stand together with the friends of their youth. The widespread high school prom features the rituals of the girl in formal gown, the boy in rented tuxedo, a limousine to the party, staying out all night indicating the breaking of curfew, one of the last vestiges of adolescence. And as the boy pins a corsage on his date when he meets her at the door of her home, the girl's parents, standing in the next room, realize she is marking an important passage.

Women's "Change of Life"

Much the way menses signals initiation into womanhood, menopause is a biological milestone marking the time a woman becomes an "elder." Some traditional societies believed that menstrual blood was the creative force of life, manifesting itself in the birth of children. When a woman no longer menstruated, the life force remained within her, becoming greater in wisdom. Whether or not this particular belief is considered valid in and of itself, it reflects the notion that at the midlife stage one does acquire a measure of wisdom not present in the earlier stages of life. Rabbi Judah tells us, "Forty is the age of *bina*, wisdom, fifty is the age of *aytza*, giving advice."[3] This rabbinic belief that one is ready for true understanding and wisdom at this particular midlife period could well apply to women as it does for men.

In this spirit some contemporary Jewish women are finding ways to make the midlife transition period a purposeful one. One such rite is a ceremony in which the woman involved carries a Torah which contains the wisdom of the Jewish people. In the joyous company of female friends, she receives a new name that recognizes her new status in life and empowers her future. Her rite of passage begins when she says, "A vibrant beauty from within marks not only an elder's accomplishments in life, but the inner enlightenment we call wisdom." Individuals and community can now be the beneficiary.

Retirement

For people who have worked all their lives, retirement is a bittersweet passage filled with uncertainty as well as satisfaction. Some have understood retirement to be a period of purposeless activity and when one simply waited for the end. Others see it as the beginning of a new era filled with opportunity. Enter the ubiquitous retirement party. Properly conducted, it is an occasion to divest oneself from the negative feelings about the competition for status, about the salary increases, the false

---

3. *Ethics of the Fathers* 5:25.

obligations, the petty distractions, the unwelcome intrusions. It can also be an occasion to reflect on one's inner stirrings of something new developing, of the deep need to continue to be useful to one's family and one's community.

The retirement party is a luncheon or evening celebration with picture taking, eating, gift giving—and speech making which articulates the retiree's letting go of the past and envisioning plans for the future. It is a ritual that reflects the person's career at work as he/she moves into the next stage of life. He/she assumes the status of an active senior and begins a new career as a constructive participant in the community.

Conclusion

We have now come full circle. Human life everywhere and through the ages has experienced important transition periods. Judaism, along with other cultures, provides sensitive and purposeful guidance for their successful negotiation. The rites of passage provide this guidance. Their essential purpose is aptly echoed by Samuel Johnson: "Life affords no higher pleasure than that of surmounting difficulties, successfully passing from one step to another, forming new wishes and seeing them gratified."

– Twenty-Two –

THE JEWISH DIETARY SYSTEM
What Are Its Purposes?

קְדֹשִׁים תִּהְיוּ כִּי קָדוֹשׁ אֲנִי ה' אֱלֹהֵיכֶם

You shall be holy, for I, the Lord your God, am holy.

–Leviticus 19:2

Zealous Vegetarians

With almost religious zeal, many Americans are becoming vegetarian. Counterculture food is distinctive and pervasive: rice, carrots, raisins, dates, peanuts, prunes; sunflower and sesame seeds; fruits and "organically" grown foods of all kinds. Consumption of meat is increasingly frowned up.

In a *Time* magazine article, the reasons for this new vegetarian trend were delineated:

- When animal flesh is consumed, people are revealed as greedy.

- Many vegetarians use the diet to become less aggressive and more spiritual. It's much easier to be tender on a vegetarian diet.

- Meat finds its way into the Zen macrobiotic diet quite simply as a concession to man's sensual desires.

- Gardening organically, grinding wheat, baking bread, preparing yogurt and making a quiet ceremony of cooking and eating are all part of the scene. For the more earnest of the cultists, the kitchen has become a holy place.

As I read this article, I was taken by the striking similarity of motivation and purpose underlying the new eating habits of some food enthusiasts today with those of the dietary system of Judaism. Indeed, both share noble aspiration, a kind of "mystic quest" about the conduct of life with regard to food. What people eat and how they prepare what they eat are processes whose objective is to ennoble life, to sensitize the spirit. In short, to develop humane men and women.

The Jewish Dietary System in Thought

Kashrut is the quest for "holiness," not health as is often asserted. In the Bible, after we are told which animals, fish and fowl are permitted and which are forbidden for human consumption, the reason is given:

- You shall be *holy to me*; therefore you shall not eat any flesh that is torn of beasts of the field.[1]

- I am the Lord your God; sanctify yourselves therefore and *be holy*, for I am holy; you shall not defile yourselves with any manner of swarming things that move on the earth.[2]

- You shall not eat of any thing that dies of itself...for you are *holy people* to the Lord your God.[3]

What is "holiness?" In the context of religious dicta, it is the process of taking the everyday, concrete aspects of life and viewing them as particulars of a higher principle, that of "holy living." Thus:

- When we relate to our spouses and children with love and compassion and understanding, we *hallow marriage*

---

1. Exodus 22:30
2. Leviticus 11:44-45.
3. Deuteronomy 14:21.

and the family.

- When we caste our ballots at election time based on the honesty and integrity of a political candidate, *we hallow our country.*

- When we file our income tax return with legitimate data and treat our employees fairly and respectfully, *we hallow our business.*

- When we refrain from sexual overindulgence, mind-scrambling drunkenness, the usage of foul language, *we hallow human life.*

- When we avoid cheating on a college exam, *we hallow the process of education.*

- And when we transform the common practice of food preparation and consumption into personal and communal refinement and sensitivity, *we hallow the act of eating.*

It is in this realm of values that the Jewish dietary system functions. The basic theme which weaves its way throughout, and its approach especially to the animal kingdom, is the pursuit of humane consciousness and behavior. This pursuit applies to individuals per se and as one relates to others and includes attitudes and actions to be affirmed and those to be negated.

Philo of Alexandria, the Jewish philosopher of the first-century CE, notes the cruel behavior of certain animal species man is to bar from his diet:

> It might perhaps be considered only fair that all wild animals that feed on human flesh should suffer from humans what humans suffer from them. But Moses enjoined that we abstain from enjoying such animals, even though they do make for an appetizing and delectable meal. But he was considering what is suitable to a gentle-mannered soul. Of [the birds] he disqualified a vast number of species, in fact all those that prey on other birds or on men, creatures which are carnivorous and venomous and in general use their strength to attack others. But

doves, pigeons, turtledoves, and the tribes of cranes, geese and the like he reckons as belonging to the tame and gentle class, and he (Moses) gives to any who wish full liberty to make use of them as food.[4]

Aristeas, the first-century BCE Jewish historian, similarly noted the proscription of the wild and carnivorous birds "who find their food at the expense of the gentle creatures among the birds who feed on plants that grow in the ground and who do not exercise dominion leading to the destruction of their fellow creatures."[5] In this same vein, the Letter of Barnabas, an early second-century CE document, reasons that the eagle, hawk and crow are forbidden "in order that man not make himself similar to those creatures who do not know how to prepare food for themselves through toil and sweat but in their wickedness plunder things that belong to others."

The thirteenth-century Bible commentator, Nakhmanides, in his analysis of the passage in Scripture dealing with the "Bird's Nest" says this:

> The reason for the prohibition (against taking the mother bird along with the young in her nest) or against killing a mother cow or goat along with her young is to teach us the trait of compassion, that we should not be cruel for cruelty proliferates in man's soul. Thus these commandments with respect to cattle and fowl are decrees to guide us and to teach us traits of good character. As Maimonides has said, if the law provides that such grief should not be caused to birds and cattle, how much more careful must we be that we should not cause grief to our fellowmen.[6]

Isaac Arama, the fifteenth-century Spanish scholar, writes that the dietary dicta concerning certain prohibited foods were not enacted because they may cause harm to the body but

---

4. Philo. *Special Laws*. 4:103-117.
5. Hadas, Moses. *Aristeas to Philocrates: Letter of Aristeas*. 1951, 144-147.
6. Nakhmanides' commentary on Deuteronomy 22:6.

because "they defile the soul and blunt the intellectual powers, thus leading to confused opinions and a lust for perverse appetites which lead men to the defeat of the purpose of Creation."[7] Others articulate the system's purpose in terms of "self-control." Thus, 4 Macabees, the first-century pseudepigraphal discourse: "When we crave seafood or fowl or meat or any other food forbidden to us under the law, it is through mastery of our passions that we abstain."[8] And Rabbi Elazar ben Azaria, the second-century BCE Tanna: "How do we know that a person should not say: I have no desire to eat the meat of a pig? On the contrary, he should say: I do, indeed, so desire, but what can I do? My heavenly Father has so ordered me. This is the meaning of: 'I have separated you from other peoples that you should be mine.'"[9] And Maimonides, the master Talmudist and philosopher of twelfth-century Spain: "The dietary laws seek to train us in the mastery of our appetites. They encourage us to restrain both the growth of desire and the disposition to consider the pleasure of eating as the end of man's existence."[10]

Again Philo of Alexandria: animals which have the finest and fattest meat thus exciting pleasure Moses (i.e. the tradition) forbad because they set a trap for slavery to the senses and produce gluttony—something dangerous to both soul and body.[11]

The essential thrust of the above is to stress that Judaism does not assume a separation between the physical and the spiritual. Nobility of spirit is entered through the stomach as well as through the body's other organs. This is to say that the spiritual in the world—that is, what we designate as "holy"—does not exist in the abstract; it is concretized in what we do and say, how we function in everyday life. The behaviors associated with eating expressed through the body encode meanings meant to act on and cultivate the ethical and spiritual dimensions of those

---

7. *Akedas Yitchak.* Shaar Shemini, 60-end.
8. 4 Maccabees.
9. Yalkut Shimoni 6:26.
10. Maimonides, Moses. *The Guide for the Perplexed.* Dover, 1956; 3:35.
11. Philo. *Special Laws.* 4:100-101.

who observe them. Eating appears to be purely physical but in the Jewish dietary scheme of things what is eaten and how one eats are inextricably bound up with ethical affirmation and moral aspiration. This is what is meant by "holiness."[12]

The Dietary System in Practice

Eating Meat: A Compromise

God has implanted within man deep feelings of kinship for all forms of life. Animals are "our friends," as it were, who, like us, emanate from God's creative powers and thus the Torah bids us to behave compassionately toward these creatures. It would seem, therefore, that vegetarianism is the ideal state for human-kind. Indeed, Scripture tells us that Adam, the first man, while in the Garden of Eden in his ideal state was told "I give you all the plants that bear seed everywhere on earth and every fruit of the tree; they shall be yours for food."[13] It was only after man sinned which brought on the destructive flood that Noah was told that man could eat meat: "Before the deluge, human beings were vegetarians."[14] The deluge revealed the stark reality that man harbored a craving for flesh as his food, and since his spiritual growth was an agonizingly gradual and tortuous process, seeking to accelerate it prematurely could prove dangerous. Rabbi Abraham Kook explains:

> When the animal lust for meat becomes overpowering, if the flesh of all living things had been forbidden, the moral destructiveness which will always appear at such times would not have differentiated between man and animal, beast and fowl and every creeping thing on earth. The knife, the axe, the guillotine, the electric current would have felled them all alike in order to satisfy

---

12. Greenstein, Edward in *Etz Hayim: Torah and Commentary*. Jewish Publication Society, 2001; p. 1462.
13. Genesis 1:29.
14. Sanhedrin 59b

the vulgar craving of so-called cultured humanity.[15]

Scripture, therefore, permits man to eat meat. It recognizes that the craving could not be totally eliminated. However, it simultaneously emphasized that it is a less than noble act. The true meaning of the phrase, "because your soul desires to eat flesh"[16] refers to a time when one's moral sensitivity about eating animals is not yet fully developed. In the interim, the authorities, recognizing the craving as tenacious, also ruled that it *should be limited, contained in significant measure.* Thus, for example, the Talmud teaches that man should eat meat only if he cannot resist the craving and then only occasionally and sparingly.[17] In addition, only the flesh of certain animals could be taken in accordance with the humane procedures of *Shechita* (ritual slaughtering process). About this the rabbis ask: "what does the Holy One, Blessed be He, care whether an animal is taken by the throat or by he nape of the neck? It is because the less brutal's purpose is to refine man; he needs to practice compassion when he takes the life of an animal."[18]

One must cover the blood of the permitted animals to dramatize the sense of shame involved in taking an innocent life and consuming its flesh. It is forbidden to eat *terafah* (a limb torn from an animal) for such an act places one in a league with those wild beasts who feed on small, helpless creatures; it would be as if man were sharing the "spoils" with them. Likewise, it is not permitted to eat *nevelah* (a dead animal) for such an act would show a desire to gleefully benefit from its death.

Rav Kook's message is that man ought never forget that meat-eating is but a concession and compromise. The merciful God of Israel would never decree that man's survival should be eternally contingent upon his butchering animals. One day mankind

---

15. Kook, Abraham Isaac in Schochet, Elijah. *Animal Life in Jewish Tradition: Attitudes and Relationships.* Ktav, 1984; p. 294-295.
16. Deuteronomy 12:20.
17. *Hulin* 84a.
18. Genesis Rabbah 44:1.

will regain its true spiritual heights and recognize the deep kinship it shares with all of existence. Then the eating of meat will be abhorred, and man and animal will coexist in peace.

In this connection, it is significant that Kook also envisioned the abolition of all animal sacrifices in the messianic era:

> In the future the abundance of enlightenment will spread and illuminate man's treatment of animal life…The gift offerings of vegetation that will be brought as sacrifices will be as acceptable as the sacrifices of ancient days.[19]

The Jewish manner of slaughter is considered to be the most humane and least painful. Great care is exercised that the knife used be perfectly smooth, without any notch which might tear the flesh. The person who renders the animal, the shochet, is carefully chosen for the task. He must not only be skilled technically but be also a person of learning and piety, for his task is a sacred one. He must recite a blessing before he performs his duties. Meat is considered "kosher"[20] by removal of the blood, as indicated, which is accomplished by a salting process ("kashering"); blood constitutes the very life of the animal and for humans to ingest it is viewed as abhorrent. Scripture emphasizes that when one takes an animal's life to satisfy one's "lust," one "must be steadfast in not imbibing the blood, for the blood is the life, and you must not eat the life with the flesh."[21] Indeed, a special benediction is pronounced when one sees spilled blood, which must immediately be covered. Blood of poultry should not be seen in the open. So evident is this abhorrence of humans ingesting blood that the Reform movement's mid-nineteenth century negation of the dietary laws contained this caveat stated by Rabbi David

---

19. *Olat Rayah.* Jersualem: Mosad Harav Kook; 1949, 2:292. Quoted in Bokser, Ben Zion (trans). *Abraham Isaac Kook: The Lights of Penitence, the Moral Principles, Lights of Holiness, Essays, Letters, and Poems.* Paulist Press, 1978; p. 23.

20. The dictionary definition of "kosher": fit, right, proper. Thus ritually fit, permitted, valid, legitimate (for human consumption). *Hebrew-English Dictionary.* Dvir Publishing Company, 1947.

21. Deuteronomy 12:20-25.

Einhorn: "with the exception of the prohibition of consuming blood and animals that died a natural death." Indeed, there is no clearer visible symbol of life than blood. To spill blood is to bring death. To inject blood is to save life. "The removal of blood which kashrut teaches," writes Rabbi Samuel Dresner, "is one of the most powerful means of making us constantly aware of the concession and compromise involved in the whole act of eating meat. Again it teaches us reverence for life."[22] And so, when we eat meat to satisfy our appetites, the least we can do is to remove the very element that gives it life—its blood.

Why are Pigs and Shellfish Forbidden?

That the pig has split hooves but does not chew its cud is the Bible's technical criterion. The underlying reason for the prohibition is not given.[23] Maimonides proffers one:

> The major reason why the law abhors pork is its being very dirty and its feeding on dirty things. You know to what extent the law insists upon the need to remove filth out of sight, even in the field and the military camp[24] and all the more within cities. Now, if swine were used for food, marketplaces and even houses would have been dirtier than latrines, as may be seen at present in the country of the Franks. You know the dictum of the sage, Rav Pappa, who said, *pi hazir k'tzoah overet damay*, "The mouth of the pig is like walking filth."[25]

The contemporary anthropologist, Marvin Harris, in effect echoes Maimonides in characterizing the abhorrent nature of the pig. He asserts that the main reason prohibiting consumption of pork was based on ecology and economics. Pigs require an

22. Dresner, Samuel H. *The Jewish Dietary Laws*. Rabbinical Assembly of America, 1982.
23. Deuteronomy 14:8; Leviticus 11:7.
24. Deuteronomy 23:13-15.
25. Maimonides, Moses. *The Guide for the Perplexed*. Dover, 1956; 3:48. Note: I have not translated the Hebrew word *tzoah* literally.

abundance of water and shady woods with seeds, but those conditions were scarce in the Middle East. And so, unlike other forms of livestock, pigs, as omnivorous scavengers who eat virtually anything they come across including dead animal meat, garbage, all manner of refuse, were thus deemed anathema. Were Middle Eastern societies to keep stocks of pigs, their ecosystem and economy would be impaired. This would appear to account for Muslim abstention from pig.[26]

What emerges from the above observations is *the abhorrent nature of the pig*: its consumption, retention and spreading of filth, its feeding on the flesh and blood of another animal, its foraging for garbage. Such a creature, in the lens of the Jewish psyche, is not fit for human consumption, but more: imbibing it into the body of a human being might well lead to their imbibing somewhat of the creature's nature.

With regard to shellfish, that these do not have fins and scales is the Bible's technical criterion for their proscription.[27] Here, too, the reason for this is not given. Nakhmanides proffers one, explaining that fish, possessing fins and scales, are permissible for consumption because they swim unfettered away from the water's bottom and are found more generally in freshwater areas. They are thus less prone to pollution of all kinds. On the other hand, those creatures without fins and scales such as the shrimp, lobsters, crabs, clams and oysters inhabit the bottom muddy waters. They are "stuck-in-the-mud" and "swarming things," they breed in swamp-like habitats, they absorb all manner of filth, they appear loathsome. Thus because of these abhorrent characteristics, the Judaic authorities, as in the case of the pig, deemed these

---

26. Harris, Marvin. *Good to Eat: Riddles of Food and Culture.* Royal National Institute for the Blind, 2005; p. 230.
27. Nakhmanides commentary on Leviticus 11:9. Note: an intriguing theory concerning the biblical categories of clean and unclean (and thus permitted and forbidden) creatures has been advanced by anthropologist Mary Douglas in *Purity and Danger,* "The Abomination of Leviticus," p. 44-58. This article provides striking analysis about this biblical category, and illumines much else about the Jewish dietary system.

creatures "abominations" and therefore unfit for human consumption. Here, too, concern that absorbing their substance into the body of humans might lead to absorbing something of their nature.

Separation of Meat and Milk

Reverence for life is also reflected in the practice of separating meat from milk and, by extension, in all things related such as refraining from eating the two at the same time, and all manner of eating paraphernalia. This regimen is rooted in the biblical prohibition of boiling a kid in its mother's milk.

רֵאשִׁית בִּכּוּרֵי אַדְמָתְךָ תָּבִיא בֵּית ה'
אֱלֹהֶיךָ, לֹא תְבַשֵּׁל גְּדִי בַּחֲלֵב אִמּוֹ

The choice of the first fruits of your soil you shall bring to the house of the Lord your God. You shall not boil a kid in its mother's milk.[28]

What follows probes for responses to two questions: what is the reason for this kid-milk prohibition? And what does cooking a young goat in its own mother's milk have to do with bringing the first fruits of the crop to Jerusalem on a festival?

The Reason for the Kid-Milk Prohibition

According to James Frazer, in the pagan world there existed the widespread practice of avoiding boiling the milk which came from the mother goat together with the young. This was based on the fear of tampering with the principle source of human subsistence—the goat. On this supposition the objection was felt about seething or boiling a kid *in any milk because the she goat from which the milk had been drawn would be injured in the process,* whether she was the mother of the boiled kid or not. Sympathy for the mother goat was involved by the vision of a boiling pot containing a kid with the milk, both of which came from the very bowels of its mother. This mother was twice as likely than any other mother-

---

28. Exodus 23:19, 34:26; Deuteronomy 14:21.

goat to lose her milk or be killed outright by the heat and boiling. Frazer proceeds to document this avoidance in a variety of cultures throughout the African continent, including Egypt.[29]

Philo writes movingly about the act of boiling a kid in its own mother's milk. He views it as terrible to nourish oneself with the sauce of a dead animal produced with the milk of that animal's very own mother. It is a sign of "unbridled licentiousness" on the part of man to slay the author of the existence of another and use it to consume the body of the other. To do this is to exhibit a poverty of feeling, a serious absence of compassion.[30]

Abraham Ibn Ezra, in his analysis of the matter, notes that the reason for the kid-milk prohibition is elusive in Scripture prompting him to speculate about its underlying rationale: such an act is *akhzoriat halev*, "cruelty of the heart," as are cases of taking a mother cow from its young, and a mother bird with its young from their nest. Rabbi Schochet understands Ibn Ezra as believing that the practice is cruel because it tends to harden a man's heart making him cruel.[31]

In our own time, Abraham J. Heschel reasoned that the prohibition might well be that the goat (for us more commonly the cow) generously and steadfastly provides man with the single most perfect food he possesses: milk. It is the only food by reason of its proper composition of fat, carbohydrate and protein that can by itself sustain the human body. How ungrateful and callous, therefore, we would be to take the offspring of an animal to whom we are so indebted and cook it in the very milk that nourishes us and is given us so freely by its mother![32]

What does cooking a young goat in its mother's milk have to do with

---

29. Gaster, Theodor. *Myth, Legend, and Custom in the Old Testament.* Harper and Row, 1969; p. 766-768.

30. *Works of Philo Judaeus* 3:445. As summarized by Schochet, Elijah. *Animal Life in Jewish Tradition: Attitudes and Relationships.* Ktav, 1984; p. 161.

31. Schochet, Elijah. *Animal Life in Jewish Tradition: Attitudes and Relationships.* Ktav, 1984; p. 217.

32. Dresner, Samuel H. *The Jewish Dietary Laws.* Rabbinical Assembly of America, 1982; p. 36.

the immediately following injunction of bringing the first fruit of a farmer's crop to the House of God on a festival?

Maimonides speculated that the kid-milk prohibition was probably related somehow to idolatry. Perhaps, he says, it was part of certain pagan festivals:

> I find support for this view in the fact that with two of the times the Lord mentions the prohibition, it is after the commandment concerning the festivals (Exodus 23:19 and 34:26). "Three times a year all your males shall appear before the Lord God" (Exodus 17:23-24; 23:17). That is to say—when you come before Me on your festivals, do not prepare your food in the manner in which the heathens do.[33]

Don Isaac Abravanel later similarly speculated about the reason for the goat-milk prohibition. In his commentary on the prohibiting passages cited, he writes this:

> It seems most plausible to suggest that it was the practice of the idolaters at their gatherings to do this, namely, to seethe a kid in milk at harvest time, believing that by doing so they would appease their god and draw near to him and he would send his blessing on the work of their hands as it is said: "and they shall no more sacrifice to the goat-demons..." (Deuteronomy 17:7). I surmise that, in reality, this is why God instructed the Israelites that when they came together on the Feast of Tabernacles (Exodus 23:16), they should not do as the heathen do and seethe a kid in its mother's milk...For this reason, the rabbis even prohibited the meat of poultry cooked in milk according to the majority of the rabbis, with the exception of Rabbi Yosi the Galilean who had a tradition that the prohibition does not apply to a species such as birds which have no milk. He therefore permitted the cooking together of poultry and milk.[34]

---

33. Maimonides, Moses. *The Guide for the Perplexed.* Dover, 1956; p. 3:48
34. Jacobs, Louis. *Jewish Biblical Exegesis.* Behrman House, 1973; p. 130-131.

Modern scholars have confirmed Maimonides' and Abravanel's remarkable intuition. The kid-milk matter was indeed a pagan practice. Ancient inscriptions unearthed in 1930 by archaeologists at Ugarit (on the coast north of present-day Israel) confirm that it was a fertility rite. J. G. Frazer, quoting a Karaite medieval author, writes, "There was a custom among the ancient heathens, who, when they gathered all the crop, used to boil a kid in its mother's milk." The purpose of the rite was to produce a liquid that was sprinkled over the fields of the Egyptian and Canaanite farmers after the fall harvest to ensure a bountiful crop from the god or goddess for the next year. Milk is that which sustains the life of the offspring and thus symbolizes fertility. In the pagan mind, then, boiling a kid in its mother's milk produced a potion to be put to good use. In his mind the potion had a magical quality and so sprinkling it on his trees, gardens and orchards would render them fruitful and induce them to bring forth abundantly in the following harvest.[35]

A second purpose of the kid-milk rite revealed by the Ugaritie find was explained by H.L. Ginzberg, the renowned Ugarite scholar who served for many years as Professor of Bible at the Jewish Theological Seminary (incidentally, a teacher of mine at its Rabbinical School). Jacob Milgram tells:

> Both the Ugaritic text and the Bible contain references to cooking a kid in milk. Ginzberg concluded that the ritual described in the Ugaritie tablet was the "same idolatrous custom that the Torah forbade." In the Canaanite ritual, the milk in which the kid was cooked symbolized the milk that the newly born gods were given when suckled by the pagan goddesses Athirst and Rahmay. The cooking of a goat in milk was forbidden in the Bible because it "symbolized the suckling (by the pagan goddesses) of the newborn gods!"[36]

35. Frazer, James George. *Folklore in the Old Testament.* Random House, 1988; p. 117.
36. Milgrom, Jacob. *The Bible Review,* 1985.

The Notion of "Separation"

Jacob Milgrom, in his Bible Review article, expands on the meaning of the kid-milk matter which is inherent in the Jewish dietary system. He takes his cue from Philo, the first-century Hellenistic Jewish philosopher and biblical exegete. Says Philo, "It is grossly improper that the substance which fed the living animal should he used to season or flavor it after its death." Hence, according to Philo, another rationale behind the kid-milk prohibition is *the Bible's opposition of commingling life and death*. A substance that sustains the life of a creature (milk) should not be fused or confused with a process associated with its death (cooking).

The kid-milk prohibition is thus another instance of the emphasis on "separation" characteristic of Jewish ideology and practice: the distinction between life and death as above, between the holy and profane, between pure and impure, between Shabbat and weekday, between light and darkness, and as the Havdalah has it, *between Israel and the nations*. Indeed, the latter notion of Israel as a distinct people is a basic element of the dietary laws. Thus Scripture declares:

אֲנִי יְהוָה אֱלֹהֵיכֶם אֲשֶׁר־הִבְדַּלְתִּי אֶתְכֶם
מִן־הָעַמִּים: וְהִבְדַּלְתֶּם בֵּין־הַבְּהֵמָה
הַטְּהֹרָה לַטְּמֵאָה וּבֵין־הָעוֹף הַטָּמֵא
לַטָּהֹר וְלֹא־תְשַׁקְּצוּ אֶת־נַפְשֹׁתֵיכֶם
בַּבְּהֵמָה וּבָעוֹף וּבְכֹל אֲשֶׁר תִּרְמֹשׂ
הָאֲדָמָה אֲשֶׁר־הִבְדַּלְתִּי לָכֶם לְטַמֵּא.
וִהְיִיתֶם לִי קְדֹשִׁים כִּי קָדוֹשׁ אֲנִי יְהוָה
וָאַבְדִּל אֶתְכֶם מִן־הָעַמִּים לִהְיוֹת לִי:

I the Lord am your God who has set you apart from other peoples. So you shall set apart the clean beast from the unclean, the unclean bird from the clean. You shall not draw abomination upon yourselves through beast or bird or anything with which the ground is alive, which I have set apart for you to treat as unclean. You shall be holy to Me, for I the Lord am holy, and I have set you apart from other peoples to be Mine.[37]

---

37. Leviticus 20:24-27.

The word *kedusha,* "holiness," employed by Scripture in the context of the dietary laws also means separation from some of the ways of the people amongst whom the Jew lives. It means adhering to a set of practices which help inculcate a sense of distinctive Jewish identity, an awareness that on a daily basis there are boundaries in communal and religious life.

Indeed, the Jewish dietary system has contributed to the perpetuation of the Jewish people and the retention of its way of life. It is particularly effective in lending Jewish atmosphere in the home which is a significant factor in resisting the negative aspects of assimilation. It contributes visible outer signs of the Jewish way that helps fortify inner attachment to and involvement with the preservation of Jewish substance and ideals. It is a discipline which unites the Jew with the historic past of this faith and links him/her with fellow Jews the world over. Milton Steinberg once wrote: "The ideas and ideals of a people may give it significance, but its group habits give it life for naked ideals are frail things that often die. The mortality risk of an idea clothed in habit is much lower. A people bound by a common law, and regular practices might well save its law, its ideas and even itself."[38]

Through the ages the Jewish people has paid a heavy price for her tenacious adherence to the kashrut dicta. Malka Simkovitch describes the curiosity of the Romans at the turn of the millennium about the unique Jewish people living among them. One instance was provided by Philo of Alexandria who went to speak with emperor Gaius Galigula as part of a delegation of Jews asking him to intervene against anti-Jewish violence that had broken out in Alexandria.

With visible annoyance and hostility the Emperor interrogated the delegation, asking them why they refused to eat pork. And later the Roman historian and statesman, Tacitus, eagerly sought to understand the reason for the Jews' abstinence from pork; he surmised it reflected their general disposition to oppose

---

38. Steinberg, Milton. *Basic Judaism.* J. Aronson, 1987; p. 39.

Roman practices, in particular eating pork which they considered a delectable dish. Such contrariness on the part of Jews rankled. And still later the fourth-century Ionian bishop Arrianus accused the Jews of caring more about avoiding pork than any other religious precept including what the Ionions considered "holy." This was a conflict, Arrianus observed, between the Jews and the Syrians, Egyptians and the Romans.[39]

Summary and Conclusion

A seminal characteristic of Judaism is to translate moral aspiration into lived experience. Abstract thought has value but ideals lived are preferred to ideas pondered.

The Jewish dietary system is designed to ennoble and refine human behavior, to tenderize and sensitize one's spirit, to mute and control man's tendency to brutality and callousness, to hallow the everyday, to nurture reverence for life—and to foster Jewish community and identity.

"Tell me what you eat, and I will tell you what you are," said an eighteenth century French gastronome. His aphorism is being taken seriously these days by the new vegetarians of America. Judaism always has.

---

39. Simkovich, Malka. "A Historical and Contextual Approach." *TheTorah.com*, March 2019, thetorah.com.

– Twenty-Three –

"A SCOUNDREL WITH THE PERMISSION OF THE TORAH"

The Hebrew: נָבָל בִּרְשׁוּת הַתּוֹרָה (*naval birshut hatorah*).
—Nakhmanides' commentary to Leviticus 19:2

Does religiosity proscribe aspects of human behavior which the Torah permits?

A Walking, Talking Religionist

In a synagogue I have attended, I encountered a striking phenomenon. He was a strictly observant Jew in the orthodox mode, an attendee of unfailing regularity at Shabbat and holy day religious services, a kohen who blesses the congregation from the synagogue bima on the designated occasions, who himself prays at attention during the Amidah and *kedusha* prayers—and who is a member in good standing in his congregation.

This man incessantly walks back and forth through the aisles during parts of the ongoing service, including, of course, the Torah reading. During his peregrinations, he engages in animated conversations with various congregants he corners. The conversations include gossip, business, the stock market, general and shul politics, and other subject matter having little to do with the prayer proceedings. Once he cornered me personally and showered me in a cascade of foul language too graphic to record here.

My question: is there anywhere in the Torah where such behavior is forbidden? Read on.

The introductory verse to the so-called "Holiness Code" [1] states this: "speak to all the children of Israel and say to them, 'you shall be holy, for I the Lord your God, am holy.'" It proceeds to enumerate what it means to be "holy," i.e. respect for parents, Sabbath observance, avoidance of idol worship, care for the poor, et al. To these, the midrash, in its comment on this verse, adds another element.

קְדֹשִׁים תִּהְיוּ. הֱווּ פְּרוּשִׁים מִן הָעֲרָיוֹת וּמִן הָעֲבֵרָה. שֶׁכָּל מָקוֹם שֶׁאַתָּה מוֹצֵא גֶדֶר עֶרְוָה אַתָּה מוֹצֵא קְדֻשָּׁה, אִשָּׁה זֹנָה וַחֲלָלָה וְגוֹ' אֲנִי ה' מְקַדְּשָׁם

You shall be holy. This means separate yourselves from forbidden sexual relations and from sin, for wherever you find in the Torah a command to fence yourself in from such relations, you also find mention of "holiness," such as in Leviticus 21:17 which mentions a harlot, a profane woman and then "I am the Lord who sanctifies you." [2]

As we read these passages from Scripture and Midrash, it appears clear that to be "holy" means adherence to specific laws which forbid various actions such as sexual immorality, etc. This is virtually synonymous with obeying the stated laws of the Torah *but has no special connotation for an extra-ordinary cultivation of sanctity.* The latter ideal, it appears, is for the saints, the holy men and women, not for "all the congregation of the children of Israel."

Nakhmanides alludes to this "extra-ordinary" cultivation of sanctity in his commentary to Leviticus 19:2 and the Midrash's (Sifra's) understanding of *hevo perushim*, "be separatists." He takes *hevo perushim* to mean *"be separatists" not only from that which is illicit, but also from what is licit, permissible, not forbidden in the Torah.* Those matters also cultivate "holiness" and are applicable to men and women, saintly or not, as well as to "all the congregation of the children of Israel."

---

1. Leviticus Ch. 19.
2. The Sifra to Leviticus 19:2.

This trenchant commentator follows the sage Rava who states that one needs to go beyond the letter of the law:

אָמַר רָבָא קַדֵּשׁ עַצְמְךָ בְּמוּתָּר לָךְ

Rava said: sanctify yourself via that which is permitted to you.[3]

There are certain so-called secondary actions, thoughts, relationships not specifically indicated either in Scripture or halakha which also reflect an indication of sanctity; these are matters one must refrain from even if the Torah permits them. Here is how Nakhmanides puts it:

> The principle is that the Torah forbids illicit sexual relations and forbids certain foods but permits the sexual act in marriage and permits the eating of meat and the drinking of wine. Consequently, the libertine would have found many opportunities for unlimited sexual indulgence, for unrestrained gluttony and drunkenness, for speaking obscene things to his heart's desire, for these things are not explicitly forbidden in the Torah. *Such a man would be a scoundrel with the full permission of the Torah.* Therefore, after the Torah had detailed those things which are categorically forbidden, it enjoins a man to separate himself from that which is permitted.[4]

Compelling religion, what Buber has called "religiosity," would not allow its followers to be, in Nakhmanides' pungent expression, "a scoundrel with full permission of the Torah." The rules and regulations of the Torah constitute the vital base, the minimum standards for decent human behavior below which none should fall. An essential part of Torah discipline is to go beyond the basic rules.

For all of Judaism's insistence on rules and laws, what the traditionist affirms as *halakhah*, Nakhmanides points us to a whole

---

3. *Yavamot* 20a.
4. Commentary on Leviticus 19:2.

area of life—the permissible—which, too, needs "holiness" to infuse it. This is a guideline for religious faith as well. With the help of one's own innate conscience and that of wise mentors this might well lead to worthy living and distance from that which pollutes the soul.

In everyday life, Jewish law permits the consumption of wine, but *drunkenness diminishes*. Jewish law permits sexual relations but *overindulgence and licentiousness hurts*; Jewish law permits drugs which soothe and heal but *addiction drags down*. Jewish law permits the consumption of meat, but *gorging demeans*. Jewish law permits, encourages dress in clean and aesthetic ways, but *filthy, bedraggled clothing offends*. Jewish law permits entertainment, but movies and television which provide *trash demean and degrade*.

And—Jewish law permits, encourages speaking one's mind, but *foul language pollutes the atmosphere*.

Kiddush Hashem, Hillul Hashem

וְלֹא תְחַלְּלוּ אֶת־שֵׁם קָדְשִׁי
וְנִקְדַּשְׁתִּי בְּתוֹךְ בְּנֵי יִשְׂרָאֵל

You shall not profane my holy name, but I am to be sanctified in the midst of the children of Israel.

—Leviticus 23:32

In the Judaic perspective religious Jews have always perceived themselves as reflecting the God who taught them how to live their lives on earth. How the religious Jew, therefore, conducts himself affects not only what others think of him, but also what others think of the God who taught him. Thus if a religious Jew acts in a manner that evokes admiration, this is regarded as sanctifying God's name (*Kiddush Hashem*). On the other hand, when a religious Jew acts dishonorably this is known as the desecration of God's name (*Hillul Hashem*). His actions alienate people not only from him, but also from the God who taught him.

Recognizing the extent to which people's attitudes toward God and Judaism are affected by the behavior of religious people, the Talmud comments: If someone studies Bible and Mishna [the Oral Law]...but is dishonest in business and discourteous in relations with people, what do people say about it? 'Woe unto him who studies the Torah...This man studies the Torah; look how corrupt are his deeds, how ugly his ways.'"[5]

To this day, when a religious Jew acts nobly, other Jews say, "That's a real *kiddush ha-Shem.*" And when a religious person acts badly, they say, "That's a real *hillul ha-Shem.*"

---

5. *Yoma* 86a.

– Twenty-Four –

THE BIRKAT HAMAZON
Grace After Meals—Its Basic Four Blessings and Their Meaning for Yesteryear and This Year

וְאָכַלְתָּ וְשָׂבָעְתָּ וּבֵרַכְתָּ אֶת ה' אֱלֹהֶיךָ

When you have eaten and are sated, you shall bless the Lord your God...lest your heart grow haughty, and you forget the Lord your God...and you say to yourself: "my own power and the might of my own hand have won this bounty for me."

–Deuteronomy 8

Eating is a biological function. That is why Judaism, with its emphasis on satisfying the physical, is especially concerned to turn the act of eating into a moment of spiritual affirmation.

It is said that Abraham and Sarah drew people into the service of God by extending them hospitality. After their guests had eaten, they would turn to thank their hosts. Abraham would reply, "Thank not us but God who provides food for all." "How shall we thank God?" "Say, blessed is the Lord, who gives bread and food to all that lives."[1] This is more than a beautiful tradition. It is a basic theme of Judaism. It is in the physical that we find the spiritual. God made the world; therefore it is in the world that we find God. And so, let us examine in some detail

---

1. *Tankhuma, Lekh Lekha* 12.

how the Jewish tradition articulated this aspiration.

The form of the Grace After Meals goes back to Talmudic times and reads as follows:

תָּנוּ רַבָּנָן: סֵדֶר בִּרְכַּת הַמָּזוֹן כַּךְ הִיא: בְּרָכָה רִאשׁוֹנָה - בִּרְכַּת "הַזָּן", שְׁנִיָּה - "בִּרְכַּת הָאָרֶץ", שְׁלִישִׁית - "בּוֹנֵה יְרוּשָׁלַיִם", רְבִיעִית - "הַטּוֹב וְהַמֵּטִיב"

The sages taught that the order of blessings in the Grace after Meals is as follows: the first blessing is "Who feeds all," the second is the "for the land," the third is "Who builds Jerusalem," and the fourth is "Who is good and does good."[2]

The authorities proceeded to establish a separate blessing for each of these four elements. Various other elements were added in post-Talmudic times. Among them are a prelude to the Grace; Psalm 126; an invitation to others to join in the recitation; prayers for Hanukkah, Purim, Rosh Hodesh, the three festivals and Shabbat; prayers for general, personal, family and collective well-being; and various concluding prayers.

What follows focuses on the four basic blessings indicated, the recitation of which fulfills the Grace obligation *halakhically* — according to Jewish law.

The First Blessing

בָּרוּךְ אַתָּה ה' הַזָּן אֶת הַכֹּל.

Bless are You, Lord, who feeds all.[3]

This blessing expresses the Jewish faith's embrace of all human beings, the universal outlook which views God as feeding all the world's children. This beneficence is not only for the worshipper's own self, his own family, his own people, his own nation. In my book about Monotheism, I sought to delineate the thought

---

2. *Berekhot* 48b.
3. For the word "feeds" the Hebrew word *hazon*, i.e. "sustenance" is used; hence the Grace After Meals in Hebrew is *Birkat Hamazon*.

of the Prophets of Israel on this perspective. These great men of expansive faith, based on the inherited mosaic notion of God's overarching sovereignty, expanded that notion to include, without equivocation or qualification, God's concern for all peoples and nations—Israelite and non-Israelite alike:[4]

> *Amos:* "Are you not as the children of the Ethiopians to Me, O people of Israel? says the Lord. Did I not bring Israel up from the land of Egypt, and the *Philistines from Caphtor and the Syrians from Kir?*"[5] Yes, God cares not only for Israel but for non-Israel as well, for He is also their God.

> *Isaiah:* The day will come when the people of Egypt will "swear allegiance to The Lord of hosts," that they will know The Lord and worship Him and that when they call upon Him, "He will hear their supplications and heal them." The Lord cares for all people.[6]

Yet more: what do we mean when we declare, "The Lord feeds all," that it is *God* who feeds people with the food they eat? What this means is that God provides the soil, the seeds, the sun, the rain which make possible for food to grow. Indeed, for these man is not responsible; rather it is a Power—not human—who is ultimately responsible for these crucial elements. Man "partners" with God, as it were, by using the soil given to him, by planting the seeds, by taking advantage of the sunlight and rain bequeathed to him. In a word: this blessing recognizes the *ultimate Source* of food that sustains all humanity.

The Second Blessing

בָּרוּךְ אַתָּה ה', עַל הָאָרֶץ וְעַל הַמָּזוֹן.

Blessed are You, Lord, for the land and for the food.

This blessing moves sequentially from the universal to the

---

4. Shechter, Jack. *The Idea of Monotheism.* Hamilton Books, 2018; p. 42-44.
5. Amos 9:7.
6. Isaiah 19: 18-22.

particular—the land of Israel and the nourishment it provides. The Bible pictures the land in ideal terms: it is good because of its natural qualities,[7] because it is a land of milk and honey,[8] because it has an abundance of water,[9] because of the positive physical efforts of its previous occupants.[10]

Now, the student of the biblical texts is aware that these praises heaped on the land are, in significant measure, exaggeration designed to portray a good and special place. Scripture, in fact, itself tells of drought and famine in the land. We know that ancient Israel in biblical times was small in size with a paucity of natural resources. It is thus apparent that the *Birkat Hamazon's* intent was to point to the true quality of the place: it is a land which nourishes the spirit of its inhabitants and the Jewish people elsewhere in the world. Indeed, scripture and the vast literature and experience of the Jewish people throughout the ages have seen the land as such.

The Land was the place in which the Patriarchs and the Prophets lived and taught. It was the destination as haven and homeland following the exodus from Egypt. It was—and is—the locale in which the Jewish people has the opportunity to *fully* act out the Jewish way, and the place on which and through which it might serve as a model for others, where she sees herself as a nation in the full sense of the word. And—it is today a nation reborn, revitalized and flourishing. It is all this and more—it is a *holy land* especially for those who resonate to the echoes of the spiritual.

The Third Blessing

בָּרוּךְ אַתָּה ה׳, בּוֹנֵה בְּרַחֲמָיו יְרוּשָׁלָיִם. אָמֵן.

Blessed are You, Lord, who in His compassion rebuilds Jeru-salem. AMEN.

---

7. Deuteronomy 8:7-10.
8. Deuteronomy 26:15.
9. Deuteronomy 11:10-12.
10. Deuteronomy 6:10-11.

This blessing moves yet further from the particular Land of Israel as a whole to the land's center: Jerusalem. It is this locale that has always been quintessential to Israel as a nation, a people, a faith. It is seen as a "holy place," revered as a locus for pilgrimage for Jews from all over the world. It suffuses all of rabbinic literature, the prayerbook, the corpus of mystic exploration and folklore. In a word, Jerusalem is embedded in the Jewish psyche and imagination. And—it is today, at long last, the capital of the Jewish state. Our blessing expresses gratitude for a people's core treasure.[11]

The Fourth Blessing

בָּרוּךְ אַתָּה ה' אֱלֹהֵינוּ מֶלֶךְ הָעוֹלָם הַטּוֹב וְהַמֵּטִיב

Blessed are You, Lord, who is good and does good.

This blessing is dated by the Talmud to the period following the Bar Kokhba rebellion against Rome circa 135 CE.[12]

The long-accepted reason for the Bar Kokhba rebellion was that it was provoked by the Romans who embarked on a campaign to eradicate Judaism; they had made circumcision and the study of the Torah capital offenses. The age's eminent spiritual leader, Rabbi Akiba, joined the rebellion's prime leader, Simon Bar Kokhba, in the struggle and promoted it by recognizing its leader as the Messiah. Other sources, it should be noted, express skepticism about Bar Kokhba's character, about the messianic claims made on his behalf, even about the legitimacy of the rebellion which they considered to be unnecessary and unwinnable.

Thousands of Jews flocked to join Bar Kokhba's army. In the revolt's early stages, his troops inflicted heavy casualty on the

---

11. Question: how and why did Jerusalem become the Jewish people's core treasure? And, most especially, a place of profound sanctity? For extensive detail in response to these questions, the reader is invited to see essay #4, "What Makes the Land of Israel 'Holy'?"

12. *Berakhot* 48b.

Roman forces, and even took control of Jerusalem. This was an important victory because the Roman emperor, Hadrian, was seeking to turn Jersualem into a pagan, Roman city. Bar Kokhba's efforts were of no avail. The vastly superior Roman army mobilized and via both subterfuge and outright might, destroyed the Jews' fortresses, razed their numerous settlements, slaughtered thousands, consigned countless numbers to starvation, fire and sword. Nearly the entire land of Judea was laid in waste. Their last fortress, at Betar, southwest of Jerusalem, was razed in 135 CE, which according to Jewish tradition, fell on the ninth of Av, the anniversary of the day on which both the first and second Temples were destroyed.

After a long delay, the Romans gave permission for the Jews to bury their dead. The sages were grateful that their people were able to salvage a fragment of consolation from the disastrous failure of the rebellion which included being initially denied the dignity of burial. And so at Yavneh the Rabbis incorporated the *Hatov v'Hamaytiv* blessing into the *Birkat Hamazon* in memory of the slain at Betar: *hatov*, "who is good," expresses thankfulness to God that the bodies of the slain did not decompose while awaiting burial. *V'Hamaytiv*, "and who does good," articulates thanks to God that the slain were ultimately brought to burial. In a word: this blessing expresses gratitude that human beings, even at the end of their lives, are to be treated with care and dignity.

– Twenty-Five –

THE HAVDALAH CEREMONY
Making "Distinctions" in
Thought and Practice

A youth who had attended Camp Ramah in Ojai, California, was once asked if he observed the Havdalah ceremony at home as he did at the lake at camp during the summer. He responded: "no, we don't have a lake at home."

The riveting and meaningful Havdalah, rich in varied spiritual and educational content, deserves attentive contemplation and regular observance whether at home or at the entrancing setting of a lake in the country. Explication here of its various facets might help in this regard.

OUTLINE OF THE HAVDALAH TEXT/CEREMONY

- **The Concept of "Separation"**
- **Evolution of the Havdalah**

  A) The Four Core Blessings

  1) Over Wine

  2) Over Spices

  3) Over (Lights of) Fire

  4) Over Cup (of Wine)

  B) Biblical Verses Added as Prelude to Core Blessings...Beginning with *Hinay El Yeshuati*

  C) Still Later Additions: Elijah Hymn as Opening and Hamavdil Hymn as Closing

- **The Full Havdalah Text as it Exists Today**
- **Analysis of Full Havdalah Text in its Present Form**

  A) The Elijah Hymn as Opening

  B) Seven Biblical Verses added as Prelude to Core Blessings...Beginning with *Hinay El Yeshuati*

  C) The First Three Core Blessings

  1) Over Wine

  2) Over Spices

  3) Over (Lights of) Fire

  D) The Fourth Core Blessing: Over Cup (of Wine)

  1) Separation Between Sacred and Profane

  2) Separation Between Light and Darkness

  3) Separation Between Israel and the Nations

  4) Separation Between the Seventh Day and Six Working Days

  E) The Hamavdil Hymn as Closing

THE CONCEPT OF "SEPARATION"

וַיַּבְדֵּל אֱלֹהִים בֵּין הָאוֹר וּבֵין הַחֹשֶׁךְ
... וִיהִי מַבְדִּיל בֵּין מַיִם לְמָיִם ... וַיַּבְדֵּל
בֵּין הַמַּיִם אֲשֶׁר מִתַּחַת הָרָקִיעַ וּבֵין
הַמַּיִם אֲשֶׁר מֵעַל לָרָקִיעַ ... יְהִי מְאֹרֹת
בִּרְקִיעַ הַשָּׁמַיִם לְהַבְדִּיל בֵּין הַיּוֹם וּבֵין הַלָּיְלָה
... וּלְהַבְדִּיל בֵּין הָאוֹר וּבֵין הַחֹשֶׁךְ

And God separated *the light from the darkness...and there was a* separation *between water and water...and He* separated *the water which was below the expanse from the water that was above the expanse...Let there be light in the expanse of the sky to* separate *day from night and to* separate *between light and darkness.*[1]

The Havdalah's central theme of separation, of making distinctions, has its roots in the creation account in the first chapter of the book of Genesis.

Originally the earth was תּוֹהוּ וָבֹהוּ "unformed and void" with darkness over the face of the deep (watery mass) and the wind of God sweeping over the waters.[2] This is a picture of what has been termed "chaos," that is, the unorganized, unstructured state of primordial matter; it had no distinct form; it was an undifferentiated, unseparated mass, an inchoate mixture. In this condition, Scripture records God saying, "Let there be light, וַיַּבְדֵּל אֱלֹהִים "and God *separated*" the light from the darkness and He called the light day and the darkness He called night. And there was evening and there was morning, the first day."[3]

From this initial creative act, God proceeds to *separate* water from water, thus fashioning the sky, the earth from the seas, *distinct* earth species, *different* animal species, *different* heavenly lights—sun and moon, and finally *different* human beings—man and woman. What God did was to create what has been termed

1. Genesis 1:4-7.
2. Genesis 1:2.
3. Genesis 1:3-5.

a "cosmos" out of the existing "chaos." He fashioned an orderly world, a structured enterprise—this all based on the fundamental act of invading, as it were, the original chaotic mass and separating it into distinct elements. Thus the process of creation is one of making distinctions, separations (הַבְדָלוֹת) imposing order when there had been randomness.[4]

Now, Scripture and Jewish tradition expanded on this notion of distinctions and separations to include numerous other matters, among them: permitted and forbidden foods, no cross-breeding of animal species, no mixing of diverse seeds, the separation between sacred and ordinary time, distinctions between "holy" and "profane" behavior—this all and more under the rubric of what has been termed "The Holy and the Profane."

To use the paradigm projected by Mercea Eliade for our purposes here, what the Havdalah does, as it brings Shabbat to its conclusion, is to carry its observer back to that original creative act of God, to the time of the world's very beginning when God concluded the work of making separations. At this time the worshipper remembers the Creator and His work of creation. In this condition *religious man's observance is an effort to capture for himself some of the spirit of the immense purity, freshness and strength of that creative act of making distinctions*—the process by which the world came into being. This, he prays, will help him face the inevitable challenges he must encounter in the week ahead.

---

4. This notion is based on Eliade, Mircea. "Sacred Space and Making the World Sacred." *Mystic Stories: the Sacred and the Profane.* Harcourt Brace, 1959, p. 29ff.

EVOLUTION OF THE HAVDALAH

A) The Four Core Blessings

The following passage in the Talmud which established the basic character of the Havdalah, is attributed to the *Anshe Knesset HaGedolah*, "The Men of Great Assembly." This institution functioned in the period between 300-100 BCE. It was an authoritative group of scribes and sages who innovated a variety of synagogue prayers, rituals and benedictions. This is what they declared was to be performed at the Sabbath's conclusion:

הַנִכְנָס לְבֵיתוֹ בְּמוֹצָאֵי שַׁבָּת מְבָרֵךְ עַל הַיַּיִן וְעַל הַמָּאוֹר
וְעַל הַבְּשָׂמִים וְאַחַר כָּךְ אוֹמֵר הַבְדָלָה עַל הַכּוֹס

When one enters one's home at the conclusion of the Sabbath, one pronounces the blessing over wine, over light (fire) and over spices, and then says Havdalah over the cup (of wine).[5]

They subsequently established the full wording of the four basic blessings as follows:

1) Over wine

בָּרוּךְ אַתָּה ה' אֱלֹהֵינוּ מֶלֶךְ הָעוֹלָם, בּוֹרֵא פְּרִי הַגָּפֶן.

Blessed are You, Lord our God, King of the Universe, who creates the fruit of the vine.

2) Over spices

בָּרוּךְ אַתָּה ה' אֱלֹהֵינוּ מֶלֶךְ הָעוֹלָם, בּוֹרֵא מִינֵי בְשָׂמִים.

Blessed are You, Lord our God, King of the Universe, who creates the various spices.

3) Over (lights of) fire

בָּרוּךְ אַתָּה ה' אֱלֹהֵינוּ מֶלֶךְ הָעוֹלָם, בּוֹרֵא מְאוֹרֵי הָאֵשׁ.

---

5. *Pesachim* 102b.

Blessed are You, Lord our God, King of the Universe, who creates the lights of fire.

4) Over cup (of wine) — the specific "separations"

בָּרוּךְ אַתָּה ה׳ אֱלֹהֵינוּ מֶלֶךְ הָעוֹלָם,
הַמַּבְדִּיל בֵּין קֹדֶשׁ לְחֹל, בֵּין אוֹר לְחשֶׁךְ,
בֵּין יִשְׂרָאֵל לָעַמִּים, בֵּין יוֹם הַשְּׁבִיעִי לְשֵׁשֶׁת יְמֵי הַמַּעֲשֶׂה.
בָּרוּךְ אַתָּה ה׳, הַמַּבְדִּיל בֵּין קֹדֶשׁ לְחֹל.

Blessed are You, Lord our God, King of the Universe, who distinguishes between sacred and profane, between light and darkness, between Israel and the nations, between the seventh day and the six days of work. Blessed are You, Lord our God, who distinguishes between the holy and the profane.

B) Seven Biblical Verses Added as Prelude to Core Blessings...Beginning with *Hinay El Yeshuati*

As indicated above, the Talmud[6] established the basic Havdalah text consisting of four blessings—over wine, spices, light/fire and "separations." The *Shulkhan Arukh*[7] quotes this passage, along with a supplementary comment by Rabbi Moses Isserles (mid-sixteenth century), to wit:

סֵדֶר הַבְדָלָה: יַיִן, בְּשָׂמִים, נֵר, הַבְדָלָה, וְסִימָנָךְ
„יַבְנֶה". הַגָּה: וְנוֹהֲגִים לֹאמַר קֹדֶם הַבְדָלָה
שֶׁעוֹשִׂים בַּבַּיִת „הִנֵּה, אֵל יְשׁוּעָתִי אֶבְטַח",
„כּוֹס יְשׁוּעוֹת אֶשָּׂא", „לַיְּהוּדִים הָיְתָה אוֹרָה וְשִׂמְחָה",
לְסִימָן טוֹב

The order of the Havdalah: wine, spices, candle (light/ fire) and "Havdalah" (separations) [and the sign of this is "Yavneh."[8] *Comment: the custom is to say prior to the Havdalah*[9] *which is*

---

6. *Pesakhim* 102b.
7. *Orakh Khayim* 296:11 (Code of Jewish Law).
8. The first letters of the Hebrew—for wine (*yud*), spices (*bet*), candle (*ner*) and the Havdalah (*hey*).
9. The four Havdalah blessings.

practiced at home, "Behold, God is my salvation," "I will lift up the cup of deliverance," and "The Jews had light and joy." (This was all for a "good sign.")

Here Rabbi Isserles pointed to the traditional practice of the German communities from the time of Rashi (1040-1105) of introducing a number of biblical verses as prelude to the original Havdalah blessings. Three verses were added to Isserles' original four, their order of recitation altered, producing the text as we have it today.

The Seven Biblical Verses

Each verse expresses the idea of *Yeshua*, "salvation," i.e. being "saved" from trouble and strife, thus gaining personal and collective fulfillment.

הִנֵּה אֵל יְשׁוּעָתִי אֶבְטַח, וְלֹא אֶפְחָד,
כִּי־עָזִּי וְזִמְרָת יָהּ יהוה, וַיְהִי־לִי לִישׁוּעָה.
וּשְׁאַבְתֶּם מַיִם בְּשָׂשׂוֹן, מִמַּעַיְנֵי הַיְשׁוּעָה.

Behold, God is my salvation. *I will trust and not be afraid. The Lord, the Lord, is my strength and my song. He has become my* salvation. *With joy you will draw water from the springs of* salvation.[10]

לַיהוה הַיְשׁוּעָה, עַל־עַמְּךָ בִרְכָתֶךָ [סֶּלָה].

Salvation *is the Lord's; on Your people is Your blessing (Selah).*[11]

יהוה צְבָאוֹת עִמָּנוּ, מִשְׂגָּב לָנוּ אֱלֹהֵי יַעֲקֹב [סֶלָה].

The Lord of hosts is with us the God of Jacob is our stronghold *(Selah).*[12]

---

10. Isaiah 12:2–3.
11. Psalm 3:9.
12. Psalm 16:12.

הי צְבָאוֹת, אַשְׁרֵי אָדָם בֹּטֵחַ בָּךְ.

The Lord of hosts, **happy** *is the one who trusts in You.*[13]

הי הוֹשִׁיעָה, הַמֶּלֶךְ יַעֲנֵנוּ בְיוֹם־קָרְאֵנוּ.

The Lord **saves.** *May the King answer us on the day we call.*[14]

לַיְהוּדִים הָיְתָה אוֹרָה וְשִׂמְחָה וְשָׂשֹׂן וִיקָר, כֵּן תִּהְיֶה לָנוּ.

For the Jew there was **light and gladness, joy and honor,** *so may it be for us.*[15]

כּוֹס־יְשׁוּעוֹת אֶשָּׂא, וּבְשֵׁם יהוה אֶקְרָא.

I will lift up the cup of **salvation** *and call on the name of the Lord.*[16]

C) Still Later Additions

Jewish tradition, being what it is, would not allow the basic blessings and verses to remain alone. And so, two hymns were added to the ceremony, one as prelude to the entire ceremony, and one for its conclusion, as follows:

אֵלִיָּהוּ הַנָּבִיא, אֵלִיָּהוּ הַתִּשְׁבִּי, אֵלִיָּהוּ הַגִּלְעָדִי, בִּמְהֵרָה
יָבֹא אֵלֵינוּ, עִם מָשִׁיחַ בֶּן דָּוִד

Elijah Hymn as Opening

Elijah the prophet, Elijah the Tishbite, Elijah of Gilead

May He soon come to us with the Messiah son of David.

---

13. Psalm 84:13.
14. Psalm 20:10.
15. Esther 8:6.
16. Psalm 116:13.

Hamavdil Hymn as Closing

הַמַּבְדִּיל בֵּין קֹדֶשׁ לְחֹל, חַטֹּאתֵינוּ הוּא יִמְחֹל

He who separates the holy from the profane, may He forgive our sins.

THE FULL HAVDALAH TEXT AS WE HAVE IT TODAY

As detailed above, the Havdalah text and ceremony developed in different time periods and thus its sequence in time was not that of the text as we have it today. What follows is examination of the text-ceremony according to its present form, which hopefully will make for an orderly exposition.

A

אֵלִיָּהוּ הַנָּבִיא, אֵלִיָּהוּ הַתִּשְׁבִּי, אֵלִיָּהוּ הַגִּלְעָדִי, בִּמְהֵרָה
יָבֹא אֵלֵינוּ, עִם מָשִׁיחַ בֶּן דָּוִד

B

הִנֵּה אֵל יְשׁוּעָתִי אֶבְטַח וְלֹא אֶפְחָד,
כִּי עָזִּי וְזִמְרָת יָהּ ה', וַיְהִי לִי לִישׁוּעָה.
וּשְׁאַבְתֶּם מַיִם בְּשָׂשׂוֹן מִמַּעַיְנֵי הַיְשׁוּעָה.
לַה' הַיְשׁוּעָה, עַל עַמְּךָ בִרְכָתֶךָ [סֶּלָה].
ה' צְבָאוֹת עִמָּנוּ, מִשְׂגָּב לָנוּ אֱלֹהֵי יַעֲקֹב [סֶּלָה].
ה' צְבָאוֹת, אַשְׁרֵי אָדָם בֹּטֵחַ בָּךְ.
ה' הוֹשִׁיעָה, הַמֶּלֶךְ יַעֲנֵנוּ בְיוֹם קָרְאֵנוּ.
לַיְּהוּדִים הָיְתָה אוֹרָה וְשִׂמְחָה וְשָׂשֹׂן וִיקָר, כֵּן תִּהְיֶה לָנוּ.
כּוֹס יְשׁוּעוֹת אֶשָּׂא, וּבְשֵׁם ה' אֶקְרָא.

C

בָּרוּךְ אַתָּה ה' אֱלֹהֵינוּ מֶלֶךְ הָעוֹלָם, בּוֹרֵא פְּרִי הַגָּפֶן.

בָּרוּךְ אַתָּה ה' אֱלֹהֵינוּ מֶלֶךְ הָעוֹלָם, בּוֹרֵא מִינֵי בְשָׂמִים.

בָּרוּךְ אַתָּה ה' אֱלֹהֵינוּ מֶלֶךְ הָעוֹלָם, בּוֹרֵא מְאוֹרֵי הָאֵשׁ.

D

בָּרוּךְ אַתָּה ה' אֱלֹהֵינוּ מֶלֶךְ הָעוֹלָם,
הַמַּבְדִּיל בֵּין קֹדֶשׁ לְחֹל, בֵּין אוֹר לְחֹשֶׁךְ,
בֵּין יִשְׂרָאֵל לָעַמִּים, בֵּין יוֹם הַשְּׁבִיעִי לְשֵׁשֶׁת יְמֵי הַמַּעֲשֶׂה.
בָּרוּךְ אַתָּה ה', הַמַּבְדִּיל בֵּין קֹדֶשׁ לְחֹל.

E

הַמַּבְדִּיל בֵּין קֹדֶשׁ לְחֹל, חַטֹּאתֵינוּ הוּא יִמְחֹל

ANALYSIS OF THE FULL HAVDALAH'S TEXT IN ITS PRESENT FORM

A) The Elijah Hymn as Opening

Elijah in Jewish tradition is the classic herald of better days. As the precursor of the Messiah[17] he proclaims a future free from pain and poverty and gloom, a tomorrow in which calm and satisfaction and peace of mind and heart pervade. He is a living presence in the religious life of the Jew—at the Passover Seder, at the circumcision ceremony and more:

- *In the Grace after meals:* "May the All-Merciful send us Elijah the Prophet (may his memory be for good) who will bring us good tidings, salvation and consolation."

- *In the blessings after the Haftarah:* Gladden us, Lord our God, with Your servant Elijah the Prophet (and with the kingdom of David Your anointed), soon may he come and make our hearts rejoice.

- In *the Havdalah ceremony:* "Elijah the Prophet, Elijah the Tishbite, Elijah of Gilead, may he soon come to us with the Messiah, Son of David." When, hopefully, that will have occurred, the prayer adds, "The Jew (will have) had light and joy, gladness and honor."

According to legend, as the day of rest departs, the Prophet Elijah prompts those who have done wrong to repent so that they may enter into the week ahead sinless. He thus enables them to begin the morrow with a "clean slate," as it were. This eases their anxieties, giving them hope and confidence as they face the tasks of the coming week.

And so, Elijah is an appropriate figure with a message of hope and confidence for the Jew at Havdalah time as he is about to confront the challenges ahead.[18]

---

17. Malachi 3:23-24.
18. For the numerous references to Elijah in legend, see Ginzberg, Louis.

B) The Seven Biblical Verses Added as Prelude to Core Blessings...Beginning with *Hinay El Yeshuati*

Each of the verses listed above contain the theme of *Yeshua*, "salvation," i.e. being "saved" from trouble and strife, thus gaining personal and collective fulfillment. (See pages 290-292 for details).

At this time of transition from Shabbat to workday, we are often filled with anxiety or insecurity about what lies ahead in the coming week. As pointed out in essay #21, "The Rite of Passage Phenomenon," transition times prompt uncertainty. Hence, in this context, the use of ritual to help ease the transition to the workday. The frequent usage of the idea of *Yeshua* reminds us of our protecting God who tells us "do not fear." He will, we pray, bless us with this goodness, His "salvation" in the period ahead.

C) The First Three Core Blessings

1) *Over wine*

בָּרוּךְ אַתָּה ה' אֱלֹהֵינוּ מֶלֶךְ הָעוֹלָם, בּוֹרֵא פְּרִי הַגָּפֶן.

Blessed are You, Lord our God, King of the Universe, who creates the fruit of the vine.

Wine has a variety of positive medicinal benefits which, in turn, promotes a sense of psychological and social well-being. It gladdens the spirit, dispels feelings of sadness and helps awaken enthusiasm for one's tasks. Thus wine has been closely associated with religious ritual as a logical and useful tool for the realization of its objective which is to promote the drives of the religious way. And so, usage of wine for this purpose was deployed by the rabbis for the Friday evening and Shabbat noon Kiddush, the Saturday evening Havdalah ceremony as here, the Passover Seder, the Purim Seudah, and other religious occasions.

It should be noted that in traditional Jewish life, small

Legends of the Jews, Volume VII and Index; p. 132-135.

quantities of wine were imbibed on those occasions, for these were not private drinking times, but rather drinking as a family or community with the aim of strengthening feelings of companionship and enthusiasm in the service of religious life.

2) Over spices

The soul of a human being helps raise him/her above animal existence, inspires her with ideals, and prompts him to choose the good and reject the evil. Since the Shabbat is such a spiritualizing force, the rabbis portrayed it as having an additional spiritual element:

אָמַר רַבִּי שִׁמְעוֹן בֶּן לָקִישׁ: נְשָׁמָה יְתֵרָה נוֹתֵן הקב"ה בְּאָדָם
בְּעֶרֶב שַׁבָּת, וּלְמוֹצָאֵי שַׁבָּת נוֹטְלִין אוֹתָהּ הֵימֶנּוּ שֶׁנֶּאֱמַר:
„שָׁבַת וַיִּנָּפַשׁ", כֵּיוָן שֶׁשָּׁבַת: „וַוי אָבְדָה נָפֶשׁ".

Rabbi Shimon ben Lakish said: an additional soul is given to man on the eve of Shabbat. And at the close of Shabbat (that soul) is taken away from him. As it is written, "He (God) ceased from work and rested." Since He ceased from work, "woe, this soul was lost."[19]

In this passage, there is a play on the Hebrew word *vayinafash*, which means "rested," "ceased from work." The prefix *va*, which is attached to the word *nefesh*, which also means "soul," creates a new concept: וַוי אָבְדָה נָפֶשׁ, "woe, the soul is lost."

The additional soul has departed at the end of the Shabbat. This soul, (combined with the original innate soul of a person) had provided extra spiritual sensitivity for the day of rest. And its leaving is cause for sadness. The Zohar then projects a reaction to this loss of the extra soul at the Shabbat's conclusion: the usage of spices:

> Come and see: smell sustains the *nefesh* (the soul of a person which remains in him after the extra soul has departed) in man...the clothes Adam was given after

---

19. *Taanit* 27b.

departing the Garden of Eden gave out a fragrance from the aroma of the Garden, and *Adam's soul was calmed and uplifted by it.* This is what is meant by the verse saying that when Isaac smelled the fragrance of Jacob's clothes, he blessed him. *The aroma calmed Isaac's spirit and the blessing could then flow from that place of serenity.*[20]

Here is where the usage of spices[21] enters the Havdalah ceremony with a blessing:

בָּרוּךְ אַתָּה ה' אֱלֹהֵינוּ מֶלֶךְ הָעוֹלָם, בּוֹרֵא מִינֵי בְשָׂמִים.

Blessed are You, Lord our God, King of the Universe, who creates the various spices.

3) Over (lights of) fire

בָּרוּךְ אַתָּה ה' אֱלֹהֵינוּ מֶלֶךְ הָעוֹלָם, בּוֹרֵא מְאוֹרֵי הָאֵשׁ.

Blessed are You, Lord our God, King of the Universe, who creates the lights of fire.

Fire is not permitted to be kindled on Shabbat. Havdalah marks the transition from the Shabbat to the weekday when we say, in effect, now we *can* kindle fire. The Talmud expands on the practice of using fire at Havdalah time.

אָמַר רַבִּי יוֹחָנָן: מְבָרְכִין עַל הָאוֹר בְּמוֹצָאֵי שַׁבָּת הוֹאִיל תְּחִילַת בְּרִיאָתוֹ הוּא

Rabbi Yohanan said: we bless the light at the conclusion of Shabbat because light was the first of His (God's) creation.[22]

---

20. Betza 16a.
21. The technical reason for the usage of spaces at Havdalah times: In the ordinary process of cooking, spices are used. Since cooking is not allowed on Shabbat, spices, as well, are not permitted. At Havdalah time we note that the weekday is at hand, hence, usage of spices is permitted. The spice blessing marks this transition. It is this usage which both the Talmud and the Zohar endowed with mystic speculation as depicted.
22. Pesakhim 54a.

It is thus appropriate to begin a new week with a blessing over fire (which produces light) by which we commemorate the first act of God in fashioning the world—the beginning of all things. We identify with that original act and seek to capture its power for our own lives in the week to come, light that dispels the darkness that ordinary days often bring.

Another explanation for the blessing: fire is the symbol of that which fosters civilization. With it man overcomes cold, prepares food, shapes instruments of labor, and more. These are weekday activities, and thus a benediction over that which makes these vital things possible is recited on the eve of their renewed activity. (In this connection note the striking suggestion by Rabbi Irving Greenberg that the Havdalah might be called the *Kiddush* for the work week.)

Characteristically, Jewish legend harbors a mystical explanation for the blessing over light/fire. The Midrash says this (I have condensed the passage):

רַבִּי לֵוִי בְּשֵׁם בַּר נְזִירָה אָמַר:
כֵּיוָן שֶׁשָּׁקְעָה הַחַמָּה בְּמוֹצָאֵי שַׁבָּת
הִתְחִיל הַחֹשֶׁךְ מְמַשְׁמֵשׁ וּבָא וְנִתְיָרֵא אָדָם
הָרִאשׁוֹן שֶׁנֶּאֱמַר „אַךְ חֹשֶׁךְ יְשׁוּפֵנִי ...
בָּא לְהִזְדַּוֵּג לִי". מֶה עָשָׂה הַקָּדוֹשׁ
בָּרוּךְ הוּא? זִמֵּן לוֹ שְׁנֵי רְעָפִים
וְהִקִּישָׁן זֶה בָּזֶה וְיָצָא מֵהֶן אוֹר וּבֵרֵךְ
עָלֶיהָ: „בּוֹרֵא מְאוֹרֵי הָאֵשׁ"

Rabbi Levi in the name of Bar Nezira said: when the sun sank at the termination of the Shabbat, darkness began to set in. Adam was terrified (thinking) that "the darkness will envelop me and come to attack me." What did the Lord do for him? He made him find two flints which he struck against each other; lights came forth and he (Adam) uttered a blessing over it: "who creates light/fire" (literally, "the lights of fire").[23]

In this ceremony we employ a multi-wick candle, and recite,

---

23. Genesis Rabbah 11:2.

Boray m'oray ha-aish, "who creates *lights of fire*," language implicit in the above midrash in which benediction is over both light and fire. It is also customary to lift the hands toward the light, by doing so one indicates usage of the light over which the benediction is recited, just as one drinks the wine and smells the spices over which these benedictions are recited. Some bend the fingers over the palms to produce shadows to symbolize the onset of evening. Yet another reason given for lifting the hands is that now that the Shabbat is over, the hands may be employed in work forbidden on the Sabbath.

D) The Fourth Core Blessing: Over Cup (of Wine)

This blessing represents the thematic heart of the Havdalah text and ceremony-making distinctions—as we have sought to show earlier in this essay.

בָּרוּךְ אַתָּה ה' אֱלֹהֵינוּ מֶלֶךְ הָעוֹלָם,
הַמַּבְדִּיל בֵּין קֹדֶשׁ לְחֹל, בֵּין אוֹר לְחשֶׁךְ,
בֵּין יִשְׂרָאֵל לָעַמִּים, בֵּין יוֹם הַשְּׁבִיעִי לְשֵׁשֶׁת יְמֵי הַמַּעֲשֶׂה.
בָּרוּךְ אַתָּה ה', הַמַּבְדִּיל בֵּין קֹדֶשׁ לְחֹל.

Blessed are You, Lord our God, King of the universe, who distinguishes between sacred and profane, between light and darkness, between Israel and the nations, between the seventh day and the six days of work. Blessed are You, Lord, who distinguishes between sacred and profane.

Note the four areas of distinctions being made in this blessing. The final distinction is a repetition of the first, though it appears to encompass them all. What follows is analysis of these four elements of distinction contained in the "separations" blessing.

1) Separation Between the Sacred and Profane Behavior

הַמַּבְדִּיל בֵּין קֹדֶשׁ לְחֹל

Blessed are You, Lord our God, King of the universe, who distinguishes between sacred and profane.

In our discussion concerning the concept of "separations," we pointed out that the essence of the process of the world's creation was the fashioning of "cosmos" out of "chaos," which is to say distinctiveness from the muddle of primordial matter. Cosmos was equated with the "holy" because God created it, and the chaos was equated with the "profane" because it was that which had been in undifferentiated state.

Rabbinic tradition applied this notion of the "holy" versus the "profane" to the behavior of people. There is "holy" behavior expected by the Creator and there is "profane" behavior the Creator denigrates. The basic guideline was that God not only created the world on the basis of distinctions, but that these distinctions rendered qualitative results as a result of the Creator's positive actions. Man, in the rabbinic mind, was obligated to replicate these actions in his own life. Indeed, it was man's purpose in life to be, in human measure, like God. This was His wish for mankind: "You shall be holy for I, the Lord, your God am holy" proclaims Scripture.[24] This is what man reaches for when in the Havdalah he praises "The one who separates the holy from the profane"; man recognizes that it is his duty to do likewise.

The attributes of God enumerated in Exodus 34:5-7, which the rabbis viewed as behaviors to be replicated by man in his regular encounters with his fellow man, are appealed to in the pseudepigraphical book of 4 Ezra in a moving plea for mankind:

> I know, Sir, that the Most High is called *rahum, compassionate* because He has compassion on those who have come into the world. And *hanun, gracious* to those who turn in repentance to His law. And *ereh apayim, slow to anger* toward those who have sinned. And *rav hesed, abounding in kindness* because He had rather give than exact. And *notzayr hesed, extending kindness* because He makes His kindness abound to those now living and to those who are gone, for if He did not make kindnesses abound, the world and those who inhabit it could not

---

24. Leviticus 19:2.

live. And *nosay avon, forgiver of iniquity,* for it He did not forgive out of His goodness, not the ten-thousandth part of men could survive. And the *v'nakay, who pardons,* because if He did not pardon those who were created by His word, and blot out the multitude of their sins, very few would be left of all the innumerable multitude.[25]

George Foote Moore comments on this passage:

The illustrations from a single compilation of "sermon stuff' tell of the humanity of God written all over the revelation as it was read by philosophically unsophisticated men; the preachers at most did no more than seek to improve less obvious texts. *They held up this side of God's character as an example of motivation for men to imitate.*[26]

When man replicates in his life the ways of God as depicted above, he demonstrates that he knows the difference between that which is "holy" and that which is "profane" human behavior: compassion versus callousness, graciousness versus hard-heartedness, slowness of anger versus impetuosity, abundance of kindness versus cruelty, extended kindness versus endless animosity, forgiveness versus blame, justice versus bias. One could extend this distinction between holy and profane behavior: moderation versus dissipation, clean versus foul language, elegance versus crudeness, order versus chaos at home or work, patience versus exasperation, charity versus hoarding.

In this construct what links man to God is his ability to make distinctions in the living of his life—to know and act on the difference between holy and profane behavior. This is what Havdalah stresses as a prime principle.

2) Separation Between Light (Knowledge) and Darkness (Its Absence)

(הַמַּבְדִּיל) בֵּין אוֹר לְחֹשֶׁךְ

---

25. 4 Ezra 62:123.
26. *Judaism: The Age of the Tannaim,* Volume 1, p. 393

(Who distinguishes) between light and darkness.

As we have pointed out, the concept of separation is basically rooted in the Genesis account of creation. What God did, as it were, was to pierce the original primordial chaos by, among other things, fashioning light from the prevailing darkness. Thus what the Havdalah does is to commemorate that initial creative act, identify with it, and recapture for the observer the initial power involved in the world's creation and use it for the ordinary weekday period of activity ahead.

As is the case with many religious rites, the initial impulses that gave rise to them were added to by rabbinic tradition through the process of interpretation. This was designed to both enrich the rite's meaning and to make it more relevant to the on-going living condition of the observer. Thus the Etz Hayyim commentary to Genesis 1:3, *Let there be light*, says this: "Light, the first thing God created, can be seen as symbolizing Judaism's commitment to clarity rather than mystery, to openness rather than concealment, to study rather than to blind faith." Light symbolizes what Jewish tradition has variously designated as *daya*, knowledge; as *bina*, understanding; as *haskel*, wisdom. It is with these tools that human beings are to conduct their lives.

The Havdalah embraces this notion. Its basic text was originally part of the evening Amida prayer recited at the Shabbat's conclusion dealing with the subject of knowledge. The text in brackets were inserted later by the rabbis:

אַתָּה חוֹנֵן לְאָדָם דַּעַת וּמְלַמֵּד לֶאֱנוֹשׁ
בִּינָה. [אַתָּה חוֹנַנְתָּ לְמַדַּע תּוֹרָתֶךָ וַתְּלַמְּדֵנוּ
לַעֲשׂוֹת חֻקֵּי רְצוֹנֶךָ. וַתַּבְדֵּל ה' אֱלֹהֵינוּ
בֵּין קֹדֶשׁ לְחוֹל, בֵּין אוֹר לְחֹשֶׁךְ, בֵּין יִשְׂרָאֵל
לָעַמִּים, בֵּין יוֹם הַשְּׁבִיעִי לְשֵׁשֶׁת יְמֵי
הַמַּעֲשֶׂה. אָבִינוּ מַלְכֵּנוּ הָחֵל עָלֵינוּ
הַיָּמִים הַבָּאִים לִקְרָאתֵנוּ לְשָׁלוֹם חֲשׂוּכִים
מִכָּל חֵטְא וּמְנֻקִּים מִכָּל עָוֹן וּמְדֻבָּקִים

בְּיִרְאָתֶךָ.] וְחָנֵּנוּ מֵאִתְּךָ דֵּעָה
בִּינָה וְהַשְׂכֵּל. בָּרוּךְ אַתָּה ה' חוֹנֵן הַדָּעַת.

*You grace humanity with knowledge and teach mortals under-
standing.*

*[You have graced us with the knowledge of Your Torah, and
taught us to perform the statutes of Your will. You have distinguished, Lord our God, between sacred and profane, light
and darkness, Israel and the nations, and between the seventh
day and the six days of work. Our Father, our King, may the
days approaching us bring peace; may we be free from all sin,
cleansed from all iniquity, holding fast to our reverence of
You,]* and grace us with the knowledge, understanding
and wisdom *that come from You. Blessed are You, Lord, who
graciously grants knowledge.*

The Talmud is the source for this addition to the Saturday
evening Amida prayer: מַזְכִּירִין הַבְדָּלָה בְּחוֹנֵן הַדַּעַת, "We mention
the Havdalah prayer *You grace humanity with knowledge.*" The
question is then asked: הַבְדָּלָה בְּחוֹנֵן הַדַּעַת: מַאי טַעְמָא? "What is
the reason for the Havdalah being included in the prayer "You
grace humanity with knowledge"? The answer is given by Rabbi
Yosef: אָמַר רַבִּי יוֹסֵף: מִתּוֹךְ שֶׁהִיא חָכְמָה, קְבוּעָה בְּבִרְכַּת חָכְמָה, "Because it requires wisdom [to distinguish between entities], they
established in the Havdalah the blessing of wisdom."[27]

The point: one needs "knowledge, understanding and wisdom" to make distinctions in the business of living, to attain spiritual insight, to live the moral life. As we engage in this prayer,
we grow in understanding, we seek better to fulfill the duties of
the human lot and station. Knowledge of what is good is to enable one to avoid evil behavior and gives one the power to do
what is right. As in King Solomon's "Grant, O Lord, an understanding mind to judge Your people, to distinguish between
good and bad; for who can judge this vast people of Yours?"[28]

Yet more: the rabbis did not look favorably on one who *had*
knowledge, but *did not use it* to guide his life in accordance with

---

27. *Berhakhot* 33a.
28. I Kings 3:9.

that possession. They put it this way:

> Knowledge does not solely refer to intellectual capabil-
> ity, but also to *one's fundamental ability to conduct oneself
> and live in accordance with that capability.* That is why the
> Gemara relates harshly to one who does not use one's
> knowledge. One fails thereby to realize one's potential
> and negates his own essence.[29]

And so, the Havdalah ceremony further calls upon its observer to use the light, i.e. the knowledge one possesses, to pierce
the potential "darkness," as it were, to know how to navigate the
inevitable challenges of the week ahead.

3) Separation Between Israel and the Nations

(הַמַּבְדִּיל) בֵּין יִשְׂרָאֵל לָעַמִּים

Who distinguishes between Israel and the nations.

In this third element of the basic Havdalah text, God is blessed
for separating the people Israel from the other people of the
world. What is the purpose of this? The idea of the covenant between God and Israel harbors the answer. The text reads:

> You have affirmed this day that the Lord is your God,
> that you will walk in his ways, that you will observe His
> laws and commandments and rules, and hearken to His
> voice. And the Lord affirmed this day that you are, as He
> promised you, *lihiyot Lo l'am segula,* to be this treasured
> people who shall observe His commandments.[30]

And Joshua said to the people that the Israelites themselves
chose to serve the Lord when they responded: "yes, we are witnesses."[31] Then, too, the rabbis pointed to Scripture that when
the Lord offered the Torah to Israel, she readily proclaimed, "we
will do and we will hear."[32]

---

29. Koren Talmud Bavli, *Berakhot* 33a.
30. Deuteronomy 26:17-19.
31. Joshua 24:22.
32. Exodus 24:7.

Why was Israel "chosen," i.e. singled out, separated from the nations? Why a "treasured possession?" The prophet Isaiah answered with words that have been embedded in the life and psyche of the Jewish people down through the ages: Israel was to be an *or lagoyum*, "a light unto the nations."[33] She is to harbor, nurture and propagate the notion of the One and Only God and the obligations specified in the covenant. Israel agreed to undertake this task. Indeed, this was God's purpose in choosing Israel. She was to influence the world to embrace the idea of Monotheism along with the principles and practices inherent in it. God's existence meant the absolute non-existence of other gods, and that the Lord was the God of all people everywhere on earth. Indeed, the book of Barukh went so far as to assert that God created the world so that Israel could and would fulfill that purpose.[34] Israel has had to pay a heavy price for such a task. That is her destiny. That's why she was "separated."

4) *Separation Between the Seventh Day and the Six Working Days*

(הַמַּבְדִיל) בֵּין יוֹם הַשְּׁבִיעִי לְשֵׁשֶׁת יְמֵי הַמַּעֲשֶׂה.

(Who distinguishes) between the seventh day and the six working days.

The precise moment when God created the world indicates the creation of time. Time did not exist in the primordial chaos from which God created the cosmos (the world). For religious man every creation, every concrete reality which exists in the world begins in time. *Before a thing exists, its particular time could not exist.* Before the cosmos came into existence there was no cosmic time. In the pre-existing undifferentiated, unformed "muddle" no specific reality which today constitutes the world obtained. Thus, for example, before a particular vegetable species was created, *the time* that now causes it to grow, bear fruit and die did not exist. It is for this reason that creation is seen as the fashioner

---

33. Isaiah 42:6; 49:61; 3:35.
34. Aprocrypha, *Barukh* 3:35.

of time itself.

It is this time that the Shabbat commemorates. Abraham Heschel puts it this way:

> The meaning of the Sabbath is to celebrate time rather than space. Six days a week we live under the tyranny of things of space; on the Sabbath we try to become attuned to *holiness in time.* It is a day on which we are called upon to share in what is eternal in time, to turn form the results of creation to the mystery of creation; from the world of creation to the creation of the world.[35]

The Friday evening Kiddush links Shabbat to creation when it declares it as "in remembrance of the activity of the beginning (of the creation)." It is the seventh day that marks the period during which God completed His work in fashioning the world during the previous six days. The Shabbat is a "holy" day because God *separated* it from the previous six days. The holy day itself and the ritual practiced during it seek to capture the thrust of that original period of divine activity, to ponder and appreciate that wondrous phenomenon.

Indeed, one can understand why the memory of that original marvelous time haunts religious man, and why he regularly each week (and each new year) seeks to return to it and capture its spirit. For at the beginning of time God displayed His great power which for man is a model of energy, abundance and creativity; it was a time when the world was fresh, pure and strong. Religious man searches for these characteristics for his own life. Rabbi Hamnuna put it this way:

כָּל הַמִּתְפַּלֵּל בְּעֶרֶב שַׁבָּת
וְאוֹמֵר „וַיְכֻלּוּ", מַעֲלֶה עָלָיו הַכָּתוּב כְּאִילוּ נַעֲשֶׂה
שׁוּתָף לַקָדוֹשׁ בָּרוּךְ הוּא בְּמַעֲשֵׂה בְרֵאשִׁית

All who pray on Shabbat evening and recite the Vayekhulu

---

35. Heschel, Abraham Joshua and Ruth Goodhill (translation). *The Wisdom of Heschel.* Farrar, Straus & Giroux; p. 304.

("And God completed," i.e., the opening phrase of the Kiddush), of him the verse says that this is as if he (man) was made a partner with God in the world's creation.[36]

And so, via the Shabbat observance one seeks to be present at the very source of the time when the world came into being— *and when the work was completed.* Thus religious man also ceases from work even as the Creator did. This enables him to disentangle himself from the churning demands of weekday labor which gives his body sorely needed rest and his mind and spirit the calm needed to contemplate the earth as a gift of divine creativity.

However, the Shabbat is not for this purpose alone; it serves everyday life. Its cultivation of the inner spirit can gradually suffuse one's consciousness in general giving one the hope of returning to the workweek with this gift of the heart. Thus, as the Havdalah rite at the conclusion of the Sabbath returns the worshipper to the concrete world, the rite might also be viewed as a kind of sanctification (a *Kiddush*) blessing for the ensuing week. Seen this way, one can take something of its spirit of repose, of calmness of heart and mind, its exodus from tension into the everyday thereby producing a degree of balance in the "business" of living.

There is another lesson here. Exodus declares as the fifth of the Ten Commandments, "Six days *shall you labor* and *do your work*, and on the seventh is a Sabbath...you shall not work."[37] About this Heschel comments: "Just as we are commanded to keep the Sabbath, we are commanded to work—*do all your work*. The duty to work for six days is just as much a part of God's covenant with man as the duty to abstain from work on the seventh day."[38] One is obliged by Scripture itself to work in the practical world to provide for oneself, family and community. A

---

36. Berakhot 66a.
37. Exodus 20:9.
38. Heschel, Abraham Joshua and Ruth Goodhill (translation). *The Wisdom of Heschel.* Farrar, Straus & Giroux; p. 308.

person is not to spend all his days "resting" as on Shabbat nor use all of life's time even in study and contemplation as some overzealous religionists do in our time. Indeed, *even as God labored in the process of creating the world, so is man to work in the process of fashioning his own world.* Indeed, even as God is the paradigm for resting from work, so is He the paradigm for laboring in the so-called "profane" world.

E) The Havdalah Hymn as Closing

As the Shabbat is ritually concluded with the Havdalah ceremony, a striking hymn provides its capstone: the *Hamavdil*. It was composed by Isaac Ibn Hayat (1030-1089), a Spanish rabbi, Bible commentator and liturgical poet. He lived in the Italian town of Lucena, where he also headed a rabbinical seminary. The hymn was originally part of the Yom Kippur Neilah service. Its first line contains its basic theme:

הַמַּבְדִּיל בֵּין קֹדֶשׁ לְחוֹל, חַטֹּאתֵינוּ הוּא יִמְחֹל

He who distinguishes between the sacred and the profane, may He forgive our sins.

As the hymn progresses, there are continual requests for forgiveness, for freedom from poverty, escape from lurking illness, for avoidance of "filthy snares," for overlooking all manner of personal shortcomings, for rest from weariness. Indeed, the hymn concludes as it began: "We are in Your hands like clay; please forgive our sins—light and grave." Why this stress on forgiveness a person requires for well-being at Havdalah time? The theme of asking to be pardoned for sinful behavior is the reason the hymn was composed for Yom Kippur. However, it is today universally sung at Havdalah's conclusion. Again: why on Saturday evening? For this we again turn to Mircea Eliade's guidelines on the subject of ritual origins, which we here apply to Shabbat time.

Shabbat commemorates creation of the world. As such, it seeks to lead the observer back to that time of quintessential origin when the world was in its pure, unblemished state, when transgression—large or small—did not yet exist, when greed and jealousy, hurt and fabrication were nonexistent. This all because man had not yet set out on life's journey. And so, what this Hamavdil hymn seeks to do is to return the observer to that pure origin in time, to dwell in it, identify with it and seek to recapture that unblemished state of purity—a time when human shortcomings were nonexistent. It thus plays an important role in healing, in human regeneration—a therapeutic purpose wherein transgression is no more. *Havdalah is, then, a time of symbolic rebirth. Religious man is here seeking a "clean slate," as it were, asking God for forgiveness of sin committed in past weeks so that he can proceed into the morrow minus the baggage of accumulated wrongdoing.* This, he prays, will give him the confidence needed to successfully confront the challenges the week ahead inevitably presents.

Twenty-Six

THE THREE SHABBAT
"MEALS OF FAITH"

אַתְקִינוּ סְעוּדָתָא דִמְהֵימְנוּתָא שְׁלֵימָתָא. חֶדְוְתָא
דְמַלְכָּא קַדִּישָׁא: אַתְקִינוּ סְעוּדָתָא
דְמַלְכָּא. דָא הִיא סְעוּדָתָא דַּחֲקַל תַּפּוּחִין קַדִּישִׁין
וּזְעֵיר אַנְפִּין וְעַתִּיקָא קַדִּישָׁא אַתְיָן לְסַעֲדָא בַּהֲדֵיה:

Prepare the feast of perfect faith,
the joy of the Holy King.
Prepare the feast of the King,
This is the feast of the Field of Sacred Apples,
The Miniature Presence, and the Holy Ancient One.
Come to feast with it.

—The Prayer Book
Before Shabbat Meals

יְהִי חֶלְקִי מֵאוֹכְלֵי שָׁלֹשׁ סְעוּדוֹת בְּשַׁבָּת

May my portion be with those who eat three meals on Shab-
bat.

—Rabbi Yosi, Shabbat 118b

Spiritualizing the Eating Experience

Shabbat meals were taken at the table of my grandparents
throughout my youth. A feature of these meals: before each
course, Grandfather had all of us at the table say *l'kovod Shabbos*,
that is, "I'm eating this food in honor of the Sabbath." It was his

way of spiritualizing the eating experience, rendering each occasion a "meal of faith." This was a practice in keeping with the tradition developed by the Hasidic movement which sought to add a dimension of "invisible light" — the presence of God — into the ordinary act of eating.

The earlier Kabbalists, the mystics from whom the Hasidim drew inspiration, had developed a number of innovations in Jewish liturgy and practice which remain in vogue in many circles to this day. Among them were recitation of a selection from the Zohar: the *Brikh Shemay*, prior to removing of the Torah from the ark; welcoming Shabbat at the Friday evening service with singing the *L'kha Dodi*; and the night-long vigil of study on Shavuot evening.

Among these innovations was a set of three passages excerpted from the Zohar to be recited at each of the three Shabbat meals. These passages were designed to introduce the three songs composed as prelude to the meals by Rabbi Isaac Luria, the Ari, the foremost Safed mystic. *The Zohar passages constitute invitations to those present to prepare for the experience of the meals about to be partaken, the virtues of which will be extolled by the Ari's songs to follow.* In each of these passages there are different terms for God's presence (His *Shekhina*), Kabbalistic designations for aspects of the Deity, and the different qualities He is deemed to bring to the experience of the diners as they consume the food. Thus, these meals are not merely physical acts to satisfy body and palate. They are, in mystical thought, "meals of faith."

Now, at each meal, all three designations are recited. However, at each, one specific term pointing to the Shekhina's presence is invoked: the *Dakhakal Tapukhin Kaddishin*, "Field of Sacred Apples," for Friday evening; the *Atika Kadisha*, the "Holy Ancient One," for Saturday noon; and the *Ze-ayr Anpin*, the "Miniature Presence," for late Saturday afternoon.

What follows seeks to explicate the meaning of these three terms and what qualitative aspect of the *Shekhina's* presence are believed to be present at the repasts.

FOR FRIDAY EVENING

A pleasant energizing presence…

אַתְקִינוּ סְעוּדָתָא דִמְהֵימְנוּתָא שְׁלֵימָתָא. חֶדְוָתָא
דְמַלְכָּא קַדִּישָׁא. אַתְקִינוּ סְעוּדָתָא דְמַלְכָּא.
דָא הִיא סְעוּדָתָא וַחֲקַל תַּפּוּחִין קַדִּישִׁין.
[וְעַתִּיקָא קַדִּישָׁא זְעֵיר אַנְפִּין] אַתְיָן לְסַעֲדָא בַּהֲדֵהּ

Prepare the feast of perfect faith, the joy of the Holy King. Prepare the feast of the King. This is the Feast of the Field of Sacred Apples *(the Miniature Presence, and the Holy Ancient One). Come to feast with it.*

The expression *The Field of Sacred Apples* (*Dakhakal Taypukhin Kadishin*) is frequently found in Kabbalistic literature to refer to *The Shekhina*—the Divine Presence. It is based on the midrashic interpretation of the text where Jacob is described as coming to his father, Isaac, for a blessing:

וַיִּגַּשׁ וַיִּשַּׁק לוֹ וַיָּרַח אֶת רֵיחַ בְּגָדָיו וַיְבָרֲכֵהוּ
וַיֹּאמֶר: "רְאֵה רֵיחַ בְּנִי כְּרֵיחַ שָׂדֶה אֲשֶׁר בֵּרֲכוֹ ה'

And he (Jacob) came close to him (Isaac) and he (Jacob) kissed him and Isaac smelled Jacob's clothes and blessed him, saying, "Ah, the smell of my son is like the smell of the field that the Lord has blessed."[1]

The Midrash comments on this passage as follows:

אָמַר רַ' יוֹחָנָן: אֵין לְךָ דָבָר שֶׁרֵיחוֹ קָשֶׁה מִן הַשֶּׁטֶף הַזֶּה
שֶׁל עִזִּים, וְאַתָּ אַמַרְתָּ: "וַיָּרַח אֶת רֵיחַ בְּגָדָיו וַיְבָרֲכֵהוּ"!
אֶלָּא בְּשָׁעָה שֶׁנִּכְנַס אָבִינוּ יַעֲקֹב אֵצֶל אָבִיו נִכְנְסָה עִמּוֹ
גַּן עֵדֶן, הָדָא הוּא דַאֲמַר לֵהּ: "רְאֵה רֵיחַ בְּנִי כְּרֵיחַ שָׂדֶה
אֲשֶׁר בֵּרֲכוֹ ה'

Rabbi Yohanan said: nothing has a more offensive smell than skins stripped from goats, yet you say, "And he smelled the smell of his raiment, and blessed him!" However, when Jacob went in to his father, the Garden of Eden entered with him and

---

1. Genesis 27:27.

*it was to this that he (Isaac) alluded with the words "See the
smell of my son is the smell of the field which the Lord has
blessed."*[2]

According to this Midrash, it was the pleasant fragrance of an
apple orchard that Isaac smelled when his son approached him.
In the context of the Friday evening meal, then, *The Field of Sacred
Apples* as a designation for the *Shekhina*, the Divine Presence,
points to a divine property that pervades the meal. *From this sacred apple field there emanates "good fragrance" bestowed on the person partaking. It refreshes him, energizes him, brings pleasantness to
the atmosphere and to his demeanor.* Indeed, this is what occurs
when one partakes of a "meal of faith."

Folk memory and country lore are rich with reference to the
apple tree's virtues. For example, Celtic myth designates Ava-
lon, the Apple Vale, as a paradise where the hills are clothed with
trees bearing flowers and fruit together that emit pronounced
pleasant fragrance. An expert on the character and properties of
the apple tree, Glennie Kindred, wrote this:

> There is much to the humble apple tree that first meets
> the eye. It has a power beyond its stature, and enhances
> abilities beyond the everyday. When we open our hearts
> to the spirit of the apple tree, we have taken a first step
> in making the journey to gain hidden knowledge which
> it holds for us.

FOR SATURDAY NOON

*A presence that brings "light" into a world that yet needs to be
fixed…*

אַתְקִינוּ סְעוּדָתָא דִּמְהֵימְנוּתָא שְׁלֵימָתָא.
חֶדְוָתָא דְּמַלְכָּא קַדִּישָׁא. אַתְקִינוּ סְעוּדָתָא
דְּמַלְכָּא.   דָּא הִיא סְעוּדָתָא דְּעַתִּיקָא קַדִּישָׁא [וַחֲקַל
תַּפּוּחִין קַדִּישִׁין וּזְעֵיר אַנְפִּין.] אַתְיָן לְסַעֲדָא בַּהֲדֵהּ

---

2. Genesis Rabbah 22:27.

Prepare the feast of perfect faith, the joy of the Holy King. Pre-pare the feast of the King. This is the Feast of the Ancient Holy One *(the Field of Sacred Apples and the Miniature Pres-ence).* Come to feast with it.

In the Zohar, *The Ancient Holy One (Atika Kadisha)* is depicted as an emanation from the *Ein Sof,* the Deity itself; it is *sefira* (a "ray") that sits atop all the other sefirot. From this sefira various lights emanate with which *The Holy Ancient One* seeks to "brighten" the world, to repair its darkness and brokenness. These lights include the sefira *Khokhma* (wisdom) and the *sefira Bina* (understanding).

And so, when at the second meal of faith religious man in-vokes the presence of *The Ancient Holy One,* he expresses his faith that it is God's will to bring light into the world and to heal its fractures. Thus human beings are obliged to use *the wisdom* God has bestowed on them to realize that the very nature of the world lends itself to "fixing," that things can be made brighter than they've been. And it means that the *understanding* capacity which God has given mankind makes humans aware that they have the ability to fix the world's brokenness.

FOR LATE SATURDAY AFTERNOON

A blurred presence, yet one who is a source of abiding hope…

אַתְקִינוּ סְעוּדָתָא דִּמְהֵימְנוּתָא שְׁלֵימָתָא חֶדְוָתָא
דְּמַלְכָּא קַדִּישָׁא. אַתְקִינוּ סְעוּדָתָא דְּמַלְכָּא.
דָּא הִיא סְעוּדָתָא דִּזְעֵיר אַנְפִּין
א, קַדִּישָׁא וַחֲקַל תַּפּוּחִין קַדִּישִׁין.] אַתְיָן לְסַעֲדָא בַּהֲדֵהּ
[וְעַתִּיק

I shall prepare the feast of perfect faith, the joy of the Holy King. Prepare the feast of the King. This is the Feast of the Miniature Presence *(the Ancient Holy One and the Field of Sacred Apples).* Come to feast with it.

The expression *The Miniature Presence* indicates that though God's Presence is everywhere, it is not readily discernible on earth where events can be understood as a result of natural causes rather than as emanating from God. The lack of clarity in our perception of the *Shekhina* is as if we observed an event through a blurred, cloudy lens. The result is that we have diminished appreciation of God's pervasive benevolence. This אַסְפַּקְלָרְיָא שֶׁאֵינָהּ מְאִירָה, a lens that is unclear through which man attempts to grasp God's influence, is thus a reference to God as *The Miniature Presence*.

This third "Meal of Faith" on Saturday afternoon is a time of particular spiritual intensity born of a sense of unease about a God who seems to be elusive at this time of transition from holy day to weekday. It has a special atmosphere as now the Shabbat is about to come to conclusion and new challenges loom. On Friday evening we experienced God as the source of special "fragrance" in our lives. On Saturday noon, we experienced Him as a "source of light," a force for life's betterment, and now on Saturday afternoon we experience Him as somewhat elusive despite our faith in Him. This produces in us a pensive mood. The melodies are more meditative, and the words of Torah at the table more inward. There is awareness that this period is the end of something and the workdays ahead tension-full, unknown and perhaps hazardous. This is a time of spiritual longing as we reluctantly prepare to leave the world-that-ought-to-be to the testing reality of the world-that-is.

`To calm and reassure us in the face of this state of mind, Psalm 23 is always chanted at the *Seudah Shleesheet*. The Psalmist speaks of "the valley of the shadow...," but then he declares, "I will fear no evil for You are with me." Chanted here toward the end of the Shabbat, these words have particular force. Indeed, even though God appears to us as a "Miniature Presence" at *Seudah Shleesheet* time—distant, elusive—we nevertheless are told to take courage born of faith that we are not to be *fearful of the morrow for "You are with me." God will help us fashion this morrow.*

– Twenty-Seven –

EATING WITH "CLEAN HANDS"

*Among the things of the day is food. One does not simply pro-
ceed with satisfying the pangs of hunger. An initial preparation of the heart is necessary, undertaken by pausing and directing one's mind to the proper benediction before engaging
in the actual act of ingestion.*

*The preparation may include a ritual washing of the
hands, if the meal includes bread; but in any case, the act of
eating is preceded by a recitation of gratitude to God for the
specific gift at hand: "who brings forth food from the earth;"
"who creates the fruit of the earth;" "who creates the fruit of
the tree;" or more generally, "for all exists through his word."
The self is embodied in naturalness, in hunger and physical
need; but covenant theology raises the worshiper's consciousness to the spiritual domain, and it is in this realm that one
lives out one's natural urges.*

–Michael Fishbane, Sacred Attunement

The Handwashing Text at Mealtime

שְׂאוּ יְדֵיכֶם קֹדֶשׁ וּבָרְכוּ אֶת ה' ... וָאֶשָּׂא כַפַּי
אֶל מִצְוֹתֶיךָ אֲשֶׁר אָהָבְתִּי, וְאָשִׂיחָה בְחֻקֶּיךָ

בָּרוּךְ אַתָּה ה' אֱלֹהֵינוּ מֶלֶךְ הָעוֹלָם
אֲשֶׁר קִדְּשָׁנוּ בְּמִצְוֹתָיו וְצִוָּנוּ עַל נְטִילַת יָדַיִם

317

Lift up your hands toward heaven and bless the Lord.[1] *And I raise my hands (i.e., I reach out) for Your mitzvot which I love, and I study Your laws.*[2]

Blessed are You, O Lord, King of the universe, who has sanctified us through your mitzvot and has commanded us concerning the washing of the hands.

The Source for the Ritual's Text

This is found in the Code of Jewish Law as follows:[3]

חֲכָמִים תִּקְּנוּ לִיטוֹל הַיָּדַיִם בְּמַיִם כְּשֶׁרוֹצֶה לֶאֱכוֹל לֶחֶם

The rabbis ruled that one must wash one's hands in water when one wishes to eat bread.

In the condensed version of the *Shulkhan Arukh* by Soloman Ganzfried, the above dictum was amplified as follows:[4]

לְאַחַר שֶׁנָּטַל שְׁתֵּי יָדָיו, יְשַׁפְשְׁפָן בְּיַחַד וְיַגְבִּיהָן נֶגֶד רֹאשׁוֹ
כְּמוֹ שֶׁאָמַר הַכָּתוּב: "שְׂאוּ יְדֵיכֶם" וגו' וְקוֹדֶם שֶׁמְּנַגְּבָן יְבָרֵךְ "אֲשֶׁר
קִדְּשָׁנוּ בְּמִצְוֹתָיו וְצִוָּנוּ עַל נְטִילַת יָדָיִם"

After one has washed both hands, he should rub them together and then raise them upward as it is written "Lift up your hands (and bless the Lord)" and then before drying them, he should recite the blessing: "Blessed are You, Lord our God, who has sanctified us with His commandments and has commanded us concerning the washing of the hands" (netilat yadayim).[5]

---

1. Psalm 134:2.
2. Psalm 119:48.
3. *Shulkhan Arukh, Orakh Hayyim* 158:1.
4. Ganzfried, Solomon. *Shulkhan Arukh.* Hebrew Publishing Company, 1961; Vol. 1 40:5.
5. The Hebrew verb *natal*, used in the phrase *netilat yadayim*, has several related meanings, so that *netila* denotes taking, lifting up, carrying. The phrase *netilat lulav*, for example, signifies *taking up for the festive lulav*. Hence, it has been suggested that the biblical phrase *se-oo y'dakhim* (lift up your hands) is alluded to at the invocation recited when washing the

To the phrase "Lift up your hands (to heaven and praise the Lord)," the Rabbis added the phrase, "I raise my hands (to reach out) for Your mitzvot which I love and I study Your laws." And these two phrases constituted a prelude to the hand-washing blessing proper.

What Are the Purposes of this Handwashing Ritual?

1) Expressing Gratitude

The first phrase of the handwashing prelude is excerpted from Psalms:[6]

הִנֵּה בָּרְכוּ אֶת ה' כָּל עַבְדֵי ה' הָעֹמְדִים
בְּבֵית ה' בַּלֵּילוֹת: שְׂאוּ יְדֵיכֶם קֹדֶשׁ וּבָרְכוּ אֶת ה',
יְבָרֶכְךָ ה' מִצִּיּוֹן עֹשֵׂה שָׁמַיִם וָאָרֶץ

Now, bless the Lord, all you servants of the Lord who stand nightly in the house of the Lord. Lift up your hands toward heaven and bless the Lord. *May the Lord,* maker of heaven and earth, *bless you from Zion.*

The reference to "hands" here, no doubt, was the initial reason for choosing this phrase for the handwashing ritual. More was involved. The rabbinic authorities had likely meant to express a vital message about the ultimate source of the food which humans consume. It is a Power—not man—who provides the soil, the seed, the sun, the rain which makes food possible. Humans use these basic resources in preparation of his food. Thus, "lift up your hands towards heaven"—to God—and thank Him for providing the resources that make your sustenance possible. Man partners with God in this process.

2) Mitzvah with Knowledge of its Purpose

The second phrase of the handwashing prelude is excerpted

---

hands before meals (*nesiat yadayim* = *netilat yadayim*).
6. Psalms 134: 1-2.

from Psalms as follows: [7]

וְאֶשְׁמְרָה תוֹרָתְךָ תָמִיד לְעוֹלָם וָעֶד. וְאֶתְהַלְּכָה
בָרְחָבָה כִּי פִקֻּדֶיךָ דָרָשְׁתִּי. וַאֲדַבְּרָה בְעֵדֹתֶיךָ, נֶגֶד
מְלָכִים וְלֹא אֵבוֹשׁ. וְאֶשְׁתַּעֲשַׁע בְּמִצְוֹתֶיךָ אֲשֶׁר אָהָבְתִּי
וְאֶשָּׂא כַפַּי אֶל מִצְוֹתֶיךָ אֲשֶׁר אָהָבְתִּי, וְאָשִׂיחָה בְחֻקֶּיךָ

*I will obey Your teaching regularly. I will walk about at ease
for I have turned to Your precepts. I will speak of Your decrees
and not be ashamed in the presence of kings. I will delight in
Your commandments which I love. I will lift up my hands for
Your commandments which I love. And I will study Your
laws.*

As was the case with the first phrase of the prelude, this
phrase was chosen for the handwashing context because of its
reference to "hands." Here again, more is involved. One theme
of Psalm 119 is expression of unflagging loyalty to the Torah and
the mitzvot: "I will obey Your teaching forever (verse 44)...I will
speak of Your decrees (verse 46)...I will delight in Your commandments (verse 47)." Yes, fervent commitment to mitzvot and
punctilious observance of them are vital in the religious life.
However, this very same Psalm 119 has a complementary take
on this mitzvah matter, to wit:

Open my eyes that I may *perceive* the wonder of Your teaching
(verse 18)...Make me *understand* the ways of Your precepts that
I may *study* your wondrous acts (verse 27)...*Teach me*, O Lord,
the way of Your laws, that I may observe them to the utmost
(verse 33).

Herein is a second purpose for inclusion of the second phrase
of the handwashing prelude, "I will lift up my hands for Your
commandments which I love" The observant religionist, by lifting his hands, is reaching for the mitzvot. He embraces them for
his religious life because he loves doing them. But then he adds,
"I will study Your laws." It is not enough to "love" the mitzvot

---

7. Psalms 119:44-48.

in the abstract, to loyally but mindlessly observe them. One must study them which renders knowledge about their purposes; one most understand the underlying reasons for them; one must grasp their implications. Indeed, there is love in understanding.

3) Performing a Mitzvah with "Clean Hands"

In biblical times when the Tabernacle ritual was in effect, the priests were required to "come clean" to their work as officiants. Thus, Leviticus tells us that when Aaron entered the Tabernacle he had to shed his vestments, *bathe his body in water,* and then bring the offerings on the altar.[8] Washing oneself here was a ritual way to cleanse oneself from contamination, which then allowed the performance of sacred work.

Washing "cleanses" one from personal shortcoming not merely in the physical sense but in nonphysical sense as well. Thus, for example, we are told in Deuteronomy that when a deceased person was found lying in the open and the identity of the slayer unknown, the elders of the nearest town were summoned to account for the terrible occurrence:[9]

> "All the elders of town nearest to the slain person *shall wash their hands* and make this declaration: '*Our hands did not shed this blood nor did our eyes see it done*...thus you will be absolved...and remove from your midst guilt for the blood of the innocent, for you will be doing what is right in the sight of the Lord.'"

Thus, washing the hands was a ritual way of disassociating oneself from evil behavior and seeking to establish one's good character. This notion is again attested to by the Psalmist, who declares that he has lived his life "without blame," did not "consort with scoundrels or mix with hypocrites," who "detested the company of evil men and did not consort with the wicked." And then he asserts: "*I wash my hands in innocence,* and walk around

---

8. Leviticus 16:23-24.
9. Deuteronomy 21.

Your altar, O Lord." Here the handwashing metaphor symbolizes *assertion of good moral character, which legitimates man's ap-*
proaching God in worship, i.e. "walking around the altar raising
my voice in thanksgiving and telling all your wonders."[10]

---

10. Psalms 26:1-7.

– Twenty-Eight –

SACRED WATERS/THE MIKVEH
From Abandoned Past to Embraced Present

Immersion in water brings a regeneration because dissolution of a person immersed is followed by a new birth when the person emerges.

-Mircae Eliade, The Sacred and the Profane

When experiencing the waters over one's head, a person enters an environment in which he/she cannot breathe and cannot live more than moments. It is the "begone" of that which has gone before. As one emerges from the gagging waters into the clear air, one begins to breathe anew—and live anew.

-Maurice Lamm, Becoming a Jew

Personal Experience

My grandfather was steeped in the Hasidic tradition, which required immersion in a Mikveh (a ritual bath) every late Friday afternoon in preparation for the onset of Shabbat. Since I was under his jurisdiction on religious matters during my youth, every Friday I had to appear at the neighborhood Mikveh to immerse myself along with my grandfather and the other adult observers of the ritual. Zayde, as he was then called, was there to meet me and supervise the proceedings. He made sure I recited the proper blessing and immersed myself in the water fully unclothed and completely underwater. I did this with him for some eight consecutive years—from age eight to sixteen— every single Friday. How vivid is my recollection of his person as we left the Mikveh building together en route to our nearby synagogue: his face with still damp beard glowed. He had been "cleansed" and was now able to proceed "unblemished," as it were, and thus able to enter into the Sabbath.

At the time I was but dimly aware of what "cleansed" in the above sense meant, what the ritual was all about. As I matured and experienced Mikveh via my wife's practice and had the occasion to actively participate in construction of a Mikveh at the University of Judaism, I delved into the matter in detail for some insight into the meaning and purpose of the Mikveh. What follows is what I discovered.

What is a Mikveh?

The term means "gathering of water." The basic scriptural text for the Mikveh is:

אַךְ מַעְיָן וּבוֹר, מִקְוֵה מַיִם, יִהְיֶה טָהוֹר

Only a spring, and cistern, a collection of water shall be clean.[1]

"Shall be clean" is understood by the rabbis to mean "shall be cleansing," that is, one who had suffered contamination remains unclean until he has immersed himself in the Mikveh. In the biblical and early rabbinic period the reference is to one who has suffered contamination by coming into contact with a deceased person, a dead animal, a bodily emission or other source of physical negative specified in Leviticus. One who was affected in these ways was not allowed to enter the temple or eat sacred food (e.g., sacrificial meat) until he had submerged himself in the Mikveh. I remember quite vividly the scene in Jerusalem where below the steps leading to the gates through which pilgrims entered the temple grounds were the archaeological remnant of

---

1. Leviticus 11:36.

numerous mikvaot in which the worshippers were undoubtedly immersed before they could walk through those gates.

After destruction of the temple, the law of Mikveh for the traditional Jew was applicable to a menstruant. After her monthly period and after counting seven "clean days," a woman had to be immersed in a Mikveh before she could resume marital relations with her husband. The Mikveh law also applied to a bride before marriage, to a woman following birth of a child, to the procedure for conversion to Judaism, and, as a custom, for men to achieve spiritual purity prior to the Shabbat, Jewish holidays, and especially before Yom Kippur.

In the twenty-first century the usage of Mikveh has been significantly expanded amongst the non-orthodox. These usages include a wide variety of life transitions and occasions, such as a groom before marriage, at birthdays, clergy ordination etc. Usage has also been invoked for "healing" — to mark the changes and challenges occasioned by illness or loss, such as after a divorce, a period of mourning, a miscarriage.

The Essential Significance of the Mikveh Experience

All religious traditions use water to denote change, transformation, rebirth, healing. Jewish tradition regarding Mikveh shares the notion.

Mircae Eliade depicts the phenomenology of water as such and how it relates to human beings. [2] Water by nature is unorganized, unstructured; it has no distinct forms; it is an undifferentiated mass, an inchoate mixture. Hence, immersion in water signifies regression to the pre-formal, to the undifferentiated mode of pre-existence, to its primordial state when time did not yet exist and creation was yet to occur. Immersion in water, then, is equivalent to a dissolution of forms, while emersion represents the fashioning of forms. This is why

2. Eliade, Mircae. "Structure and Aquatic Symbolism," *The Sacred and the Profane*. Harcourt Brace, 1959; p. 129-132.

the symbolism of the waters implies both death and rebirth. Contact with them brings regeneration—on the one hand because dissolution is followed by rebirth, and on the other because immersion engenders and multiples the potential of life. Thus immersion in water is equivalent not to a final extinction but to a temporary reincorporation into the indistinct, followed by a new creation, a new life, a new person.

Maurice Lamm, in explaining the purposes of Mikveh, applies Eliade's paradigm. He writes:

> Jewish tradition prescribes a profound symbol. It instructs the conversion candidate to place himself or herself in a radically different physical environment—in water rather than air. This leaves the person floating— momentarily suspended without breathing—substituting the usual forward-moving nature and purposeful stride that characterize his or her waking movements with an aimlessness, a weightlessness, a detachment from the former environment. Individuality, passion, ego—all are submerged in the metamorphosis from the larval state of the present to a new existence.[3]

This is the function of the Mikveh for those who use it for a variety of purposes—traditional and contemporary—enumerated above. As a religious act, *sub*merging oneself, naked and fully under the water, touches the whole person. It symbolizes for some internal change, for others altered status, for yet others ridding oneself of the old and *em*erging into the new. In a word, it "swallows up," as it were, the old and gives birth to the new.

This is why Mikveh marks transitions in a person's life. Anthropologists refer to these times as "liminal" or "between times." This state in life is common in virtually all persons and societies. It represents a move from past status to a new one as an individual, as a family member and as a member of society. Entering marriage from singlehood, for example, requires a

---

3. Lamm, Maurice. *Becoming a Jew.* Jonathan David Publishers, 1991.

tunnel of time, a rite of passage—in this case Mikveh immersion—which eases the passage and acknowledges the change taking place in one's self-identity, behavior and attitude.

As Maurice Lamm has put it, immersion in the Mikveh's pool of water represents the spiritual drama of "death and rebirth" in one's life. Experiencing the waters over one's head, one enters an environment in which one cannot breathe and cannot live more than moments. It is the "death," the begone, of that which has gone before. As one emerges from the gagging waters into the clear air, one begins to breathe anew—and live anew.

ADDENDUM
A Conservative Mikveh: A Tale of Origins

A lifelong inclination of mine has been to seek to translate personal experience and reflection about religious ideas into concrete undertakings. Such has been the case with the Mikveh matter depicted in this article. An illustration of this is the following I wrote when serving as dean of continuing education at the University of Judaism in Los Angeles:

Often in the cloudy mists of time, important events take on fanciful form, even legendary character, and obscure what actually happened in real time.

Such is the case about the origin of the Mikveh at the University of Judaism in Los Angeles. This article seeks to tell its story for the record. I tell it also not only because it is admittedly in part a personal one, but because it is a story that reveals a significant development in the religious life of Los Angeles Jewry during the past two decades.

In 1983, the University was about to construct its second building on its campus on Mulholland Drive in Los Angeles' Bel Air. At the time, I served as dean of continuing education and, as such, responsible for the Conversion-to-Judaism program on behalf of the Conservative Movement. Integral to the conversion process was the requirement of immersion in a Mikveh. And so, though the orthodox Mikveh was not built to welcome people to Judaism, we had been using it uneasily out of necessity. At times the Mikveh's sponsors' ambivalence about our usage and the scheduling constraints imposed forced us to use the ocean off the Santa Monica shores. The matter suddenly, though not unexpectedly, came to a head: the Mikveh's authorities ruled definitively that our conservative conversions were illegitimate and we could therefore no longer use their Mikveh.

Since at that very juncture the University of Judaism was about to build its new structure on Mulholland Drive, I saw an opportunity. Perturbed as I was by the orthodox decision, I came to Dr. David Lieber, president of the university at the time, and urged that we incorporate a Mikveh of our own in our new structure. I stressed that this would give us unfettered jurisdiction over our conversion process, that we would be certain that it conform to the highest halachic standards, that it would be an aesthetic place, warm and welcoming, and also a major contribution not only to the Conservative Movement, but to the Jewish community as a whole. Above all, we would be free from our unacceptable dependence on the orthodox once and for all.

Dr. Lieber's response: "If you want a Mikveh, Jack, then put it in a closet in your office." Needless to say, I walked away from that encounter dismayed. Dr. Elliot Dorff, the UJ's provost and professor of Jewish thought, told me that Dr. Lieber's negative attitude about the Mikveh reflected the posture of many of his colleagues of his era, including Jacob Agus, a leading Baltimore conservative rabbi, author of a work on Rav Kook and other scholarly works. When Dr. Dorff had occasion to discuss the matter as a possibility at the UJ, Rabbi Agus indicated how outdated and uncalled for was a Mikveh at a "modern" religious institution.

A few months later, Dr. Gerson Cohen, then chancellor of the Jewish Theological Seminary and at the time also of the University of Judaism, was visiting in Los Angeles. I told him about the orthodox authorities banning us from using their

Mikveh. I explained that even though we conformed to the halachic requirements and procedures in the conversion process and usage of their facility, we had been banned simply because our activity in this realm was conducted by us conservatives. Dr. Cohen was perturbed.

The chancellor then proceeded to urge of Dr. Lieber that the UJ incorporate a Mikveh in our new building. He assented. As I sat in his office discussing the matter, Dr. Lieber picked up the phone and called Jack Gindi, who was in charge of constructing the new building, and told him to incorporate a Mikveh into the project. Mr. Gindi agreed then and there. Thus was born a Mikveh at the University of Judaism.

We then proceeded to plan the facility. Eager to be certain that it conform to precise halachic standards, I supplemented my own experience with the matter by bringing into the process Rabbi Ben Zion Bergman of the UJ Talmud faculty, a respected halachic expert. Together we surveyed various mikvaot around the country for the necessary physical and procedural requirements. We personally visited a traditional Mikveh in Long Beach where we directly observed the water flow system, the ice compartment adjacent to the main water pool, the required amount of water for the pool, etc. We recorded our inquiries and observations, which equipped us to proceed. We then met with the architect and builder, who incorporated our concepts into the Mikveh project. Our approach, I need to add, included heavy emphasis on ample, comfortable, well-equipped elements for the place as well as striking aesthetic features.

A humorous aside: when the place was about ready to be used, to Rabbi Bergman's astonishment, I personally tested the Mikveh by immersing myself into the water to examine the aperture between the adjacent ice compartment and the pool proper to be sure that it was open, thus making possible the two waters to mingle—an halachic requirement.

For the next decade the Mikveh at the UJ operated under the aegis of the Department of Continuing Education in the context of its Introduction to Judaism program. This enterprise was expanded considerably when Louis Miller, a devoted UJ supporter, agreed to my proposal to fund a full-time program director in the person of Rabbi Neil Weinberg. Thus, the "Louis and Judith Introduction to Judaism Program" came into being. In 1993 supervision of the Mikveh became the responsibility of the conservative Rabbinical Assembly and the Introduction to Judaism venture became the responsibility of the Conservative Ziegler School of Rabbinic Studies.

Throughout these twenty-five years, this Mikveh facility has become a mecca for thousands of converts who have adopted the Jewish way of life. It has served as a powerful spiritual experience for brides-to-be, for marital purity purposes, for men and women during crucial times of transition in their lives, and for a variety of other human situations in which inner calm and healing have been sought. And this all in an attractive, well-appointed setting in accordance with the principle of *hiddur mitzvah* (the aesthetic enhancement of the mitzvah), along with a warm and welcoming approach toward all who have come to avail themselves of the facility.

And finally, though always open to the community at large, to soon-to-be-converted Jews and Jews of all or no denominational persuasion, this Mikveh throughout the years has functioned in accordance with full adherence to the dictates of traditional Jewish law, yet with an openness to all—a distinctive hallmark of the Conservative Movement.

– Twenty-Nine –

THE HUMAN BRAIN AND THE FIVE SENSES IN RELIGIOUS EXPERIENCE

Robert Fulghum, author of All I Really Need to Know I Learned in Kindergarten, *was, among other pursuits, a high school teacher and a wise mentor for adult living. At one class session he had a human brain brought into the room. The startled students were asked to see it up close and touch it, whereupon Fulghum explained:*

> *I have one of these things between my ears. It is made up entirely of raw meat at the moment. It is fueled by yesterday's baloney sandwich, potato chips, and chocolate milk. And everything I am doing at the moment—everything I have ever done or will do—passes through this lump. It is the most mysterious thing on earth.*
>
> *I've come to understand the mechanical work of the brain—stimulating, breathing, moving blood, directing protein traffic. It's all chemistry and electricity. A motor.*
>
> *This three-pound raw-meat motor also contains all the limericks I know, a recipe for how to cook a turkey, the remembered smell of my junior high locker room, all my sorrows, the ability to double-clutch a pickup truck, the face of my wife when she was young, the Prologue to Chaucer's Canterbury Tales, the sound of the first cry of my firstborn son, the cure for hiccups, the words to the fight song of St. Olaf's College, fifty years' worth of dreams, how to tie my shoes, the taste of cod-liver oil, an image of Van Gogh's Sunflowers, and a*

working understanding of the Dewey Decimal System. It's all there in the MEAT.

One cubic centimeter of brain contains ten billion bits of information and it processes five thousand bits a second. And somehow it evolved over a zillion years from a molten block of rock, Earth, which will itself fall into the sun someday and be no more. Why? How?

That's what I think.

"Oooo-wow," chorus the students. The teacher is in a groove.

Once again the brain is passed from hand to hand, slowly and solemnly. Once again it is very quiet. The Mystery of Mysteries is present, and it includes us.

In the Service of Religion

The truly miraculous character of the human brain which the person of faith believes only God could have planted in the human body in the process of man's creation is depicted quite graphically in this Fulgham classic. It is this wonderous physical entity that organizes, records and prompts expression of a person's experiences with the senses God has bestowed.

The rabbis knew this well for purposes of the religious enterprise. The Talmud tells us this:

טַעֲמוּ וּרְאוּ כִּי־טוֹב ה' ...
שְׁלֹשָׁה מְשִׁיבִין דַּעְתּוֹ שֶׁל אָדָם וְאֵלוּ הֵן: קוֹל וּמַרְאֶה וְרֵיחַ

Taste and see that the Lord is good (Psalm 34:9). Three things influence a person's sensibilities, and these are: sound, sight and taste (our additions: smell and touch).

—Berakhot 57b

Here are but three of the five senses which God has embedded in the body of a human being; the five are: *sight, smell, sound, taste* and *touch*. The vignettes which follow, gathered together from my own personal experience, seek to illustrate the tangible power of these physical senses in the pursuit of the religious life. The depictions of the physical character of the five senses as such which caption each "sense" are taken from a volume about human anatomy in my library.

SIGHT

The human eye is an exceptional tool for gathering light; it can distinguish among 500 shades of gray and spot the light of a star millions of light years away. Seeing is a function of the brain which makes sense of shapes and symbols putting them together like a jigsaw puzzle, organizing fragments into a coherent whole.

Stained Glass Windows

As one looked out upon the stately, magnificent stained-glass windows that rim the circular back of the sanctuary of Congregation B'nai Israel in Pittsburgh where I served as rabbi for a decade, a striking scene confronted the observer. One was moved by the riot of color, the undulating design, the jewel-like luminous flow that brought streams of light into the place. The windows expressed the eternal values of Judaism as exemplified by the lives and teachings of its greatest sons.

The roll call began with Abraham, idol breaker and father of monotheism. It rose to the incomparable Moses, Prince of the Prophets, then proceeded from Isaiah to Jeremiah, from Amos to Micah, and from Hosea to Jonah. The last window was reserved for Elijah, who by tradition has been endeared to his people as herald of the Messianic Age.

Shabbat and Festival Paintings

Shelley Blumenthal, a member of our Pittsburgh congregation, was an artist of great skill and imagination. At my prompting she produced a set of striking and captivating paintings of Jewish religious practices, objects and scenes: the candlesticks on a Shabbat table setting, the spice box and *havdalah* settings, the scenes of Passover, Shavuot, Sukkot, Chanukah and Purim. Reproductions of these paintings have been on the walls of our home through the years as well as on those of our three sons. Significantly, as well, Shavuot, Sukkot and Chanukah reproductions grace the chapel walls of our Etz Chaim synagogue in Thousand Oaks, California, presented by Leah and me in honor of our grandchildren's B'nai Mitzvah occasions. "A sight to see."

A Sukkah: From Persia to America

While yet a student in Rabbinical School, I served as student-rabbi in Mexico City for a fledgling congregation. My diary recorded an experience with a Persian sukkah transplanted to Mexico. Invited to visit during an intermediate Sukkot evening, I was startled upon entering the scene of the huge enclosure. Intricately designed, colorful Persian rugs constituted the wall coverings throughout as well as the floor. A riot of fresh fruit and vegetables hung everywhere from the slatted roof. Colorful plastic balls surrounded the lit bulbs, giving the whole place a multicolored glow. The aroma of burning incense pervaded the place. A variety of exotic foods graced the colorful covered tables. The required Hebrew liturgy for the sukkah along with rabbinic quotes and pictures of the Land of Israel adorned the walls and hung from the sukkah top. Some two dozen Sephardic Jews were all dressed in their finest—the men in suit and tie, the women in their best outfits and sparkling jewelry. The *ushpizin* (the imagined ancestral guests) were invited into the sukkah and the blessings over the food chanted with the traditional moving Sephardic lilt.

As I stood in that sukkah, my eyes beheld a scene that seemed to picture some kind of Persian Shangri-La. The experience made an indelible impression, clearly retained somewhere in my brain. And so, when later, as a full-fledged rabbi in Pittsburgh, I determined to make a "big deal" about our synagogue sukkah, something like the Persian one—American-style.

I persuaded our sisterhood women to expand the place in size and elaborate its decorative elements. Fred Siger, one of the congregants, was in the wholesale produce business, beginning his working day at 4:30 a.m. in the downtown wholesale market. He provided the women with a massive amount of colorful fruit, vegetables and flowers with which they adorned the place. Fred's wife, Thelma, who served as chairwoman of the sukkah enterprise, supplemented Fred's contribution with colorful lighting and rugs along with an array of varied additional decorative items. The place was a sight to see, its color and aroma drawing many a congregant into its space.

SMELL

Because aromas are processed by the same part of the brain that handles memories and emotions—the temporal lobe—we respond to them with rare intensity. Decades later, a passing scent may summon memory of our first-grade classroom, one so vivid that we seem transported across time and space.

Aroma Permeates a Summer Camp

Rabbi Zalman Schachter (no relation to the author), one of our era's leading innovators of religious practice, once held the post of "Religious Environmentalist" at Camp Ramah in Connecticut when I served as "Prayer Specialist" one summer. One of Zalman's goals was to transmit to the campers some of the sensory, non-verbal experiences that go with the adjective *shabbosdik* (the Shabbat feel, atmosphere). Every Friday in the late afternoon, for example, as the campers were dressing for Shabbat and the special Friday night meal was cooking in the kitchen, he arranged to take all the available fans and set them up to blow the aroma of the food all over the camp, so as to permeate the air with a Shabbat feel. Zalman felt that linking this non-verbal experience to Shabbat would store the experience in a much deeper place than would words alone—a place, the incredibly retentive brain—where the smell of special food would be stored for good; this could well cause the kids to recollect and re-experience Erev Shabbat later in life.

A Redolent Odor

I was ten years old. The sexton of a synagogue in my Brooklyn, New York, neighborhood "employed" me each Friday afternoon at the munificent "salary" of three cents. My task was to gather the scattered prayerbooks and Bibles throughout the sanctuary and put them back neatly in the designated shelves—this in preparation for the forthcoming Shabbos services. As I did my work, I remember well the awesome atmosphere of that empty sanctuary—the silence, the imagined echoes of the chanted prayers, and especially, the redolent odor emanating from the worn prayer shawls, the constantly fingered books and Bibles, and the musty smell of the old rickety shelves.

When I grew up, I was the Rabbi of a synagogue in Pittsburgh whose cemetery I had to visit, alas. In the early years, services for the deceased were conducted in the chapel on the cemetery's grounds. In my day, that practice was discontinued with the services conducted at the funeral home in the city. Hence, the cemetery chapel was abandoned, alone and forgotten and though deteriorating, remained intact.

During these visits I could not resist the urge to open the place's creaking door, enter and walk around exploring. I would sit for a few minutes in quiet meditation gazing at the old seats, the still standing though bended bookshelf, the empty ark with its tattered lion figures crowning it, while inhaling the places redolent musty odor. These chapel visits reminded me of the "holy work" of a ten-year-old.

SOUND

In South Sudan, near the border of Ethiopia, a tribe known as the Mabaan reportedly live in a place of such quiet that their ability to hear has become astonishingly acute. Legend has it that even the oldest Mabaan can make out the words of another tribesman whispering to him from across a wide field.

The Trombone and the Shofar

On Shabbat afternoon I was in the habit of strolling through various neighborhoods adjacent to where I lived. One such stroll was through the Larimer Avenue section of East Liberty in Pittsburgh—a heavily black enclave. A set of ruminations took hold of me as I observed the people and mood of the place.

The cluttered streets, the boarded-up windows, the cracked pavements, and the neglected trees testified to the neighborhood's run-down condition. It was a sunny, warm afternoon. Children played languidly in the streets; young mothers cradled their infants on the front steps; men sat in sleeveless undershirts on rickety porches; old folks stared aimlessly from open doors leading directly on the sidewalk.

In the midst of this quiet, dreamy atmosphere, I heard a band playing in one of the backyards. It was muted, rhythmic, pulsating music. The electric guitar, drums and trombone played in beautiful harmony. The whole block seemed to be listening to the soulful music, attuned to its beat, focused on that spot in the backyard.

I stood and listened…and listened. I could not help thinking that in the midst of all this poverty and misery, this band was sounding the heart of these people. Its restrained yet passionate rhythm sounded like a cry for help, the trombone especially like a fervent plea: "Save us from these wretched surroundings! Extricate us from this desolation!"

I headed home for the Mincha afternoon service into our cool, carpeted, richly paneled, immaculate chapel. Instead of reveling in the stark contrast between the Larimer and East Liberty neighborhood locales, I thought about the soon-to-be-observed High Holy Days, and could not help but envision a connection between the Larimer condition and the Jewish religious one, between the piercing trombone and Rosh Hashana's chief symbol, the shofar. For we Jews, too, are mired in a somewhat dilapidated spiritual condition. Many of us remain consumed with hostility and jealousy; some are lonely and friendless; others are torn by warring inner impulses; some parents have lost connection with their children; religious practice show signs of neglect; learning and piety are increasingly declining.

And so, I thought about the shofar soon-to-be sounded, its signals transmitted from the eardrum to their designated section in the brain. I mused that we Jews need to listen to its soulful blasts and attune ourselves to its staccato rhythm. For the shofar is, in a real sense much like the Larimer trombone—a cry for help—a Jewish cry—a plea to extricate ourselves from our rundown spiritual condition. And then I prayed that even as the Larimers of America have thankfully spawned urban renewal, so may Rosh Hashanah spur inner Jewish renewal.

Ever since hearing those Pittsburgh shofar sounds, whenever I hear a shofar sound, I'm transferred back to the Larimer Avenue section of East Liberty in Pittsburgh.

A Shabbat Song

There are special Shabbat *Zemirot* (table songs) one of which is for Friday evening, the *Kol Mekadesh Shevee-ee* ("all who fittingly sanctify the seventh day…will have great reward"). This song was chanted with unfailing regularity every Friday evening at our table in its traditional melodic form. I once calculated the song as being at least one hundred and fifty years old.

When in college my son Judah once heard the *Kol Mekadesh Shevee-ee* at the Shabbat table of a family he had been visiting. It was in the same melodic chant he was reared with. His familiarity with that table song and the melody in which it was chanted—far away from his own home—brought him back to Shabbat at home with his family. When Judah told this to me, I was reminded of the biblical passage in which Jacob tells his sons (one of whom was Judah!) to take *mizimrat ha-aretz* "from the choice products of the land" as a gift to the vizier of Egypt.[1] Jacob meant honey, wine, nuts and almonds. The sages, however, interpreted the words *zimrat haaretz* to mean *zemirot haaretz*, "songs of the land."[2] Take with you your favorite melodies from your father's table, Jacob was saying, and they will remind you of your home while you are away.

TASTE

There are more than ten thousand taste buds spread over the tongue, palate and inner cheek. The buds send a signal to the brain which then determines whether the food is "safe" or not. In a part of the brain, tastes get fixed to an emotional reaction — to "distaste" for a rotten apple or delight in a sweet apple pie.

Eating in Honor of Shabbat

Shabbat and festival meals were partaken at the table of my grandparents throughout my youth. That the food was abundant was to understate the case. A feature of these meals: before each course, all of us at the table had to say, *l'kovod shabbos*, that is, "I'm eating this food in honor of the Sabbath." This was said before the fish course, before the soup, before the chicken, before the dessert. I can produce witnesses to testify to the truth of that ritual.

A Breakfast

Once in a conversation with a Chabad rabbinic couple, I contended that much of Chabad's success was due to its *kugel* (noodle pudding delicacy) and ample food offered to its followers, not its "theology." To which the Chabad rabbitzen (rabbi's wife) responded, "The kugel is our theology."

It did not take a rocket scientist to get the point. And so, I introduced "A Theology of Food" into our morning minyan

---

1. Genesis 43:11.
2. Genesis Rabbah 10:11.

experience. With the financial backing of Mr. Sam Deaktor, the owner of a chain of Giant Eagle supermarkets in Pittsburgh and a minyan regular, we instituted a full-blown breakfast following each service. The food fare was more than adequate to start the day with. John and Ann Harris, our resident caretakers, prepared the repasts and were a benign presence in our midst. Sam provided a shot of whiskey for everybody each morning. (An aside: when at the beginning stages of our breakfasts, Sam offered me a drink from his colorful whiskey bottle. I demurred, saying "I don't drink that stuff, I don't like the taste." To which Sam responded, "What kind of rabbi are you?" From then on, I drank from Sam's bottle—as little as I could get away with!).

Camaraderie developed each morning around the table. Animated discussion about affairs of the day and religious matters was constant. Often arguments over a variety of subjects took place. Cantor Heiser, our sexton Reverend Mordecani Haalman and I served as Jewish and religious "resources" for the group about the morning and other prayer services. The mourner's kaddish phenomenon was analyzed in some detail by me. Special guests, visitors in the city and non-synagogue members were regularly present. An average of thirty worshippers attended the daily minyan throughout the ten years of my tenure in Pittsburgh.

This all primarily for the taste of food!

TOUCH

Of all the senses, touch is the most difficult to fathom. With hundreds of nerve endings in every square inch of the skin, the body functions like an antenna receiving a constant stream of information. Take the fingers alone. They are, in effect, living sensors having some dozens of receptors in just one-sixth of a square inch. Moreover, these receptors are varied, each having its own function, enabling a person to feel texture, temperature, wetness, vibrations, pressure and pain. The human finger is the most sensitive touch sensor in existence.

"O, God, There You Are"

The Hasidic sage, Nakhman of Bratzlav, once said that if you want to know God, are lonely for Him because you are out of touch with Him, you can always touch your own pulse and realize, "O, there You are!" This is a "touching" practice I have long since adopted.

The pulse and the heart rate are the same. When one touches the pulse, one experiences the reality of the physical heart. The heart is a vital organ, absolutely essential to our physical lives. In a basic way, it is the center of our bodily being because it pumps life-sustaining blood throughout the body. As Scripture says, "The life of the flesh is the blood,"[3] and "Above all else, guard your heart, for it is the wellspring of life."[4] This all the work of God, "It is You who created my innards."[5]

Yes, God gave man life, and so, when one is in search of Him, to acknowledge and thank Him for the very gift of life and for much else, one needs but touch one's own pulse and say, "O, there You are."

A Small Talis

The Shabbat and holiday services with my Zayde (grandfather) at our synagogue featured, among much else, "tzitzis inspection." This little drama required me, a preteen, to prove that I was wearing under my shirt the required four-fringed garment (*talis katan*, "small talis") to be kissed at the designated passages in the prayer service—a sign of one's loyalty to and affection for the good God. And so, I unbuttoned my shirt, drew the tzitzis out, showed them to Zayde, he nodded in approval, I rebuttoned the shirt. I passed the test.

Ever since, whenever I touch and kiss the fringes of my adult talis, I am transported to a grandfather's "tzitzis inspection."

---

3. Leviticus 17:11.
4. Proverbs 4:23.
5. Psalm 139:13f.

Thirty

OLD WINE IN NEW VESSELS
Religious Creativity

Creativity leaves us when we are imprisoned by precedent. It is in daring—to be outrageous, to play with the least probable possibilities, the ones more weird and spiritual—where we may find answers.

These possible forms dance before the mind's eye and from that vision emerges an unexpected form with its creative proposal and therefore its new way to understand and to map reality.

–Zalman Schachter

The Unusual

One day some years ago during a summer at Camp Ramah in Connecticut, I suddenly beheld an unusual sight: there he was, a rather tall man dressed in a long black caftan, bearded, with side curls and a *shtreimel*, a round headpiece atop his luminous face. It was Rabbi Zalman Schachter, the Scholar-in-Residence for the summer at our Conservative summer camp.

It was Friday, late afternoon, at the Camp's Shabbat worship service, which he conducted. He swayed from side-to-side, forward and back, his arms reaching upward, his resonant voice chanting the liturgy, his *niggunim* (wordless melodies), engulfing the entire camp population. The usual orderly, dignified and carefully orchestrated assemblage seemed stunned and puzzled—and appeared to be deeply affected.

The next day's Shabbat morning service repeated the Friday evening experience with an added touch: instead of the congregants standing still and erect for the *amida* (the silent prayer), Reb Zalman invited those who wished to go off into the shaded tree area surrounding the worship setting and stand there as long as they wished in prayer—silent or otherwise.

The Havdalah service Reb Zalman conducted was equally unusual. This was ordinarily quite moving at Ramah, only this time the singing and swaying had additional quiet passion as Zalman's sonorous voice carried all of us away with him. An unusual feature was added to the ceremony: an empty coke bottle was used to hold the Havdalah candle. Some smirked at this so-called innovation. Zalman later explained that this kind of ritual artifact was a way to connect an old religious ceremony with an object of contemporary familiarity so as to creatively integrate the traditional with the modern. Some were persuaded by his explanation, some were not.

There were a number of other unusual rituals and comments Zalman delivered to campers and counselors during that summer (and elsewhere throughout the years). Their purpose was to synthesize the traditional with the contemporary in order to revive and revivify Jewish practice and idea for our time, to make them relevant and compelling for the modern Jew, "It's no good," Zalman urged, "educating youngsters to be Jewish for 1815! We have to give up nostalgia. We have to reinterpret our tradition for our new and ever-changing society."

More of the Unusual

At times, we might chant the prayers in English, Zalman suggested. This helps give the worshipper a sense of really talking with God because he is speaking directly with words he himself grasps. Rabbi Nahman of Bratzlav had urged his Hasidim to sometimes chant their prayers in the Yiddish vernacular, their native language. Most of us pray through a "glass darkly," and so it appears legitimate to use the understood vernacular periodically. And more:

Our ritual can be harnessed to teach social values and awareness of others. Blessings, for example, can be used, not only as a
way to foster gratitude to God, but also to fellow man. Thus; when
we bless the food we are about to eat, we might include the
farmer, or the baker, or the truck driver, who were involved in the
process of getting our food to the table.

If recitation of the entire Amida is too much, either because of
length or constant repetition, pick just one passage that you identify with and focus on it alone. Example: the one about *malshinim*,
slanderers who you wished would stop using their hurtful words.

During one of Zalman's lectures to the staff, he suggested a
new ritual dealing with personal spiritual development. Why not
adapt the biblical seven-year cycle of nature to our own lives?
Each seven years after our Bar or Bat Mitzvah, he suggested, we
conduct a ceremony of re-initiation with which we renew our
pledge to God to study, practice and affirm the faith of Israel. In
this way we'd keep in touch with our own personal spiritual development.

At one point during a weekday service, Zalman made a striking suggestion. He quoted Reb Nahman of Bratzlav, who said that
if you want to know God, you need only to listen to the beat of
your heart. One need never be lonely for Him or out of touch with
Him who fashioned your heart. You can always touch your pulse
and say, "Oh, there you are!"

An approach to a written prayer suggested by Zalman: hold a
copy of the twenty-third Psalm, peering at oblique words, recited
mechanically in a sad setting such as a funeral service. Zalman
proposed how one can bring these words alive and make them a
real experience. For example, the Bible's David was being followed by the Philistines, who were out to kill him. He was able to
elude them, making his way to a pastoral place where he was safe
and secure, and gets to eat something. He then reflects on how
God has helped him, and begins to sing, "The Lord is my shep-
herd, I shall not want." The way he sings these words is full of his
experience. Now the prayerbook's black-and-white print in front
of the worshipper is taken closer to the experience that David had,

"walking through the valley of the shadow of death"…yes, he was afraid. Yes, he had trust, but now he eats despite the fact that if it were up to his enemies, he wouldn't get anything to eat. "Thou preparest for me a table *despite my enemies.* (Note Zalman's different translation of the usual *"in the presence of my enemies"*)

From that summer experience with Rabbi Zalman Schachter, as well as subsequent contacts with him personally and via his recordings and writings, I learned a great deal. Indeed there are abiding spiritual notions and experiences in ever-changing forms of expression.

A Seder in a Circle

The following limns a personal experience which adds to the substance of Zalman Schachter's emphasis on spiritual aspiration in changing forms of expression.

It was during a *shiva* call in a house of mourning. From the moment I walked through the door and throughout the evening's conversation, a young man's face was riveted on mine. We were talking about the purposes of various religious observances, such as Jewish mourning practices, the dietary laws, ritual in general. The young man was in his twenties; his Jewish education and religious interests had been minimal; he was now married and living and working on a farm.

When I sought to explain the system of *kashrut* as designed to sensitize the Jew to the value of human life and to ennoble the simple act of eating, that consumption of meat was a "concession," as it were, to man's weakness, the young man reacted. He told me that he and his wife were vegetarians. The basic purposes I was talking about were essentially the reasons they were vegetarians, he said, with quiet fervor and obvious conviction. With eyes sparkling, the young man with his earring dangling urged me to try vegetarianism, that it was good for the spirit.

Then and there I sensed that I was in the presence of a kindred spirit, and I began to understand the focus on that young man's face.

The conversation moved on to the Passover Seder. I made the point that the root purpose of the ritualized Seder was to recall a particular ancient event that emphasized the notion of the Jewish people's—and by extension all people's—yearning for freedom. Whereupon our young man described the Seder he, his wife and friends inaugurated recently in their home: they sat in a circle on the floor, sang freedom songs to guitar music, selectively recited some of the traditional text along with contemporary prose and poetry, used some of the Seder symbols such as the matzah and horseradish, and followed the haggadah in their own unconventional way.

All this was designed, the twenty-something said, to give expression to emotional impulses, to articulate the yearning for freedom, for liberation from the often oppressive shackles of modern society. And, yes, he and his friends recognized that some sort of form for the Seder was necessary to effectively express these feelings.

As the young man continued to talk with such clarity and passion, I realized increasingly that I was indeed in the presence of a kindred spirit. I now more fully understood the riveted intensity on his face as he listened and spoke to me.

I walked out of that *shiva* home that night exhilarated—for reasons more than personal. I realized that this young man, until recently an estranged, indifferent Jew, was emotionally, psychologically and spiritually somewhat in sync with the inner rhythms of the religion of Israel, even as more conventional folk should be.

Some Jews—young and not so young anymore—observe the rituals of Jewish living in unconventional fashion. Others do so in more conventional ways. So be it. What is important in either methodology of observance is the "religiosity" of ritual practice— their underlying purpose and spirit.

– Thirty-One –

ON EMBRACING DISAGREEMENT:

Hillel/Shammai…Buber/Rosenzweig…
Kaplan/Heschel

כָּל־מַחְלֹקֶת שֶׁהִיא לְשֵׁם שָׁמַיִם סוֹפָה לְהִתְקַיֵּם וְשֶׁאֵינָה לְשֵׁם שָׁמַיִם
אֵין סוֹפָה לְהִתְקַיֵּם אֵיזוֹ הִיא מַחְלֹקֶת שֶׁהִיא לְשֵׁם שָׁמַיִם
זוֹ מַחְלֹקֶת הִלֵּל וְשַׁמַּי וְשֶׁאֵינָה לְשֵׁם שָׁמַיִם זוֹ מַחְלֹקֶת
קֹרַח וְכָל־עֲדָתוֹ

A disagreement which is for the sake of heaven (in pursuit of valid exposition of the Torah) shall in the end be preserved (as legitimate). But a controversy that is not for the sake of heaven, shall not in the end be preserved (as legitimate). Which disagreements were for the sake of heaven? The disagreements between Hillel and Shamai. Which were not for the sake of heaven? The ones between Korakh and his company (who merely sought power for themselves).

–Pirke Avot 5:20

Hillel and Shammai

The Talmud records several personal disputes between the sages Hillel and Shammai. With time, the disagreements between their respective "schools" (Beit Hillel/Beit Shammai) multiplied dramatically.[1] Their clashes concerned vital matters about ritual practice, theology, ethics, as well as politics. In general, Beit Shammai's positions were stricter than those of Beit Hillel who

---

1. Shabbat 15a; Hagigah 2:2; Eduyot 1:2-3; Niddah 1:1.

was more flexible and tolerant. Thus, for example, Beit Shammai believed that only worthy students should be admitted to study Torah, while Beit Hillel believed that all should study in the expectation that they would become worthy. Shammai, with irritation, rejected prospective converts while Hillel patiently welcomed them. Beit Shammai sided with the zealots in his time who strongly challenged the Roman authorities while Hillel cautioned that such zealotry would be counterproductive. Yet though, by and large, the positions of Beit Hillel prevailed as authoritative, the relationship between the two schools remained accepting of each other in friendship and mutual respect. The Talmud tells us:

> Come and hear: although Beit Shammai and Beit Hillel are in disagreement on the questions of rivals, sisters, an old bill of divorce, a doubtfully married woman, a woman who her husband had divorced but who stayed with him over the night at an inn, money, valuables, the value of a *perutah*, Beit Shammai did not, nevertheless, refrain from marrying women of the families of Beit Hillel, nor did Beit Hillel refrain from marrying those of Beit Shammai. This is to teach you that they showed love and friendship towards one another, thus putting into practice the Scriptural text in Zecharia 8:19, "Love ye truth and peace."[2]

Indeed, Beit Hillel and Beit Shammai together helped steer the Jewish people through a tumultuous and troubling period in its first century BCE history.

Particularly significant for the specific purpose of this essay is this: both schools studied each others' opposing views in depth, and not only did Beit Hillel actively teach Beit Shammai's views, but presented them openly and first before its own.[3]

Embracing disagreement.

---

2. Yevamot 140b.
3. Eruvin 13b.

Fast Forward to Martin Buber and Franz Rosenzweig

Martin Buber, a leading Jewish theologian in twentieth-century Germany, famously dismissed Jewish religious law and practice as effective routes to true spirituality, what he termed "religiosity." Torah is correctly understood, he maintained, as Divine instruction that is continually revealed in the ongoing flux of life. Nothing is incapable of becoming a reception of revelation or continuing Divine instruction. The "primal creative forces" in Judaism are engendered by the human response to that instruction—not Jewish law, but Jewish teaching which leads to access to those primal creative forces informing the spiritual biography of the Jewish people. Thus Buber insisted that "revelation was not legislation," that the Jew must be free from the law and prevailing ritual patterns which he claimed freeze and impede access to fundamental "religiosity" as opposed to "religion" which law and ritual constitute.[4]

This position prompted Franz Rosenzweig, a friend and collaborator of Buber, and a profound Jewish thinker in his own right, to compose an open letter of rebuke of his older colleague. Rosenzweig contended that "the constructive growth of the law is entrusted to our loving care." As heirs to the covenant that God made with our forebearers, Rosenzweig writes, we have the responsibility to bear the mantle of the law, "to become builders" of Jewish life.

Moreover, in contrast to the contemplative act of reading a body of literature, the cognitive significance of the mitzvot can be learned only from within the process of performing them. Also, it is only in their observance that the mitzvot can possibly be known not merely as laws (Gezetze) but also as Divine commandments (Gebote), addressed personally and directly to the individual in the here and now. The commanding voice of God can be heard only from within the lived experiences of observing the mitzvot. And then Rosenzweig concludes: "I could not

---

4. Flohr, Paul Mendes. *Martin Buber: A Life of Faith and Dissent.* Yale University Press, 2019; p. 151-153.

believe that you, Martin Buber, who has shown us again the path to the Torah and its teaching as documented in its literature, should be unable to see what moves us as well today along another path—the law."[5]

Now, Buber was the longstanding editor of Der Jude, a major journal of Jewish thought at the time. Rosenzweig had sent the letter to Buber to see before he planned to make it public. Whereupon Buber urged Rosenzweig to allow him to include it in his journal. The vigorous letter of disagreement with Buber was indeed published in the August 1924 issue of Buber's own Der Jude!

Embracing disagreement.

Fast Forward Again to Mordecai Kaplan and Abraham Joshua Heschel

Mordecai Kaplan, the seminal Jewish thinker in mid-twentieth-century America, famously articulated the notion of God as "the Power that makes for salvation" i.e. human fulfillment. His formulation has long been considered a major departure from the traditional Jewish conception of the Deity. God is not a "person," Kaplan contended, in the sense that He is an independent being to whom we pray and hope for response. Rather God is a "process"; in the universe there exists a complex of forces and relationships and patterns which make for the fulfillment of man as a human being—and it is this process which we term God. Reason leads us to perceive God as personal only in the sense that He manifests Himself in human personality. Thus God is not an independent, "transcendent" entity who can be grasped by man through some act of human intuition or faith or of God's own self-revelation to humanity at Mount Sinai or at any other given point in time.[6]

Abraham Joshua Heschel, a great theologian and fellow

---

5. Glatzer, Nahum (ed). *On Judaism: Martin Buber*. Schocken Books, 1967; p. 149ff.
6. Kaplan, Mordecai Menahem. *Questions Jews Ask*. Reconstructionist Press, 1972; p. 102-103.

faculty member of Kaplan at the Jewish Theological Seminary, wrote a far-reaching essay, "Faith," in which he directly contradicted Kaplan's rationalism and his notion of God. "Faith is a force in man lying deeper than the stratum of reason, and its nature cannot be defined in abstract terms." Intuition, not reason, is the path to religious insight. "Each of us has at least once in his life experienced the momentous reality of God. God is in search of man," Heschel asserted, and assumed that human beings could conceive of themselves as *objects* of God's concern. "Faith opens our hearts for the entrance of the holy." Thus God is, in a real sense, an independent entity who can be grasped by man via an act of faith for God is ever in search of man who needs to respond to His embrace and to His expectations.[7]

Take note: Mordecai Kaplan was the editor of his highly influential periodical, The Reconstructionist. *And it was Kaplan himself who solicited Heschel's "Faith" essay and published it in his very own journal of Jewish thought!*

Embracing disagreement.

---

7. Heschel, Abraham J. *God in Search of Man*. Jewish Publication Society, 1956; p. 136-143.

ACKNOWLEDGEMENTS

There are a number of people long since departed from the land of the living who yet live on in the pages of this book. They helped me a great deal in many ways through the years for which I am grateful:

Rav Frankel, my fifth grade Yeshiva teacher: "Yankel, you have a good head. Use it;" Pinchas Schechter, my "Zayde," spiritual and learning guide of youthful years; Louis Shechter, my father, who envisioned a bright future for his son; Alexander Litman, a challenging college professor; Nahum Sarna, embracing scholar and mentor; Wolfe Kelman, an inspiring leader of rabbis; Simon Greenberg, Seminary leader: "You were created for this work, Jack;" Mordecani Kaplan, practical visionary; Abraham Joshua Heschel, spiritual visionary.

One cannot possibly write, edit and publish a book without the decisive help of collaborators. And so, I must thank wholeheartedly those who have assisted me in this endeavor:

- My wife, Leah, whose discerning eye has approved, disapproved and improved so many of its pages.

- My son Judah, whose critical analyses of the text located passages where greater accuracy and clarity were required.

- My longtime typist and technical expert, Terri Nigro, who, alas, has departed from our world. She prepared the early drafts of the manuscript with consummate care and skill. May she rest in peace.

- My highly competent aide, Jamie Pagett, who took over this task from Terri and executed it with accuracy, good judgement and patience.

INDEX

A

Aaron, 40–41, 321

abiding principles, in changing categories, 125; "My Sons Have defeated Me," 131–32; permanent truth, in transient phrasing, 127–29; prayer then - and now, 132–33; Rabbi Akiba articulates Moses' principles, 129–31

Abraham, 23, 39–40, 240–42, 279

Abravanel, Don Isaac, 267–68

absence of land. *See* Jewish survival miracle

Abulafia, Abraham, 35

Acre, 77

Adam, 72, 144, 145, 192–93, 260, 298

adolescence, Jewish rites of passage for: *aliya* relating to, 243; *Bar Mitzvah*, 238, 243–45; *Bat Mitzvah*, 97, 243–45; between childhood and adulthood, 242–43; *minyan* relating to, 243; *tefillin* relating to, 243

affirmation of faith, *kaddish* as, 228–29

African paganism, 220–23

Aggadah, 69, 131, 235

Akiba (rabbi), 12, 58, 76, 120–21; Moses' principles articulated by, 129–31

Albright, William Foxwell, 99

Alef-beis of *Torah* and Judaism, 215, 216, 217

aliya, 111, 195, 243

All I Really Need to Know I Learned in Kindergarten (Fulghum), 331

amen specialist: coming to synagogue early, 178–84; fourteen morning blessings and, 177–84; one-hundred-blessing obligation, 177–78

Amida, 76, 124, 199, 303–4, 345

Amos, 75, 105, 281

ABOUT THE AUTHOR

For two decades, Jack Shechter, Ph.D., served as Associate Professor of Biblical Studies and Dean of the Department of Continuing Education—renamed *The Whizen Center for Continuing Education*—at the University of Judaism (now the American Jewish University). Prior to his tenure at the University of Judaism, he served as Executive Director of the New England Region of the United Synagogue of America, followed by a decade as the Rabbi of Congregation B'nai Israel in Pittsburgh. He was ordained at the Jewish Theological Seminary and received the Ph.D. in Biblical Studies from the University of Pittsburgh, and is the author of *The Land of Israel: Its Theological Dimensions* (2010) and *Journey of a Rabbi* (2014), both published by the University Press of America, as well as *The Idea of Monotheism: The Evolution of a Foundational Concept* (2018), Hamilton Books.